T0305974

Good Night,
Beloved Comrade

LIVING OUT

Gay and Lesbian Autobiographies

David Bergman, Joan Larkin, and Raphael Kadushin
SERIES EDITORS

Good Night, Beloved Comrade

The Letters of
Denton Welch to Eric Oliver

Edited and with an introduction by
Daniel J. Murtaugh

The University of Wisconsin Press

The University of Wisconsin Press
1930 Monroe Street, 3rd Floor
Madison, Wisconsin 53711-2059
uwpress.wisc.edu

3 Henrietta Street, Covent Garden
London WC2E 8LU, United Kingdom
eurospanbookstore.com

Printed in the United States of America

This book may be available in a digital edition.

Library of Congress Cataloging-in-Publication Data
Names: Welch, Denton, author. | Murtaugh, Daniel J., editor, writer of introduction.
Title: Good night, beloved comrade: the letters of Denton Welch to Eric Oliver
/ edited and with an introduction by Daniel J. Murtaugh.
Other titles: Living out.
Description: Madison, Wisconsin : The University of Wisconsin Press, [2017]
| Series: Living out : gay and lesbian autobiographies
| Includes bibliographical references and index.
Identifiers: LCCN 2016017722 | ISBN 9780299310103 (cloth: alk. paper)
Subjects: LCSH: Welch, Denton—Correspondence. | Oliver, Eric, 1914–1995—Correspondence.
| Gay authors—Great Britain—Correspondence. | Gay artists—Great Britain—
Correspondence. | Gay authors—Great Britain—Biography. | Gay artists—Great Britain—
Biography. | Gay couples—Great Britain—Correspondence. | Authors, English—
Correspondence— 20th century. | Artists—Great Britain—Correspondence. | Authors,
English—Biography—20th century. | Artists—Great Britain—Biography.
| Accident victims—Great Britain—Correspondence. | Accident victims—
Great Britain—Biography. | Conscientious objectors—Great Britain—Correspondence.
| Agricultural laborers—Great Britain—Correspondence.
Classification: LCC PR6045.E517 Z48 2017 | DDC 823/.912 [B]—dc23
LC record available at https://lccn.loc.gov/2016017722

To

Patricia Clarey Murtaugh, Freda Clarey, and **Anna Mae Murtaugh**

my mother and grandmothers, who introduced me to a world of books
and reading, making it possible for me to travel—then as now—to places
otherwise out of reach; havens of tranquility, passion, and imagination.

ℒ♥

To

James Methuen-Campbell and **Michael De-la-Noy**

for their championing of Denton Welch's writing and art, and for their
invaluable research, advice, and encouragement.

ℒ♥

And to

Dr. Barbara Judd

my friend and mentor.

Contents

Acknowledgments

I would like to acknowledge the cooperation and kind attention of the staff at the Harry Ransom Humanities Research Center, both during my initial manuscript research at the Center and during the permissions process for this book. In particular, I wish to express my thanks to Richard B. Watson, Head of Reference Services, and to Ariel Evans, Public Services Intern.

I also wish to thank Raphael Kadushin, Amber Rose, Adam Mehring, Carla Marolt, Sheila Leary, and Sue Breckenridge of the University of Wisconsin Press, for their commitment to this book and for their great care and dedication in making its publication possible.

I would be extremely remiss if I did not also mention Professors Peter Casagrande and Haskell Springer of the University of Kansas, for their invaluable guidance and advice in the initial drafting and editing of the manuscript.

Editorial Policy

The letters of Denton Welch to Eric Oliver are included in their original handwritten form in the collection of Denton Welch papers located at the Harry Ransom Center for the Humanities, the University of Texas, Austin. All of Welch's personal correspondence, journals, and manuscripts were sold to the Ransom Center in the late 1960s by Welch's executor and heir, Eric Oliver. There are no other published editions of Denton Welch's letters. Before I transcribed this selection, I first read all of the originals at the Ransom Center, making numerous annotations concerning provenance and style. The final transcriptions were made from verified photocopies of the letters supplied by the research center.

The majority of the letters were written in blue or black ink on unmarked sheets of stationery or on leaves from notebooks. A few letters have the Pitt's Folly address letterhead, which is noted in the pertinent transcriptions. In some cases inkblots have obliterated portions of the texts, and paper deterioration (tears, dents) further impedes a clear reading. In all such cases, I have noted the editorial difficulties or the fact that the text is illegible.

Extensive excerpts from journal entries and from Welch's autobiographical fiction are included in the annotations. These fragments, when aligned with the letters, "flesh out" and illustrate emotions and events related to them. Denton Welch was—in his correspondence, journal writings, and fiction—quite consciously *writing his life*. He was in a sense annotating and embellishing his letters with contemporaneous journal entries, and revisiting with Eric Oliver the events of his youth as related in his fiction. Excerpts from the fiction are given in the annotations where they illuminate or explain some aspect of his developing relationship with Eric. The full import of his feelings for Eric, and of his attempts to explain the difficulties he was experiencing in relating to his friend, would not be possible without information gained from the journals and autobiographical accounts of his early life contained in the fiction.

The complete correspondence of Denton Welch to Eric Oliver comprises fifty-one letters, dating from 1943 through 1946, all of which I have elected to include in this collection. This decision is based on the fact that the entire correspondence is neither voluminous nor overly repetitious, and on the realization that the story of their developing relationship—with all of the obsessive quirks, emotional rants, and anguished self-doubt—could not have been fully told in fragments or arbitrary selections. It should also be noted that only one letter from Eric Oliver to Denton Welch is extant, the remainder having been destroyed by Oliver shortly after Welch's death. This leaves *only* Welch's description of their relationship, a conversion of his literary yearnings (seen intensely portrayed in his journals, novels, and short fiction) into a kind of Wildean imitation *in life*. The autobiographical nature of Welch's writing, as evidenced in the close parallels of the letters to his journal entries, necessitates the inclusion of the entire Oliver correspondence as, without it, we would not get a clear impression of how Denton *intentionally* wrote and recorded his own life. This is not only a record of a relationship but also of an advancing illness that would eventually end a remarkable artistic and literary career. Finally, each of Welch's letters illuminates his times, including details of daily life in wartime England, and of the lives of fellow painters, writers, and editors.

As Denton Welch's correspondence with Eric Oliver records the development of an intimate relationship and a working partnership—without which Welch's last novel, *A Voice through a Cloud*, would not have seen publication—I have chosen to preserve the integrity of the emotional turmoil and the intensity of feeling that characterize them.

I have therefore left misspellings, irregularities in punctuation, use of ellipses, hyphenation, and paragraphing as they appear in the original manuscripts. The letters are rife with frustration, self-distraction, and outright resentment at Eric's vacillating, noncommittal reaction to Welch's urgings of love and affection. This is conveyed not only in syntax and diction choice—or outright errors in both—but in Denton's staccato use of underscoring and punctuation (particularly of exclamation points). Hence, I did not want to interfere with the reader's understanding of the nature of the letters by including bracketed notes on such irregularities. For guidance in these matters, I have examined—and to some extent followed—the form of two editions of selected letters, *Your John: The Love Letters of Radclyffe Hall*, edited by Joanne Glasgow (New York: New York University Press, 1997), and *Song of Love: The Letters of Rupert Brooke and Noel Olivier*, edited by Pippa Harris (New York: Crown, 1991). Both of these editions track the course of romantic relationships revealed in the correspondence of the writers; both attempt to maintain the immediacy of emotion related in the letters by way of reportorial transcription of the written texts.

There also exists in the correspondence a peculiar mix of British public school diction and phrasing (characteristic of Welch's English middle-class upbringing) with an attempt to "roughen up" his writing by ignoring conventions of mechanics and style. He clearly wants to convey the *raw self* of his emotions, desiring not to present himself as effete and unmasculine; this is a sensitive point, as the letters indicate a distinct awareness of how this background of restraint might interfere with establishing an emotional and sexual relationship with Eric. It would then be unjust and truly insensitive to force a false conformity onto the free expression of sexual desire and of the elemental need to be loved. Welch felt the necessity of emending his identity in a desperate bid for Eric's affection, of making his language conform to what he believed— perhaps mistakenly—was more Eric's style of speaking.

As these letters comprise some of the most intimate of Welch's written work, I believe it incumbent on me to render them in as close a form as possible to the originals. To alter their form—either mechanically or stylistically—would erode their immediacy and authenticity as a record of difficulties (both emotional and physical) Welch had to daily endure. As the correspondence provides a highly personalized portrait of an artist depicted against the backdrop of wartime Britain, a close adherence to the anxiety evinced in the structure of the letters is essential. Denton and Eric's attempts—with a large degree of success it must be noted—to locate a "safe territory" for their romantic partnership did after all take place against a backdrop of general uncertainty and fear, channeled into the strained and yearning prose of Welch's love letters.

All references in the introduction and notes to James Methuen-Campbell's *Denton Welch: Writer and Artist* will be designated simply as *Writer and Artist*. All references to Michael De-la-Noy's *Denton Welch: The Making of a Writer* will be found as *Making of a Writer*. References to *The Journals of Denton Welch*, edited by Michael De-la-Noy, are noted simply as *Journals*.

Good Night,
Beloved Comrade

Introduction

The genesis of this collection of the letters of Denton Welch to Eric Oliver was a result of pure happenstance. Some years ago, I ran across a copy of *The Journals of Denton Welch* (edited by Michael De-la-Noy) on the sale rack of the University of Kansas bookstore. The dust jacket is illustrated with a self-portrait of the artist: he peers at the observer with seeming curiosity, warily sizing up and analyzing him through his horn-rimmed glasses, perhaps—as some of his friends and acquaintances have noted about his relationships with others—considering whether his new admirer would be worth cultivating as an eventual subject for his fiction, poetry, or painting. Denton is stylishly dressed in a green sweater and a jersey under which he's tucked a deep red scarf; self-aware, discerning, and detailed, much like the autobiographical personae found in his writings. I was quite taken with him at once, leading me on the journey that culminated in this volume of letters.

As I read the journals, I became fascinated with Welch's short but remarkable literary and artistic career, spanning the period from 1940 through 1948. I was drawn to the writer's unique manner of reporting his times, interwoven with his emerging homosexual identity, the devastating impact of chronic illness upon his potential relationships and artistic and literary aspirations, and the conditions of life on the British home front during the Second World War. His was a sensitive, minutely personal approach to wartime insecurity and prevailing fear, to his sense of

3

a "fractured" or "ruined" life, to his sexual yearnings and experiences. James Methuen-Campbell describes Denton's solitary walks through the Medway Valley while he was living near Tonbridge in 1936, where he would "customarily be on the lookout for some young farm worker to chat with" (*Writer and Artist*, 84). He goes on to create a poignant picture of a young man plagued by physical injury who was erotically attracted to naked young sunbathers or to sweating, shirtless laborers he encountered on his rambles, and who are so ravishingly described in *The Journals* and in his fiction: "His romantic image of the 'naturalness' of the working man was undiminished—indeed one suspects this had been heightened as a result of having his own body ruined by the accident—and it was a thrill for him to come upon someone responsive and willing to make contact. . . . One does not really know the extent to which Denton ever became involved with such people. There are references in letters to Marcus Oliver that suggest that he did have the occasional sexual fling" (84). But particularly the journals, the letters (a portion of which are the subject of this book), and the short fiction record the development of the only *and last* intimate relationship of his life: his first meeting with Eric Oliver, the tempestuous beginnings of their friendship and love for one another, and their more domestic and settled outcome. These writings also contain the psychological acuity of his observations on sexual identity, and his sophisticated commentary on the social and cultural context of wartime experience.

My research initially focused on a traditional gay studies and literary analysis of Welch's writings (his journals, fiction, poetry, and essays), particularly as these were—in whole, or in part—an autobiographical retelling of his life story. However, as my approach to the material seemed now to be following a truly psychosexual and biographical course, I was led to do manuscript research into Welch's letters. Michael De-la-Noy's references to the correspondence in his biography, *Denton Welch: The Making of a Writer* (1984), and in *The Journals*, left much unrevealed about Welch's creative and personal development. And though James Methuen-Campbell, in his sensitive and thorough biography, *Denton Welch: Writer and Artist* (2002), does excerpt and quote some of the Welch/Oliver correspondence, few of the letters are included in their entirety.

All of Denton's letters to Eric Oliver were in the latter's possession at the time of the writer's death. They were subsequently sold in the 1960s, along with Welch's other correspondence and manuscripts, to the Harry Ransom Center for the Humanities at the University of Texas, Austin, by his heir and executor, Eric Oliver. A substantial portion of the correspondence was that of Denton Welch to Oliver, over the period from November 1943 through October 1947, and I soon realized that this portion of the Ransom Center collection more poignantly and sincerely underscored the themes of Welch's life, career, and times, than did the more self-conscious autobiography of his journals and fiction.

Welch's literary career was launched in 1942 with a *Horizon* article on the English painter Walter Sickert and furthered by Edith Sitwell's praise for Welch as a "born writer" with the publication of his first novel *Maiden Voyage* (1943). In fact, Dame Sitwell wrote the foreword to *Maiden Voyage*, in which she says: "This is a very moving and remarkable first book, and the author appears to me to be that very rare being, a born writer . . . I feel that Mr. Welch may easily prove to be, not only a born writer, but a very considerable one" (Welch, *Maiden Voyage*, vii–viii). Despite intensifying health problems, he continued to write numerous short stories, many poems, and two more novels (*In Youth Is Pleasure* and *A Voice through a Cloud*) in the intervening years before his untimely death in December 1947, at the age of thirty-three. What is most remarkable about his career is that he accomplished so much—both artistically and literarily—in something less than eight years, and this under a near-constant pall of pain, discomfort, and persistent fevers, as a result of a serious physical injury suffered when he was eighteen years old, and from which he never fully recovered. Edith Sitwell's praise for Denton Welch's writing rings particularly true in that Welch did not learn to read until he was nearly nine years old, due to the largely unstructured nature of his early education and to his having been as a child shuttled back and forth between Shanghai (where his father, Arthur, was a partner in a rubber exporting firm) and England. James Methuen-Campbell notes that, at that point in his life, "books were only of interest to him if they had pictures" (*Writer and Artist*, 9). Methuen-Campbell goes on to relate that the writer's first mention of any book was in his recounting of a Christmas party in Shanghai when he was eight years

old, where he received a gift of a book of Greek mythology; the young
Welch was taken by a nude depiction of Prometheus chained to his
rock that, as is asserted by the biographer, perhaps revealed that Denton
regarded this as a sort of homosexual awakening (9).

Even the character and duration of his formal education (a school
for British children in Shanghai, a Christian Science day school in
Queen's Gate in London, and St. Michael's prep school in Sussex, during the period 1923 through 1929) were not necessarily conducive to his
development as a writer, though he received considerable encouragement as an illustrative artist while at Repton School between 1929 and
1931. Welch, unlike his older brothers, William and Paul, did not follow the middle-class agenda of a university education at Oxford, but
instead convinced his father to send him to Goldsmiths School of Art
in London. His remarkable ability as a writer must be attributed to his
independent—and voracious—reading habits as he moved into adulthood, and to precise, minute observation of every detail of his remembered experiences, and of antique and exotic objets d'art and curiosities.
Methuen-Campbell attributes "the lack of sympathy" of Arthur Welch
for his son to Denton's "unusual behavior . . . his passion for collecting
trinkets" upon which he "would lavish hour upon hour of loving attention" and "a choice selection would travel with him wherever he went"
(2–3).

Many of Welch's short stories, novels, and journal entries deal un-
apologetically with homosexual attraction and his desire for men, but it
is in his letters to Eric Oliver that the integrity of his emotional need
and the crippling, discouraging effect of his injury on the fulfillment of
that need are most clearly revealed. In fact, they map the fatal progress
of his illness, with its counterpoint of developing intimacy and attach-
ment for Eric; the wrenching conclusion threading its way through the
narrative. Though Eric Oliver's early indecisiveness concerning intimacy
with Denton (probably resulting from Eric's bisexuality and his lack of
physical attraction to Welch) infuriated the writer, he appears to have
come to some understanding of the nature of things when he remarked
to his artist friend Noël Adeney: "How does a person of his divided
personality expect to find complete love with anyone, whether man or

woman? Will he find it with me? . . . Will he find it with the youths he works with, or the innumerable landladies' daughters? It seems extremely doubtful to me" (letter to Adeney, February 9, 1944; quoted in *Making of a Writer*, 199).

Though Denton's early, troubled relationship with Eric is agonizingly recounted in the letters of 1943–44, the last years of Welch's life would remarkably be made more blissful and creatively productive as a result of Oliver's dedication and affection for him. In his journal entry of January 8, 1945, Welch described his life as "a great unfoldment of many marvelous things. . . . I would not have thought that I would be damaged and ill so soon (twenty) or that so comparatively late (twenty-eight and a half) I should find someone with whom I could live in almost complete peace. . . . In my heart are hung two extraordinary pictures: one is called 'Accident and Illness' and the other, exactly opposite, tilted forward as if to meet it, is called 'Love and Friendship'" (*Journals*, 181).

Denton Maurice Welch was born in Shanghai on March 29, 1915, into a family whose wealth—on both the English paternal and American maternal branches—had for some years been connected to the China and East Asia trade. His upbringing was colonial middle class, but with some unusual variants, partially attributable to the early death of his mother and the relative independence of action given to him by his father and older brothers after this event, and to his family's seeming tolerance for Denton's eccentricity and emerging homosexual identity (which if his autobiographical fiction is to be believed began to exhibit itself in late childhood). In 1924 Welch was enrolled in an English grammar school, St. Michael's in Uckfield, Sussex. Before this, he had been the near constant companion of his mother, Rosalind Bassett Welch, both in China and on their infrequent trips to England. Rosalind suffered from Bright's Disease, a kidney ailment that led to frequent episodes of fatigue and illness, during which she relied on her youngest son for companionship and support. Denton's early education was therefore sporadic and undisciplined. This however did not impede—and, in fact, probably enhanced—his amazing capacity for observation and a curiosity about the minutiae of life. Many years hence, he would record his solitary experiences in such marvelous stories as "At Sea" (recounting an ocean-liner trip back to England with his ailing mother and his early homoerotic feelings toward another adolescent male passenger), "The Barn" (occurring during a family trip to Sussex, mostly dedicated to erotic descriptions of a young vagrant whom Denton imagines as his lover, sleeping next to him in a barn on their rented estate), and "The Coffin on a Hill" (a disturbing story of a Chinese funeral ritual, observed on a river outing near Shanghai).

Rosalind Welch died of nephritis in March 1927, due in part to her reluctance to seek medical treatment: she was a devout Christian Scientist. She had in fact placed Denton in a grammar school (St. Michael's) that was managed and taught—to a substantial degree—by fellow devotees of Mary Baker Eddy's religious philosophy. As Michael De-la-Noy notes in *Denton Welch: The Making of a Writer*: "Many of Rosalind's friends, whom Denton was to know for the rest of his life, were Christian Scientists, and the most formative years of his childhood were spent in the company of a fervent believer—his mother—struggling with an incurable illness. He was later, through intellectual scepticism, to discard any formal allegiance to the faith, but its influence, perhaps because it was so strongly associated with his mother, never entirely left him; on the whole, while making use of doctors in later life, he disliked and distrusted them" (31). This theme is echoed repeatedly in Welch's journal entries and in his correspondence with Eric Oliver, concerning the lingering effects of—and potential treatment for—his injuries and subsequent illness.

Welch's disposition bridled at the traditional educational and professional expectations of his class. He, like his brothers, was eventually sent to Repton School in 1929, where he developed a distaste for the worn-out conventions and sexual hypocrisy of the English public school regime. He later described his time at Repton as a "*sordid* and fearful time" (*Making of a Writer*, 41–42). Nonetheless, it was here that he finally learned the mechanics for his eventual career as a writer, and where he received encouragement from his art teacher Arthur Norris to continue his training as a painter: "When he called in at the art school for the last time the art master said, 'Well, good-bye, Welch. Go on with your drawing. Don't let them make you do anything else.' Denton felt flattered, and decided there and then that he wanted to be a painter" (*Making of a Writer*, 57). James Methuen-Campbell concludes that "Denton's work in the Art School was his only real accomplishment" at Repton (*Writer and Artist*, 24). Though Denton had friends at Repton who shared his homosexual orientation, his journals or autobiographical fiction don't indicate that he either engaged in a great deal of sexual experimentation while at the school or that he made any secret of where his true desires lay. Michael De-la-Noy puts it succinctly: "Even while in the throes of adolescent homosexuality it is normally obligatory for boys at least to pretend to an interest in girls, but such was Denton's individualism that he seems, at an early age, to have shut his mind to the possibility of heterosexual experimentation" (*Making of a Writer*, 43). This unabashed and unapologetic approach to his sexual identity reveals itself again and again in his fiction and in his journals. In fact, it took a great deal of determination and courage—both on his part and on that of his publishers (Routledge and the magazines *Horizon*, *English Story*, and *Cornhill*, to name a few) to submit and publish his more risqué writings. When Welch's first novel, *Maiden Voyage*, was published, Winston Churchill's private secretary Eddie Marsh happened to read a review of the book in the *Sunday Times*. He wrote to a friend that "someone was telling me about it [the book] in London" who said "it was rather unfortunate, as the book was reeking with homosexuality. . . . I think I must get it" (quoted in *Making of a Writer*, 149). Marsh had worked for Churchill during the Great War, and he had been a high-ranking official in the British colonial civil service. More to the point though, he was unabashedly homosexual and was an astute admirer and friend to many talented and "beautiful" young men, including the poet Rupert Brooke and the Bloomsbury-connected artists Duncan Grant and Mark Gertler. Not surprising then that he was so enthusiastic about *Maiden Voyage* and could perhaps be counted as one of Denton's first "fans," as the writer would later come to call his admirers.

Perhaps, during the Second World War, some English publishers were finding the prewar moral standards concerning homosexuality to be both outmoded and socially counterproductive, and thus were willing to make a defensive stand for Welch's writings. However, attesting to the fact that old attitudes die hard, the first edition of Welch's journals, published by Jocelyn Brook in 1953, was heavily edited, omitting the more explicit sexual episodes and descriptions. It was not until 1984 that an unedited version was published by Michael De-la-Noy.

It was during his holidays from St. Michael's and Repton, and finally during a return trip to China in 1932, that Welch began to experience and note for his journals (written from memory during the early 1940s) and fiction, the voyeuristic and "cock-teasy" sexual interludes (E. M. Forster used this expression to describe the manner in which Denton described his sexual experiences) of this period in his life. Most notably—and discussed in some detail in the annotations to the letters—Welch refers to sexual play with a young scout master and his charges during a summer vacation with his father and brothers, and to sexual advances and fits of temper by his fictional eldest brother, Charles Pym (in the novel *In Youth Is Pleasure*); to a poignant episode of companionship, hero worship, and intimacy, with a gay Oxford undergraduate while on a ski trip to Switzerland (in his short story "When I Was Thirteen"); and to his inviting a soldier over to his father's flat in Shanghai for vaguely sexual purposes (in the novel *Maiden Voyage*). Welch details the experiences, as well as the consequences. He was brutally punished by his brother Bill for his contact with Archer, the fictional veil for his Oxford friend, and brow-beaten by Paul (his other brother) for bringing the soldier to their home in Shanghai.

Not only are sexual experiences related in these stories and novelistic portrayals, but Welch reveals a true wealth of observation concerning the very different cultural milieus in which he lived his youth. These observations move across time from early childhood through adolescence, and record in minute and breathtakingly beautiful detail the physical and human landscapes of rural England and of China.

When Welch returned to China in 1931, he spent nearly a year collecting the observations and experiences that would make up *Maiden Voyage*. I speak of "collecting," as he was an inveterate collector of minutiae and curiosities (both of physical objets d'art and of detailed mental notations, recalled many years later in his fiction, journals, poetry, and painting). He not only spent time in the Europeanized cantonments of

Shanghai, but he also made a lengthy journey with one of his father's friends into the Chinese interior, to a settlement called Kai-feng Fu. It was here that he noticed the increasing animosity of Chinese nationalists to Europeans (he was threatened with the butt of a rifle and verbally abused by a Chinese sentry), the traditional trade networks of the Chinese mandarin class, the day-to-day brutality of life among the peasant poor, and the fate of Chinese political "undesirables" (he stumbled across a decapitated head outside of Kai-feng Fu). The Shanghai episodes recounted in *Maiden Voyage* don't follow an exact timeframe, as they include both childhood recollections (before the death of his mother and his return to England) as well as his late-adolescent search for sensual and erotic pleasure (he evidently spent a good deal of time "cruising" the military district of the city, though perhaps these episodes are creatively embellished in Denton's memory).

No matter his early troubled relationship with his father and with his brother Bill, his family provided support—both financial and personal—and encouragement for his career as an artist, and ultimately as a writer. Rather than force Denton to attend Oxford (for which his son would have had little aptitude and even less interest), his father agreed in 1932 to send him to Goldsmiths School of Art at New Cross in London. The choice of art schools was arrived at through the recommendation of Arthur's sister, Dorothy Welch (referred to by Denton as Aunt Dolly). Dorothy had been introduced by chance to Gerald Mackenzie, a senior art student at Goldsmiths, who when told of her nephew's interest in becoming an artist suggested that she send him to Goldsmiths, as "students were accepted at well below university entrance age, but more importantly, the staff took an enthusiastic and enlightened approach to teaching, and the general atmosphere was quite relaxed" (*Writer and Artist*, 42). Not only was Mackenzie instrumental in helping launch Welch's training as an artist but he would remain a mentor to him while he was at Goldsmiths and a lifelong friend.

Denton's entrance into Goldsmiths School of Art gave him the opportunity to immerse himself in the eccentric and truly unconventional world of the London prewar art scene. Some of his more important connections and friendships developed during this time (including Evie

Sinclair, who would eventually become Denton's housekeeper and
caregiver, and fellow art students Betty Swanwick and Joan Waymark),
to an immensely liberating effect. Welch seems to have determined that
he could make a career for himself as an illustrative artist and painter, and
the sense of sexual freedom and acceptance gained from his acquaintances
cleared the way for his uncharacteristically honest portrayal of the bohe-
mian London art world and of the unabashed depictions of homoerotic
attraction and gay identity contained in "A Novel Fragment" and "The
Party." These autobiographical stories contain hilarious descriptions of
the Sinclair household at 34 Croom's Hill, where Welch boarded while
at Goldsmiths, particularly of Evie's father, a feeble and inept cellist,
of raucous and campy art-school parties, and of Welch's first tenta-
tive approach to an openly gay life (his literary persona, Robert, "rubs
shoulders" with a life model, engages in sexual give-and-take in a dark-
ened bath at a costume party, and reads Oscar Wilde's *De Profundis*—
admittedly not the most affirming of gay documents). However, just as
Welch was coming of age both creatively and emotionally, he experienced a life-changing catastrophe.

On June 7, 1935, while bicycling to his uncle's home for the Whitsun
holiday, he was run over by a motorist and severely injured. Welch describes his return to consciousness in his novel *A Voice through a Cloud*;
a policeman's voice came "through a great cloud of agony and sickness."
Denton's spine had been fractured, causing temporary bladder failure.
For a time, he was paralyzed from the waist down, and though he was
eventually able to walk again, he did so with difficulty (due to lingering
nerve injury). The injuries to his spine and bladder, however, made him
chronically vulnerable to infections of the kidneys, bladder, and pelvis;
fevers; high blood pressure; and a degree of sexual dysfunction. From
the age of eighteen until his death at thirty-three, he suffered from the
physical and emotional impact of his injuries. His anguish and resentment at having been deprived of his youth and of the opportunity for
normal, physical relationships (he above all, regretted not having met
Eric prior to his accident) are poignantly related in his correspondence
and in the journals.

Welch's lengthy recuperation from the accident is recounted in his
last autobiographical novel, *A Voice through a Cloud*, the last portion of

which remained incomplete at the time of his death in 1948. Eric Oliver helped see the book through to publication at John Lehmann Press in 1950. The novel recounts in startlingly clear—and objective—detail the humiliation and pain Welch suffered during his initial hospitalization, his gradual—but partial—recovery at Southcourt Nursing Home in Broadstairs, his remarkable drive to regain physical independence, and his intense infatuation for his attending physician, Dr. John Easton (Dr. Farley in *A Voice*). These wrenchingly frustrating and at times pathetic episodes involving Dr. Easton are referred to in detail in Welch's journals and in his later letters to Eric Oliver. The most important, actual contribution made by Dr. Easton was his encouraging the young artist to again take up painting. Interestingly, however, it was not Dr. Easton, but his associate, Dr. Hugh Raven, who inadvertently set Welch on the path to becoming a writer. Dr. Raven attempted to set up a visit to Welch at the nursing home by the painter Walter Sickert. Though Sickert declined this invitation, Denton was later able to visit with the painter at his home near Broadstairs. This episode would be hilariously recounted in Welch's first published piece, "Sickert at St. Peter's" published by Cyril Connolly in *Horizon* in 1942.

When Denton left Southcourt Nursing Home in July 1936, he moved into a flat at 54 Hadlow Road, near Tonbridge, where he hired Evie Sinclair as his housekeeper (an association that would continue intermittently until Welch's death). Part of the reason for this move was so that he could be close to Dr. Easton, who had moved there from Broadstairs during the previous year. Welch's attempt to "act out" his infatuation for Easton led to some embarrassing episodes, related in excruciating detail in the letters and notes. However, while he was living in Tonbridge, Welch was once again drawn to painting and to acquaintances with eccentric personalities. James Methuen-Campbell reveals much about Denton's artistic endeavors while in Tonbridge, including exhibiting at the Mitre Theatre Club's annual art show, completing no fewer than seven self-portraits, and incorporating many of his collectible porcelains into "quite arresting pictures through the skillful juxtaposition of the artefacts he had chosen" (*Writer and Artist*, 82). One particular painting, described by Methuen-Campbell, was of a group of three male nudes drying themselves after bathing. He makes special note of Welch's "sensitive feeling for skin texture" in the painting, and that if "the genitals and nipples appear to be shaped with greater care than any other part of the body, then one must see this as a reflection of Denton's homosexuality and also of the fact that for the span of his convalescence he had been deprived of gazing on the beauty of the male form, which previously he was able to admire at leisure in the life class [at Goldsmiths]" (82).

While living on Hadlow Road, Welch heard talk of a Russian émigré by the name of Lieutenant General Prince Serge Belosselsky-Belozersky, who had fled Russia during the 1917 Bolshevik Revolution and was living nearby. Denton sought him out, and in fact painted his portrait. According to Methuen-Campbell, the relationship soured when "Denton offended the venerable nobleman by offering to buy some of his mementoes from Czarist Russsia" (*Writer and Artist*, 79). A much more fruitful acquaintance made during this time was with Marcus Oliver, who would become a dedicated friend and lifelong correspondent. Arthur Welch, who was on a honeymoon trip to England with his second wife, was introduced to Marcus by his son and Gerald Mackenzie in November of 1936. Though his father seemed to be impressed with Oliver's "manly conversation" (82), with his admirable aptitude for bridge, and with the fact that the young man's brother was a famous mountaineer, he found him to be "very polite, but rather Jewish" (quoted in *Writer and Artist*, 83). No matter what Arthur Welch's opinion, it was through Marcus Oliver that Welch was able to establish the network of gay acquaintances and associations that would transform the remainder of his life. It was also at this time that Denton completed a large-scale Gothic panel of Hadlow Castle, which through Jack Miller, a friend from Goldsmiths, and Jack Beddington of Shell Mex, was accepted as a travel poster by the company. It was included in a "series of lorry posters, 'Visit Britain's Landmarks,' it featured as No. 496," and was the first painting the young artist sold (83).

Soon after the sale of his Hadlow Castle panel, Arthur bought Denton an automobile, a Baby Austin. Methuen-Campbell emphasizes the importance of this event: "The Baby Austin turned out to be an invaluable asset in broadening his [Denton's] spheres of interest," enabling him to explore "the Kentish countryside, with its picturesque views of oast-houses and the beauty of the North Downs seen across the patterned rows of hop-fields and apple orchards," the Medway Valley where "there were endless churches that could be visited. And Denton now had the freedom to attend any odd private auction that took his fancy" (*Writer and Artist*, 83).

From 1936 through the outbreak of war, Welch made many other useful acquaintances, both in the publishing/literary world and among the cultural and social "lights" of Tonbridge. Chief among these were Herbert Read, Edith Sitwell, Peggy Mundy-Castle, and May Walbrand-Evans. Having taken the initial steps in furthering his artistic and literary careers, Denton turned his attention to finding a new place more conducive to painting and writing (54 Hadlow Road was quite dreary and dark). He used his mother's influential friends—Cecilia Carpmael, Mary Sloman, and particularly May Walbrand-Evans—to locate comfortable accommodations, first at a modern cottage called the Hop Garden at St. Mary's Platt (which escaped an exploding German bomb, only to be burned in a fire accidentally caused by his Evie Sinclair in early December 1941) and then at Pond Farm, near the Medway River, where he and Evie rented rooms in a large house owned by Cecil Gardener and his wife, Jane (together with whom Denton had visited many auctions in search of fine porcelain). Ultimately, however, Denton found it impossible to get along with his friend-turned-landlady, so early in 1942, he and Evie moved once again, this time to Pitt's Folly Cottage, rented by Mary Sloman (the estranged wife of the Tonbridge School's headmaster), who arranged for them to live in the former chauffer's quarters above the garage (*Writer and Artist*, 111–13). By June of 1941 Welch had completed the manuscript for *Maiden Voyage*, written several short stories, and finished some paintings, including a portrait of Lord Berners (an English composer, artist, and writer) as a boy, dressed in a Robinson Crusoe costume. Denton had done his painting from a photograph of the author contained in his reminiscence, *First Childhood* (*Making of a Writer*, 133), and he met with Lord Berners in an unsuccessful attempt to sell the work. From 1942 forward Welch placed numerous paintings in the Redfern and Leicester galleries, published illustrations and articles in *Vogue*, and completed some private commissions, including one for

Lady Ottoline Morrell's daughter, Julian Goodman (that of her pug, mentioned in the letters and notes). However, his painting career was soon to occupy a secondary position to the writing.

Welch initially requested advice concerning the publication of *Maiden Voyage* from Margot, Lady Asquith (widow of Prime Minister Herbert Asquith), herself an autobiographical fiction writer. She was encouraging but provided little concrete assistance. His first, failed attempt to publish the novel with Jonathan Cape was followed by yet another rejection by Arthur Waugh of Chapman & Hall. Finally, after a memorable meeting with Herbert Read at his London club in September 1942, Welch received word that Read's publishing house, Routledge, would accept the book. Notably, by this time Welch had been corresponding with the Sitwell family and had sent Edith a copy of his *Horizon* article about Walter Sickert. Edith wrote to Welch, "I cannot tell you how much my brother . . . and I enjoyed your alarming experience with Mr Sickert. . . . We laughed till we cried—though really in some ways it was no laughing matter. But one thing came out very clearly, and that is, that you are a *born writer*! . . . As I say, we were full of admiration for the *writing* of your adventure. . . . I hope, very much, that we shall meet one day. I'll promise not to sing, or to dance!" (qtd. in *Making of a Writer*, 144–45). Meet they did, for a luncheon memorialized in Welch's journals. By this time Edith had become Welch's literary champion, having written a foreword to *Maiden Voyage* (published in 1943 and containing Welch's own jacket art, frontispiece, and chapter-heading illustrations). Sitwell's praise is unfeigned and premonitory of a notable career in the making: "This is a very moving and remarkable first book, and the author appears to be that very rare being, a born writer. . . . Mr Welch uses words as only a born writer uses them. He never fumbles. . . . I feel that Mr Welch may easily prove to be, not only a born writer, but a very considerable one" (*Maiden Voyage*, ii).

Unfortunately, the serious lingering effects of his injuries often hampered his creative output in painting, illustration, and writing. Nonetheless, *Maiden Voyage* met with significant critical success and opened Welch up to literary and homosexual contacts (he refers to them as "fans") from around the world, including men in the United

States, Canada, and India. Most notable of these contacts was Hector Bolitho, who wrote a biographical "at home" article on the artist/writer for the American magazine *Town and Country*. Welch's chronic condition mercifully abated at times, allowing him to write, paint, and go on walking and bicycling trips around the Sussex countryside. The extensive excerpts from his journals and fiction in the notes to this book attest to a fascination and vibrant love for his world; the pastoral beauty of rural England interrupted by war and inhabited by its castaways and soldiers (Italian and German prisoners of war as well as off-duty English and American servicemen are often described by the writer), the intense attractiveness of young men, particularly of the working classes or of the military, and to the writer's insatiable appetite for bits of culture or tradition captured in collectibles (tableware, porcelains, doll houses, lacquered screens, sculpted angels, and architectural details).

Though Welch was of an extremely independent disposition, he yearned for companionship, ironically of a sort that the "disruption" of his youth had in part deprived him. Though he had frequent disagreements—and insulting exchanges—with his housekeeper, Evie Sinclair, he was in fact dependent upon her. Evie, however, could never fulfill his need for physical and emotional love. His desire is achingly revealed in his descriptions of the men he encountered in his hikes along river banks, in the fields or woodlands of Sussex, and in his fiction, recording a history from childhood to early adult life of searching for a comrade with whom to share his aspirations and sexual life. That individual came belatedly—but fortuitously—into his life on November 6, 1942. While Denton was ill in bed at Pitt's Folly, Francis Streeten brought Eric Oliver, a "new hearty land-boy" by to meet him (qtd. in *Writer and Artist*, 139). This chance occurrence would ultimately make the last years of Welch's life more productive, happy, and fulfilled as Oliver took over the more onerous aspects of keeping at bay the annoyances and day-to-day activities of existence at Pitt's Folly and Middle Orchard.

Denton had met Francis Streeten while still living at 54 Hadlow Road. As Welch was leaving the public library in Tonbridge, he encountered Francis and they struck up a conversation. Methuen-Campbell describes

Francis as "the typical dilettante. . . . He was the black sheep of the family,
spending his time dabbling in literature and anarchist politics" and "incapable of settling into any sort of work" (*Writer and Artist*, 84). Streeten
had apparently sought out Welch, as "the young artist with a reputation
for strolling around and talking to any available young rustic" (84).
Once the pair initiated a friendship, Streeten "quickly achieved the status
of Denton's most prized oddity," and Gerald Mackenzie observed that
"Denton frequently liked to be both attracted and repelled at the same
time. Streeten was a pathetically inadequate person, indecisive and physically broken," but "whatever his failings might have been, Streeten certainly possessed an agile mind and could be entertaining on a number of
topics" (85). His greatest gift, however, was his introducing Eric Oliver
to Welch on that auspicious day in November 1943.

The letters and annotations tell—much more accurately and poignantly than any textual or biographical summary—the course of the
developing relationship between Denton and Eric: the early episodes
of uncertainty, hesitation, and resentment caused by Eric's diffidence
about his sexuality, by his aimlessness, and by his serious bouts of drinking. Great good fortune allowed James Methuen-Campbell to get to
know Eric before the latter's death in 1995. Oliver clearly remembered the
circumstances of his being introduced to Welch, Methuen-Campbell
remarks, even though it had been nearly fifty years in the past:

> I had met Francis Streeten when I was working for the land army. I
> hadn't known him for long when, one rainy day—it was too wet to
> work—he came up to me and asked in his rather squeaky voice,
> "Would you like to meet a friend of mine?" I seem to remember we
> were working at East Farleigh and we got onto trains and buses and
> eventually came to Pitt's Folly near Tonbridge, where Denton lived.
> Francis really hadn't told me anything about Denton beforehand. And
> first of all Miss Sinclair opened the door and said that Denton couldn't
> see anybody, because he was upstairs and wasn't alright; and then he
> must have changed his mind, because he called us back and that was
> the first time I saw him.

I didn't think of him being ill. I just thought that I had never seen anybody like him before. I knew at once he was something out of the ordinary. Yes, I was interested in Denton right from the word go, although I don't think I was physically attracted towards him. (qtd. in *Writer and Artist*, 139)

From 1943 until the late summer of 1944, Welch and Oliver spent an increasing amount of time together, usually characterized by Eric's spending weekends or leaves with the writer at Pitt's Folly or in London. (Eric was doing alternative agricultural service, as he had been exempted from active military service due to high blood pressure.) Eric was intelligent and extremely handsome and had been something of an athlete during his school days. However, he had spent most of his early adulthood as an itinerant laborer, and he showed every likelihood that he would continue along this unsettled path indefinitely. Methuen-Campbell explains how the unlikely relationship between Denton Welch and Eric Oliver may have come about:

The contrast in their looks, for instance were extreme. Denton, though well-proportioned, was small in height, had tiny feet and walked with a slight limp. He had rather "doggy" eye-teeth, restless, darting eyes, a high and aristocratic forehead with unusual tightly-curled dark auburn hair and ears that turned down at the top. . . .

Eric on the other hand, had strong and handsome features. . . . [H]is overall physique was muscular and well-developed. . . .

But apart from the very obvious physical attraction, Denton soon discovered that his new friend was highly sensitive, acutely observant of other peoples' personalities and, above all, intensely insecure. As such, Eric posed no threat to him. A wonderful gentleness and an inability to intrude upon another person's thoughts or way of life were qualities Denton came to value highly as the friendship deepened. . . .

Denton saw his friend as a poignant figure, naïve, otherworldly and lost. He took it upon himself to comfort him and to make his life more interesting and purposeful. Each of them was obsessed with

death—it was something embedded in their psyches—and the obsession
itself became an unusual spiritual bond. In the moments when Denton
faced the ghastly limitations of his own life, he found that Eric was the
ideal person to talk to. His sympathy was instinctive. (*Writer and Artist*,
140, 144)

On July 8, 1944, Eric arrived at Pitt's Folly to tell Denton that his
hostel at Appledore had been destroyed by a German V-2 rocket and
asked if Denton would "put him up for awhile" (*Writer and Artist*, 153).
Eric eventually decided—to Welch's great joy ("great and wondrous
things")—to move in with the writer first at Pitt's Folly and then at
Middle Orchard (a house in Crouch, rented from Denton's artist friends,
Bernard and Noël Adeney). By this point, the friends had become sexu-
ally intimate, though, as Methuen-Campbell learned, "this aspect of the
relationship quickly fizzled out, and Eric later denied quite firmly that
he and Denton were ever 'lovers,' at least in the sense of being sexual
partners. What is more, he hardly found the description flattering, especially since Denton had to use a plastic sheet in bed so as to cope with
incontinence. In short, it was Denton who was physically attracted to
Eric, but not *vice versa*" (140). Nonetheless, Eric settled easily into the
role of caretaker, partner, and assistant. As Welch's relationship with
Eric gradually stabilized, his second novel, *In Youth Is Pleasure*, and a
number of short stories were accepted for publication (*In Youth* by
Routledge, "When I Was Thirteen" in *Horizon*, "At Sea" in *English
Story*, and "The Coffin on the Hill" and "The Judas Tree" in *Penguin
New Writing*). The degree of intimacy and cooperation between Eric
and Denton is clearly demonstrated in the letters and annotations, but
most poignant are Welch's concerns for his lover's welfare while he was
away on service. Both individuals experienced "near misses" from V-2
rocket attacks. In fact, one of Eric's friends had been killed in a rocket
explosion at the workers' boarding house near Appledore.

With the end of war came new ambitions and opportunities for
Welch, both domestic and creative. Though Denton and Eric began a
search for a home of their own in 1945, they were continually frustrated
in this ambition by a lack of funds. Welch had not received a hoped-for

legacy from his father's estate (Arthur Welch had died in a Japanese internment camp in 1943), and his commissions—either literary or artistic—were not enough to underwrite this project. They ultimately settled for an offer by the Adeneys to stay indefinitely at Middle Orchard.

Welch's popularity was growing: *In Youth Is Pleasure* (pub. 1945) had been enthusiastically reviewed by W. H. Auden in the *New York Times*, he was interviewed by Hector Bolitho for *Town and Country*, commissioned to do illustrations for *Vogue*, and invited by Michael Ayrton (of the BBC program *Brains Trust*) to exhibit his paintings at Heal's Gallery with sixteen other painters in a publicized exhibit of post-war works, and he had received an invitation to discuss his work over the BBC. From 1945 to 1947 Welch continued to write short stories and to paint, receiving a flow of commissions, including an offer by Hamish Hamilton to publish a collection of his short fiction, to be entitled *Brave and Cruel* (published posthumously in 1949). He had also begun work on his last novel, *A Voice through a Cloud*, which recounted the events of his injury and recuperation from 1935 to 1936.

The words "brave" and "cruel" could in fact be used to summarize the last two years of Welch's life. As his reputation grew, his health deteriorated. During the winter of 1946–47, his increasing bouts of fever and headache (caused by kidney and bladder infections, as well as a type of tubercular condition of the bone) were hampering his creative drive. In Welch's journal entry for February 2, 1947, he wrote, "The snow is still thick, and it falls fitfully, the flakes floating down, or driving more fiercely mixed with a little rain. As I lie in bed, only getting up twice a day, I feel I shall never walk about again. The effort seems tremendous. My legs sway and my head swims. . . . I wish to have stories and poems in many magazines. I want to finish my story [Michael De-la-Noy notes that this is probably *Brave and Cruel*] and my book [the novel *A Voice through a Cloud*] and get them to the publishers. I want to be a sausage machine pouring out good sausages, savoury and toothsome, delightful, desirable. I want pleasure and interest to flow out of me" (*Journals*, 320). In spite of his declining health, Welch tirelessly worked on proofs for the short stories to be included in the Hamish edition, as well as on paintings and illustrations for the Leicester Gallery and for *Brave and*

Cruel. As De-La-Noy points out, "It is hard to imagine how, in spite of ever more frequent and more painful bouts of illness, Denton managed to keep up the flow of work" (*Making of a Writer*, 279). The fact is that Eric's constant and affectionate attention made it possible for Welch to continue his work, against the inevitable force of fatal illness.

Attempted treatment for his condition had only resulted in increased pain or distress. On February 7, 1948, Welch related his pleasure in taking a drive with Eric, but also that this outing was hampered by "the difficulty I had in moving. Ever since Jack's [Dr. Easton, returned to practice following the war] lumbar puncture last year I've had to move about with painful care. If I don't, terrible pains shoot through me. . . . I should feel easier if I thought it was melting away, but it isn't. It has been there for about nine months and it is still fiery torture if I sneeze, cough or move about suddenly. And to be sick is quite out of the question—one just feels as if one was being torn apart by wild apes" (*Journals*, 350).

As a tribute to Welch's literary achievement (as it turned out, the last of his life), he received an invitation to visit Vita Sackville-West and Harold Nicolson at Sissinghurt on August 31, 1948. Welch's journal entry for the date seems, however, to be more interested in the Elizabethan architecture and appointments of the manor house and gardens than in the aging writer and her diplomat husband. Regardless of Welch's impressions of them, both Vita and Harold would take an active interest in his legacy as a writer. It was Harold Nicolson who wrote a review of *A Voice through a Cloud* for the *Observer* in 1950. He stated to Eric Oliver that "it is certainly an unforgettable work. . . . I should like to feel that he was remembered by this book above all the others, since I think it shows far greater power and assurance" (quoted in *Making of a Writer*, 288). Welch sent an advance copy of *Brave and Cruel* to Vita in November of 1948, for which she wrote a thank you on the day of his death, December 30, 1948 (*Making of a Writer*, 288). When she read Welch's obituary in *The Times*, she wrote to Eric, "I had so hoped that you and he would come here again next spring, and now it is not to be. . . . [I]t is dreadful that so brilliant a talent should be lost to the world. I know how good you were to him, and what care you gave him" (quoted in *Making of a Writer*, 288).

James Methuen-Campbell relates in painful detail the last hours of Denton's life:

> The morning of Thursday, 30th December was one that Eric would never forget. Much of the time Denton was distraught, crying out in fury and frustration that he was not ready to die. A letter had come from Paul [Denton's brother], but when Eric showed it to him, he just waved his hand aside, too weak to take an interest in it.
>
> Finally, Denton achieved some calm. He told Eric that in his mind's eye he could see children climbing over a gate. It was the last thing he said. Eric was sitting beside the bed when at two o'clock in the afternoon Denton died.
>
> On the mornings that followed, Eric, unable to face the reality of the situation, found himself running upstairs to Denton's room to show him what had arrived in the post. (*Writer and Artist*, 200–201)

Vita Sackville-West's sentiments in her note to Denton were couched in terms of grief at a truncated career and in gratitude for Eric's service to Denton during his partner's lifetime. However, Oliver's efforts to preserve the legacy of Welch's writing and art work extended well beyond the writer's death. As executor for Welch's estate, Eric Oliver not only took steps to preserve the manuscripts and many of the unsold paintings (now located at the Harry Ransom Center for the Humanities, University of Texas) but he tirelessly worked to see that Welch's unpublished work would in fact be eventually recognized. This he did either by himself, seeing through to publication certain of the manuscripts (including *A Voice through a Cloud*, *Brave and Cruel*, and *A Last Sheaf*), or by unselfishly assisting others in compiling editions of previously published or unpublished works, and in completing biographies of the author, including Jocelyn Brooke for the *Denton Welch Journals*; Jean-Louis Chevalier for *Dumb Instrument* (a collection of Welch's poetry and illustrations) and *I Left My Grandfather's House*; Michael De-La-Noy for his *The Journals of Denton Welch* and for the biography *Denton Welch: The Making of A Writer*; and James Methuen-Campbell for his biography, *Denton Welch: Writer and Artist*.

My sole regret in editing the letters of Denton Welch to Eric Oliver is that I was myself not able to meet and interview Eric, who died in 1995. It is, however, my privilege—and a measure of my debt to him for preserving the manuscript writings of an author I have grown to treasure—to transcribe and annotate this correspondence with what I hope is the sensitivity and understanding it deserves.

Denton Welch at Hadlow Road, Tonbridge, 1937. (photo by Gerald M. Leet, reproduced with permission of James Methuen-Campbell)

Denton Welch with baroque angels at Hadlow Road, Tonbridge, 1937. (photo by Gerald M. Leet, reproduced with permission of James Methuen-Campbell)

Top right: Denton Welch and Eric Oliver at Middle Orchard, 1946. (photo by Derrick L. Sayer, reproduced with permission of James Methuen-Campbell)

Bottom right: Denton Welch with his shells. (Harry Ransom Center, the University of Texas at Austin)

Denton Welch at his harpsichord. (Harry Ransom Center, the University of Texas at Austin)

Eric Oliver at Middle Orchard, 1946. (photo by Derrick L. Sayer, reproduced with permission of James Methuen-Campbell)

Denton Welch with his Victorian Doll House, 1946. (photo by Derrick L. Sayer, reproduced with permission of James Methuen-Campbell)

Denton Welch at Middle Orchard, 1946 or 1947. (photo by Derrick L. Sayer, reproduced with permission of James Methuen-Campbell)

Eric Oliver, 1990. (photo by James Methuen-Campbell)

Eric Oliver at Brighton, 1992. (photo by James Methuen-Campbell)

The Letters of Denton Welch
to Eric Oliver

Pitt's Folly Cottage Hadlow Road
W. Tonbridge Kent
November 17th Wednesday 1943

Dear Eric

Francis has just been in on his way back to Maidstone. I said that it was a pity I was ill when you both called, as it couldn't have been very amusing for you; but that I hoped you'd come in again another time.[1] He seemed to think that you might like to, when you felt at a loose end; so I am simply writing to say, look in when you're passing. If you're doing nothing this <u>Friday</u> or <u>Sunday</u> and would like to come to tea, please do so. I shall be in both days.

I wonder if you remember how to get here. You just take the Tonbridge 'bus from Maidstone & ask to be put down at Cuckoo Lane (the small stop before the larger one, Three Elm Lane.) <u>Don't</u> go down Cuckoo Lane, but retrace your steps towards Hadlow down the Hadlow Rd until you come to two lions on top of brick pillars. Walk down the drive and turn in at the <u>side</u> <u>door</u> <u>of</u> <u>the</u> garage when you will see another door on your left. This is mine. What a lot of instructions![2]

Sincerely yours
Denton Welch

ℒ♥

29th November

Dear Eric,

Hope you got home safely without a rear light. I saw a most enormous lorry pass me just after I'd left you. So nice to have you come over & so looking forward to seeing you again this Sunday. It is such a happy change for me to have someone to talk to after working most of the week.

ℒ♥

Thursday 30/11/43

My dear Eric,

I was so delighted this morning to get the book and your letter. It was very good of you to think of me and do what you said you'd do so punctually. As you can see, I wrote to you on Tuesday, but didn't post it at once. I also have found another letter I wrote to you after your second visit here. I don't know whether I shall send it now or not; I'll see. I also have the letter about Christmas day here. I put it in my pocket. It seems I have annoyed you by its coldness and dullness, so perhaps I won't send it back to you either. Dear Eric, do believe me when I say that I never intend to be cold or dull to you. You are the last person in the world I want to be that to. It is just training that makes me matter-of-fact and bald in letters. I also don't care of the idea of other eyes than the ones intended seeing them, and I know you have a naughty habit of leaving your letters about or showing them.[3] Even the most boring letter of mine I don't care to have exhibited in this way. This is just my particular fad. There is also such a great deal that cannot be said in a letter; it is too difficult.

Your letter to me I liked <u>so</u> much, but I could have wished that it had been much longer. I think in some ways it <u>must</u> be a good thing that we met and became friends. We both ought to be able to help each other somehow; but just at the moment I feel so cut off, far apart from you, as if you were someone a long way off at the end of a long, long telescope. It makes me sad that we are such different people and so cannot share my interests; and yet what I suppose I like in you and admire are the qualities I lack myself. Perhaps one day, if neither of us goes and dies suddenly! We shall gradually gain common experiences which we can share. Perhaps not; perhaps we drift quite apart. <u>I hope not</u>.

But whatever happens, know that I will always be your true friend, and that a part of me loves you and thinks about you as if you had been my brother. This letter is not supposed to be either dismal or sentimental. I only want to say what is in my mind. I shall love reading the book. Write to me again, saying anything you like. Your letter's privacy will be respected.

My love, D.

℘

p.m. 21 Dec. 1943 Kent

Dear Eric,

I don't think I shall be going away after all (at least not on Christmas day, perhaps the next) so do come over for lunch if you've nothing better to do and if you don't mind meagre fare. There may be nothing but Christmas pudding!

If you decide to come, I hope you'll be able to come, I hope you'll be able to get over. Someone tells me there won't be any buses on Christmas day, but perhaps you can borrow a byke.

I've been reading the transcript of my book all this morning,[4] so feel quite addled.

Noël Adeney and her son turned up here yesterday suddenly. If she turns up again at Christmas when you're there I think you will like her; but she may be up in London with her family.[5]

Hope to see you Christmas Day
Love D.

ℒ♥

1943 Dec 28th Tuesday

My dear Eric,

How I hope you got home safely after Christmas celebrations! I thought after you left that I should not have let you go; but in one way perhaps it was just as well, as yesterday I woke up with a particularly bad feverish attack and lay all day languishing with a most appalling headache. I am better today, thank the Lord, but still rather groggy, and am staying in bed. Isn't it awful to be at the mercy of bodies in this way! I do hope that you aren't feeling ill or worn out too. You must drink less Eric, else I feel that you'll absolutely ruin your health. You'd so hate to be invalidish. Do take warning. I feel so terribly sad about your drinking, perhaps there is no need, and you won't thank me for it, but there it is. I think, as you suggest, better not come over for a little, as I would be telling you this all over again, and the one thing I will not be taken for is a bore and a lecturer. It just isn't my line.[6]

We both as very different people, have to muddle our way thro' life as best we can. I probably at times get messed up and in a turmoil just as much as you do.

You know I would do whatever I could for you if you ever got into any unpleasant jam, so don't feel to [sic] lonely unless you want to!

Love D.

ℒ♥

Monday Jan 10th 1944

My dear Eric,

Thank you so much for nice letter. Yes, do come over, either on Sunday 23rd or this coming Sunday, whichever suits you best. I shall so look forward to seeing you.

I thought my last letter rather preposterous and almost decided not to send it, then I thought as an antidote to the Christmas one which (although you may not remember) you told me at the time was chilly, indefinite, and altogether vague and unsatisfactory; I don't seem to be able to strike the happy medium, do I! For heaven's sake, if you haven't already torn the last letter up, bring it with you when you come over. I will keep it here, if you want it preserved. I hate to think of your inquisitive landlady going thro' your pockets and cackling at my extravagances! and I won't have it, so please remember what I say![7]

I have been thoroughly enjoying the book you lent me. I read it all in one day or two. Very sound I think, but not much solution offered for general difficult problems.

I shall be going up to London soon to see another doctor about myself, but I think that very little can really be done about these high temperature attacks. I must simply lead a very quiet life, then they are less frequent.[8] Come to lunch about 1 o'clock if you can, otherwise I'll expect you in the early afternoon.

Love D.

∞♥

Sunday, January 16th, 1944

My dear Eric,

Thank you so much for sending the book, for your letters, and for doing what I asked you so punctually. I will keep them here for you, if you should ever want to lay your hands on them again. I have found an excellent place for them.

I wonder if you had a nice time with your mother this weekend; or whether it was hell; or whether it all fell thro' at the last moment as it did the last time.[9] I have just been here quietly writing a new book.[10] Yesterday Rosemary appeared with her mother. She was rather self-conscious and hardly dared mention your name. This amused me. I think she thought I'd be thoroughly annoyed and put out.[11]

Do you still work at Mereworth or have you moved on somewhere else?[12] I was over there the other evening. I bicycled, and went and walked about the churchyard in the moonlight. It is lonely there except for all those wretched bombers circling overhead and those peculiar lights which flash from the hillside.[13]

I have your book here for you when you come over. Come as early as you can won't you, then there's no rush. Marvellous about not going into the pub this year! You really seem able to do what you say you'll do, when you make up your mind.

Next Sunday it will be exactly a month since we've met, as you arranged! Looking forward to seeing you. To lunch 1 o'clock if you can manage it.

Much love D.

℘❤

January 16th 1944

My dear Eric,

So sorry to miss you this afternoon. I've just come in and Miss Sinclair's told me that she came back and found you looking very nice in grey suit![14] And that you were very polite & apologized for rowdy Christmas behaviour. You evidently went down very well with her!!

It is a curse you didn't come a little earlier. I had only gone into Tonbridge to post letters, buy stamps etc., and on the way back I sat by the wayside & had tea out of a thermos & read! Extraordinary weather for picnics! If I hadn't stopped, I would perhaps have been back before you left.

The late afternoon is the very worst time in all the day to catch me in; I nearly always go out. But the early afternoon—anything up to <u>three</u> or so—will generally find me here.

I rather wish you'd waited a little longer tonight, or perhaps you wanted to get back, or perhaps you thought Sinclair wanted to get on with the supper. Anyway, see you on Sunday for certain by first 'bus, unless you borrow a byke. Did you have a good time with your mother? Be good, and take care of yourself.

Love D.

𝓛♥

Jan. 30th 1943[15] <u>8:45</u> p.m.

Dearest Eric,

You have just gone and I am sitting over my supper, waiting to go in next door, & listening to "I will give you the keys of Heaven" on the wireless.

I want to say so much and I don't know where to begin.

<u>11.0 p.m.</u>

I have just come back from next door. My God, Eric; I feel just like you did at Noël's; blown out and completely fuddled. The conversation!!—like half-witted pea-hens screaming. They <u>would</u> talk in what they imagined to be a sophisticated way, and the result was painful to the extreme. O my dear; I really feel as if I'd been beaten all over. It makes me feel so ashamed & hot and cold when other people talk complete balls for two hours. The only nice thing was one of the women said "I only caught a glimpse of your friend, but I did think him extraordinarily handsome"!! This is <u>you</u> (when you were pumping Evie [sic] byke last week) in case you don't know! It pleased me very much that she said this. I expect she wanted to hear a lot more about you which was <u>not</u> forthcoming.[16] The man I was asked to meet was appalling;

about 20ish and so vapid and conceited that I felt uncomfortable for him. An actor going out to Near East & Italy, just like your sister.[17] I loathed him—and she said she thought he was of my persuasion & we'd get on so well! I can't stand those egoistic buggers. He could do nothing but cap everything that was said by repeating some ghastly made up story about his own exploits.

They are playing lovely Mozart music now on the wireless. It is such a relief after all that bloody silly talk. I wish you were here. You have a soothing effect on me and I feel rubbed up the wrong way. Don't mind if this letter's ga-ga. I'm drunk without wine as Evie says. A little "with" too, I think.

I have written three poems for you, may I, later, if I publish them, put your name or initials at the top? Tell me if you don't want me too [*sic*] and I won't, but I would like to.[18] I would like to dedicate my new book to you; but perhaps better not, as I think it should really be dedicated <u>publicly</u> to some highly respectable and eminent woman![19] Besides you may not like it as <u>you haven't</u> read it yet. I want to write all about you, so that years afterwards people will read it and think about us. They'll read how we had tea together or went for a walk in the moonlight wood. When we're in our cold cold graves, they'll be sitting cosily by the fire turning the pages! I'm always thinking of this. I want people to read about us 500 years from now.

If you want me to look after any things for you, bring them next week (if you come next week). I will take great care of them. But don't come next week if you don't want to (even if you aren't going to your brother's). It would be <u>awful</u> for me if I thought you come without particularly wanting to. All that month you stayed away it seemed perfectly right to me. I don't know why it did, and I don't know why I didn't miss you <u>much</u> more, consciously; but there it is—something seemed to make it quite right. I suppose you felt so too, else you wouldn't have done it. I wish I knew why exactly you did. I hope you didn't think I was thoroughly fed up with you, because I wasn't. I was only tired and felt everything was <u>hopeless</u> and I got sadder and sadder. In the drive when you said "shall I come back in a month" & I didn't answer, I thought, "Better not ever see him again, nothing's any good. Everything gets in more & more of a muddle." I felt I couldn't reach you at all and you were killing yourself. It's awful for me to think that you're killing yourself. It makes me wish I'd never met you. Everybody's life is so sad—yours is—mine is—we're all falling to bits. One is young for so short a time and it all rots away. I get this on the train sometimes and I get so alone feeling that I could burst.

When you were tight on Christmas, you brought this all out in me. Because I wasn't tight too; it worried me. I thought it was so terribly bad for you & you'd probably get run over & killed peddling about in the dark. O Eric don't get killed—don't booze too much—and know that I'll always do anything I can for you.

This is a drunken letter, but I'll send it to you with my love. P.S. Come, Sat. & spend the night & we can go out the next day; or come Sun. if you prefer; or don't come at all if you're going to your brother's, or you need a change of scene. I'll understand perfectly.

♌︎❤

Wednesday Feb. 9th 1944

My dear Eric,

How right and truthful you are. Your letter is <u>good</u>.[20] I am <u>quite</u> conscious, I think, of the true nature of your feeling for me. It is just, that you think I'm all right, I won't trip you up or double cross you; but that I'm not <u>really</u> down your street, and sometimes, just a bit hysterical. You find the barrier of our different temperaments much more insurmountable than I do. It is just that you <u>are</u> different that I like you. You wouldn't touch my imagination in the very least if you approximated more to my type.

But apart from this difference, I think there <u>are</u> some points which should bind us together, and I think they would, if you would allow them to. You seem so distrustful of your emotions & feelings that you appear to tear them to pieces every now and then.

You may be incapable of sustaining a feeling towards anyone for long, perhaps you are, I don't know; (from what you told me, your past certainly does sound a bit iffy and changeable!)

I don't think I <u>am</u> incapable in this way; and I can quite truthfully say that, apart from Jack Easton (for whom I had a quite overpowering obsession)[21] I have not been as fond of <u>anyone</u> as I have been of <u>you</u> over the last few months. But I think this feeling would die in a moment if I thought you really didn't give a damn for me. In fact let me explain once and for all dear Eric, that it is not your lusty body that is your chief attraction (I have seen many as lusty or lustier and they've not been of the slightest interest) but your essentially good nature. Your real self is surprisingly honest, generous, sensitive and affectionate. I could also reel off a list of your faults, but what is the point? You know them all, and they are not so important. The important thing is what is good in you, and what is good in you shines out very clearly. <u>I mean this</u>.

It would be unspeakably sordid in me, if you only came to see me or kept up with me because you thought I expected it of you. The whole idea of your trying to please me against your own inclinations is quite <u>disgusting</u>; and you would do it <u>so</u> badly Eric, because you're so truthful, so please don't ever try. I have the unpleasant fear that you may have tried, while you've been here. <u>How</u> unnecessary! I assure you (in spite of what you may think) that I am a very realistic and unsentimental person, and quite willing to believe that I am not in the <u>least</u> desirable or inspiring to you or to anyone else. It's easy to me to see that I'm probably quite grotesque in some people's eyes. This doesn't worry me. I have lived for so long without love—or rather without love of the right kind from the right person (there has been plenty of love from the wrong person)—that I am quite capable of going on living for the rest of my life without it. In some moods I would quite ruthlessly sacrifice all the lovers in the world to my work. I want to get something done, and shall do, I hope if I don't die. From this point of view it can be seen that love is probably not so overwhelmingly important to me as it is to some people. But in other moods, I am just as much in need of it, of course, as anyone else. But it seems to me that the most natural thing is to be devoted to one's work and yet be able to have great friendships as well. But if nobody is capable of loving one one must simply go without, and work instead. That is my philosophy. So don't ever think that I'd go crazy for lack of love. One can not force what isn't there. And it's no good my screaming at you or anyone else "Love me!" if it's impossible.

Perhaps it was rather naughty of you to tell Francis that you were attracted to me, if you <u>weren't</u>; and perhaps it was rather unthinking to be <u>very</u> determined at our first tea party, but these are things that everyone does, I suppose, and I don't hold that against you in the least, except that they put me in the difficult position of supplying goods that are not really needed!! However I shan't do it again & you may come and see me in the utmost safety, that is if you should ever want to in the future.

You've no idea how reserved and lighthearted and just ordinarily friendly I could have been with you if you hadn't so baldly and abruptly cleared the deck for action, as you did.

If you break down a person's defenses, you must not complain if they behave with unreserve towards you.

I would agree with you absolutely, over 100% love affairs being <u>very uncommon</u>, but doesn't that apply to everything in life? Aren't all our feelings, however strong, never quite as strong as we <u>think</u> they might be? Aren't they always mixed with some doubt; and aren't we always torturing ourselves and wasting time thinking, can this be love?—Am I really fond of that person?

I think that what is important is that one should be able to love another person <u>even</u> a tiny little bit. Usually one is quite incapable of the first step in this direction. Most people are of the utmost indifference to one. I am always delighted when I can feel a genuine interest, however mild in <u>anyone</u> else. I don't pretend that I would ever have loved you as insanely and unreasoningly as I love J. E.[22]—that sort of thing only happens when one is very young, very ill, and very inexperienced (besides, you wouldn't have liked it at all!)—but I do know that I would have been capable of loving pretty deeply, if you had wanted it. My feeling for you began just as an attraction and a liking, as these things always do, but I quickly felt, in spite of slight misgivings, that I accepted the essential <u>you</u> as something that I admired and respected, and this made me <u>very</u> happy. Usually I don't have this feeling, at all; whatever my association with the person may have been, I still feel indifferent, unmoved by their real self.

It seems to me that we are all going to die so soon, that we ought to snatch at everything we can, and swallow it gratefully. Love or no love, I'm grateful for having known you and I don't suppose anything else ought to really matter. No harm has been done.

How horribly pompous and gloomy this all sounds! All I want to say is, I wish you'd just be happy and gay if you've enjoyed knowing me <u>at all</u> and not <u>bother</u> whether you <u>love</u> me or not. It ought to be quite obvious by now that I have felt love for you; but I also felt love for my Siamese cat and have got over it now that it is dead!

Although I may be slightly younger than you, you make me feel so old, so immensely old, like a stone image on a mountain watching small boys play; then another time it is completely different and I'm the small child and you're telling me what to do. My whole attitude to you is this mixture of wanting to protect and wanting to be protected. It is all utterly hopeless I suppose. Usually I am never caught like this. I am far too wary to take anyone at his face value (ask Francis, he thinks I'm awfully metallic & heartless) but I suppose I was rather misled by your affectionate disposition. You <u>do</u> rather slap it on Eric—and if you mean to steer clear of entanglements you <u>must</u> keep a <u>colder</u> exterior. No wonder the landlady's daughter rubs your back with embrocation! Which reminds me that Rosemary[23] wrote yesterday asking me to tea on Sunday and saying that if I had anyone staying with me for the weekend, would you bring them too! This <u>is</u> a hint isn't it!

Right to the end she put "I hope Eric kept his vow about not boozing too much." The poor girl is longing to be pounced on again. I told her that unfortunately you'd been moved to Appledore. This bloody letter will go on forever, if I don't stop, and I have wasted all morning writing it. It will probably bore you stiff, but I suppose sometimes one has to try to get certain things said.

I <u>am</u> aware of your state of mind, but of course your letter has made it clearer, leaving no possible room for doubt.

It was a good letter, your very best, both interesting & unusual. You have a thoughtful and practical mind. Always write like that, if you ever do again. Christ! If you told me you loved me, when you didn't, I should be sick.

It is useless for you to go on thinking that I can't understand you or sympathize with you or enter into your feelings, or love you, because I can. I don't have a fancy picture of you before my eyes. I am perfectly shrewd, almost cynical about you. You're no angel, nor am I. We're just two human beings that have to flounder thro' life as best we can. If you don't want to flounder any of the way with me you'd just better say so, not put the blame on me. If I hadn't felt any love for you, I just wouldn't have taken any notice of you. I don't care a fuck for most people; they're just like so many peas in a pudding to me. Casual acquaintances, I feel I never want to see again too.

I am very annoyed with you now, because I think you are utterly shallow and not worthy of any deep feeling at all; but perhaps this is just because my vanity is piqued, who can tell? At any rate, deep down I feel glad that you wrote like that because frankness however painful does clear the air. I have been wearing the signet ring (I hope you don't mind) but now I have taken it off and put it away somewhere safe with your snuff box. Don't forget you've left them here will you? I can send them to you, whenever you want them.[24]

It is difficult now, and perhaps not worth the trouble, to go backwards step by step in our relationship till we have reached the coolest of cool friendliness; so God knows whether we'll be meeting in the future, or what will happen. It really all depends on your true state of mind (with no monkey tricks or pretences). I have already stated mine with embarrassing clearness and sincerity.

You have humiliated me; but you like doing that, and I can stand it, if you really have any feeling for me behind the surface cruelty; but if you haven't, for God's sake bugger off somewhere else. I have enough difficulties emotional, physical, mental, on my hands without the added wrong of a totally one sided affair. I go quite hot with shame to think you may only have come to see me, because I wanted you to. And there was I, fussing and arranging, and scrounging food & drink because I thought you liked coming! It is too ludicrous, like one of those silly plots for a farce or musical comedy.

I would never expect to have 100% of your love. I think you are constitutionally incapable of being constant, faithful, persevereing [*sic*], what-you-will. But it seems that I made myself very ridiculous in expecting even 1%. Why on earth didn't you make all of this clear at our first meeting? No doubt you are attracted to thousands of people. But why give me the impression that you are attracted to me <u>at all</u> (and you did give me this impression) if you really find me quite repulsive in mind and body? It's all such a bloody mess, and I mustn't write any more. I have already written too much.

I suppose I should have realized at once that the whole set-up was extremely phoney and not likely to last a moment; but I didn't; I was cuckoo enough to imagine that two people had met who, although different, might sometimes be a comfort or a help to each other.

Don't be annoyed if I appear to abuse you in this letter. I am really abusing myself. (don't laugh) You will realize that it is not the letter to have about for the 17 year old boy to see or anyone else. Please destroy it at once, or put it in this envelope & send it back to me. You needn't trouble to write yourself.

I am unable to put 'Love' 'yours ever' or any of those things; they seem to mean nothing at all for the moment. I don't even particularly want to sign my name; but no doubt if you're very clever you'll be able to guess who its [sic] from!

D.T.O.

P.S.

I have a very low fountain-pen that I found on my bed after a friend & his girl had been lying there! I was out, and they waited for me in my room but then went off before I returned, leaving the pen behind them! It's not very nice but it works, so if you need a pen I'll send it. I don't want it. I always write with this Parker Duofold. It might be easier to have fountain pen by you than always to have to pinch a post office one! Where did you pinch the ink from? You'll be in gaol yet.

The rain is pouring down in great gusts and its getting dark and I'd like to knock your teeth down your throat, if I knew that it wasn't such an impossible wish.

✐

Pitt's Folly Cottage
Nr Tonbridge
Kent

Saturday Feb 12th 1944

Dear Eric,

Please forgive insolence and rudeness in last letter, if there was any, and I feel there must have been; but I suppose I was a bit upset because you didn't seem to care about anything at all.

Perhaps you are right, and it's really bloody silly to make a fuss about love and friendship and everything else; but just sometimes one has the feeling that it's awful to go through life so <u>absolutely</u> alone, and one longs there to be contact with another human being. I think you make a mistake when you feel I can't understand your different states of mind. You must remember that I have a great many difficult states of mind to deal with myself since my accident. I have been terribly ill, and nearly dead, and terribly unhappy, and feeling that I'd go quite dotty with it all. This surely wouldn't make me blind to your problems, although they might be different ones.

If I talk very little about illness and appear not to notice your quick changes of mood, it isn't that I'm blind, it's simply that I feel we've all got to behave as normally as possible and get on as best we can; otherwise we might all sit down and go quite cuckoo. There is no need for you to pretend in the <u>least</u> thing with me; and I will try never to pretend with you.

Yesterday evening I bicycled to Penshurst and thought of you as I passed the house and village. I thought of you winning the prize in the race there. I think I must have been in Tonbridge at the same time as you were there. I wish we'd met then. It was the worst time in my whole life. And it would probably have helped me to know someone like you.[25]

I went back the other way thro' Leigh and wondered if I passed anywhere near where you lived.

The wireless always seems to be playing Mozart when I write to you. It is doing it again! I don't know whether it makes me write much better or worse.

I hope you find your new place bearable, with pleasant companions not too noisy, when you don't want them to be. Is the work the same or different?

I don't think I'll write to you any more after this, as you must find it an awful curse feeling that you have to answer. You can't be very fond of writing in your spare time.

Once more let me say how sorry I am if you found my last letter a silly and unwanted and rude outburst. I just felt a bit frustrated; as if you'd treated me rough and thrown my feelings back in my face, because you thought they were bogus.

I can't help thinking of you a bit now; but I don't suppose I'll mind a bit soon.

Goodbye for now,
Denton.

𝒟♥

10 p.m. Tuesday Feb. 15th 1944

Dear Eric,

You don't feel far away, unless you want to, will you?—The fleabag's always here for you; so just come and use it when you get fed up with your hostel and want some peace, or a change of scene. I <u>shall</u> enjoy hearing your news.

Ever yours
Denton
I'm always here.

ℒ♥

Feb. 18th 1944

Dearest Eric,

For heaven's sake don't fuss! Your letter made me cry <u>literally</u>. I can't bear you to spoil everything by all this wrong. What <u>does</u> it matter if you pinch anything of mine or not! I give it to you beforehand. So if you want anything just take it as a present. Remember that you can't lift anything of mine because it automatically turns into a present. Remember too that I would gladly send you anything you need (If I can) wherever you are. You only have to write.

I am <u>not</u> right and tight and smug and prim. I judge <u>nobody</u>. You don't have to put a "proper" act on with me, because I'm not "proper"! I need no living up to <u>at all</u>. Of course I'd be upset if you drank too much & hurt your health, but that's just common sense—nothing to do with thinking drink's wicked.

In many ways I should love to be able to drink more myself with no awful after effects. I have <u>always</u> felt this way. Unless you simply want to get rid of me, I can see absolutely <u>no</u> reason for your behaviour. Perhaps you do just want to do this and I should just take the hint; but I feel I can't do this without explaining myself completely to you, so that there can be no misunderstanding:

I make absolutely <u>no</u> demands on you at all. You don't have to be fond of me, write to me, or pay me any attention at all, unless you feel like it! And I understand completely when you <u>don't</u> feel like it.

But if and when you do feel the least bit fond of my company, or, in need of a change, it would have been wicked and pointless to me if you just cut yourself off from me, because you thought our lives and our circles of friends were too different to mix well.[26]

I would gladly swop [*sic*] all my circle of friends for you, and if you really don't even want to meet my middle-aged women you needn't. It gives me the greatest pleasure to lock them out and be only with you.

You <u>don't</u> interfere with my work, unless, at the moment, you make me thoroughly unhappy and muddled by your seeming to want to cut me off from you completely.

There seems absolutely no reason for this (unless of course you find me utterly boring and distasteful). Life is so terribly short we <u>must</u> love each other a little, else what's the good of living at all? And think of the long time when we'll be dead and utterly alone.

Do please <u>think</u> before you decide to cut yourself off from me in this ruthless way.

If you decide to, I suppose I shall just have to submit to it, but it seems to me <u>terribly</u> unnecessary and cruel, and I would never be able to forget it.

I know I love you. I'm not beglamoured or silly about you, I just love you and accept you, just as I accept and love my brother Paul, or anyone else I'm fond of.

Do <u>please</u> try to accept me, just as the person I am with <u>all</u> my <u>faults</u> and foibles. Things would be so much easier if you just took me for granted and didn't worry about the situation at all.

We've all done shoddy things in our time, I suppose. If you say I don't really know what things you're capable of, I can say the same about myself. In certain moods we're all absolute bastards at heart, but that doesn't seem to matter very much to me. The real self is much better than that and that's what is important.

I really couldn't take such presents as your ring & your snuff box; I have done nothing to merit such valuable presents and, although it is wonderfully generous of you to offer them to me, I must send them straight back to you, if you <u>really</u> never want to see me again. That would make it even more impossible for me to accept them.

I can't believe that you value love and friendship so lightly, that you can just cut yourself off from them capriciously, but if you do and can, and you really want to make this a complete split, don't you think that you should at least leave it in the air until we can meet again and talk utterly frankly about it? Letters are so unsatisfactory and I feel that whatever is said may be taken up wrongly by either party.

You know you can come here <u>whenever</u> you want. I would offer to come & see, but this doesn't seem so suitable, as I might not be allowed into your area and there probably wouldn't be anywhere to talk.

Dear Eric, don't let's be tragic and gloomy about our affection for each other. Our lives are already much too full of unpleasant possibilities and problems. Can't we snatch just a little pleasure for ourselves, and not think of tomorrow or the next day? Circumstances will probably be only too ready to divide us and keep us apart. Isn't it for us <u>not</u> to be destructive and critical? Shouldn't we at least try to have some moments of understanding and gaiety? Neither of us need demand or expect anything of the other. I don't demand or expect your love or any part of it.

Christ, Eric please don't spoil everything so wilfully. It really breaks my heart (whatever that phrase means.)

I swore never to burden you with this sort of letter again, nor would I, if I felt I did not have to make my position absolutely clear. You owe nothing to me, and I fully realise this. We are two separate persons. But does this mean that we're never to meet or find any enjoyment in knowing each other? Must we really be absolutely lonely all our lives? If you care anything for me at all, won't you make some sort of effort to see me fairly soon, or tell me what effort you'd like me to make, so that we can talk instead of writing these terrible frustrating letters.

Don't bother to answer this, just wait until we meet again.

If you'll let me know the time of the train, I'll go into Tonbridge to meet you.

Do come to see me very soon, this weekend, or next, or any time, if only to get this thing settled.

Now that I've written this, it looks as if I'm trying to make you do what I want. — You will of course only do what <u>you</u> want. I am powerless to influence you and wouldn't want to, even if I could. You must only do what your heart wants.

At any rate you know now what I think.

I love you and trust you,
Denton

✐

Feb 23rd 1944 Wednesday

My dear Eric,

I was so <u>delighted</u> to get your letter. Yes—do come on Saturday, as soon as is convenient for you.[27] I shall be here. You know how to get here do you? If you take a train to Tonbridge, then get on Hadlow or Maidstone 'bus (No 7) outside station. They go just after the hour & half hour, I think.

If you'd like me to meet you in Tonbridge, tell me time of train and I'll be on platform.

I'm sorry you're hating the hostel and the boys; I thought you might be enjoying it from your first letter. Perhaps you'll be able to talk about it more when we meet. Sods to hold your ration books to ransom! But I'm glad you didn't go after all.

I'm so happy to think you're coming that I can't write any more. It seems ages since you went, although it's not yet three weeks.

On Monday I was in the Checquers at Ightham drinking gin all alone. It was terribly gloomy. The gin reminded me of you, for some reason, and I thought you'd disappeared for good.[28] But it wasn't true after all. I shall see you Sat.

Meanwhile, my love, D.

✐

Saturday March 4th 1944

Dear Eric,

Here's your shirt. I did it myself, as I think the little man in the town has packed up. I do hope it will be alright and that it doesn't look too unprofessional. I am not exactly a trained needleman! At any rate, I think it ought to be strong while the cloth lasts, as I sowed [*sic*] it with tough thread and did a good deal of knotting and licking & going over and over.

Nothing much has been happening here. I was sick the other night when bombs began to drop. The bombs didn't make me sick, but it just so happened that everything began at once. I am all right again now.

I've been v. busy trying to get a short story done & my decorations for the book.[29] I think it was all this work that made me sick.

Someone is coming to see me tomorrow whom I don't particularly want to see. To keep the person at bay I shall have to be very bright & talk a lot and sit rather a long way a way [*sic*]; unless I get Miss S. to chaperon [*sic*] me![30]

However I don't know why I should be mentioning this to you, since you always think I'm silly in suffering people when I don't want to. This can't exactly be avoided tho,' as I've just had the letter announcing the visit.

I've been wondering what sort of week you've been having. Fairly good, I hope.

I rather liked John. He seemed quite nice & sensible. I think somehow though, that he should insist on his girl <u>not</u> walking home with the dough boys, or she'll probably be garotted one night. I thought he took it <u>much</u> too calmly when he said that the man probably had a brainstorm.[31]

What I really wanted to do in this letter was to thank you for being so very good to me last Sunday when I felt weak-kneed. I hate showing you that side of myself, but your sweetness in trying to put me right just seemed to save my face. There can be nothing much wrong with you, if you can do impulsive good things like that.[32]

Ever your D.

March 7th 1944. Tuesday.

My dear Eric,

It was fine to have your letter this morning. I was beginning to wonder whether I should hear from you again. I did not write to you last week (although I wanted to) because I thought that you didn't much like hearing from me, as you felt you had to answer. You never have to, of course, but you sometimes give me the feeling that I worry you; and that is what stopped me writing.

I waited until Saturday & then just sent the shirt off with a small note. I hope you got the shirt and that it's all right and not done too unprofessionally!

I suppose (if I must tell you the truth) I was unhappy last time we met because I felt very fond of you and yet not much good to you. I had the feeling that you'd probably much rather be with another, different type of person, and I was just rather a strain and a nuisance. I felt that you couldn't really like me, and I wanted you, like anything, to like me.

I suppose too I was in that state because, as you say, I pity myself sometimes. I feel that all my youth since 19 has been wasted on being ill and getting a little better & being ill again. It's made everything such a terrific strain and effort. That's why I'm jittery and nervous, and self-conscious.

And I wish like anything that this wasn't so and that I could have enjoyed myself and done a lot of silly things like anyone else. I feel that all my earliest days, which should have been best, have been spoilt for me; and I lie down and wallow in it sometimes!

However, I don't mean to again with you, if I can help it! I should hate to repay you in that way for being so kind to me.

I've never had a friend like you before, and I don't suppose I ever shall again. I say this just straight out, because it's true. You've done something for me quite different.

I don't know what I'd do if you walked out on me. I suppose I'd just go on living as I do now, but I know I'd distrust people more & more and I'd think that things were worse than they are.

(Don't you wish you could read all those crossed out words!) (They're not very interesting really.)[33] O God, Eric, I always seem to get gloomy and full of the state of my own feelings when I write or talk to you, and all I really want to do is to amuse you or make you feel happy!

Come Saturday; it will be <u>fine</u>. Shall I expect you sometime in the afternoon? I shall be here all the time so just turn up. Lovely!—I will get some beer in.

The sod who came to see me on Sunday drank some of the last lot. God! and wasn't I bored and disgusted with him! I suppose I was comparing him with you all the time, which didn't exactly work out in his favour. He didn't seem to be a real person at all—just a lump of dough. But we needn't talk about him.

My pictures' [*sic*] come out in this month's 'Vogue' with a little bit about me. Absurd, isn't it! I look rather hearty in the picture and rather peculiar all together, I'll show it to you, if May let's me keep the 'Vogue'![34]

My eldest brother, Bill, the one I'm rude about in the books, is coming home! I hope he won't bring a libel action or come down to Pitt's F.C. with a revolver or anything! If he does, will you come and be a thug for me and help to put him on the mat?![35]

"Goodnight, Beloved Comrade" (These are the words of a Negro song I heard) I like them. They say what I want to say to you.

D.

ℒ♥

Tuesday March 14th 1944

Just a line, <u>dear</u> <u>Eric</u>, to say that I hope you got a connection soon in Tonbridge & did not have to wait because the weekday trains are not the same as Sunday ones.

I <u>did</u> so enjoy having you for the weekend, although I felt <u>absolutely</u> exhausted last night, and slept this morning almost solidly till quarter to nine!

I expect the gin on Sunday helped, by upsetting my guts a bit, but I don't think I'll have any bad effects if I take it easy today & tomorrow.

Anyhow, I'm glad I had it, for I think it made our talk in the wood more possible—and the talk was a good thing, don't you think? Even my boozy, weepy state was a good thing because it helped me to talk about what gnaws at me rather—the fear, I have that it is absolutely impossible for you to find anything to like in me at all. I feel so lonely and deserted when I have this fear that I'm at my very worst. I'm sort of defenceless then, and that makes me try to cling on to you too desperately.[36]

When I'm bad like that, if you could just reassure me a bit, as you did in the wood, you'd put me right. I'm so conscious of the quality I lack—you've no need to tell me—it hits me in the eye everyday when I wake up. And this knowledge makes it difficult for me to believe that you care anything for me at all. I feel awful, and absolutely left out in the cold, if I can't believe that there's some little bit of me somewhere that might vaguely resemble your cup of tea. I suppose I should not allow you to see this longing that I have for a little bit of your affection. Worldly-wise people would certainly tell me that it is the very worst possible way of going to work; but it seems that I have to be <u>quite</u> truthful with you. I even have to admit it when I have told you that I am nearly 27 when I am nearly 28. And for me to have to confess that I've told a silly, petty, pointless, vain lie like that is <u>very</u> difficult.

I have also had to tell you things about my accident which never cease to give me pain, humiliation and embarrassment.[37]

I can tell anyone hardly about these things, and I try to go on from day to day pretending to everyone that I'm really perfectly all right. It puts a pretty good strain on me, and I sometimes feel fit to bust.

The fact that I used to be so hardy and free from all that sort of thing makes my present messed-up state very hard to bear with a good grace. It's given my conceit and pride a smack which it won't ever forget, and I have to use quite a lot of will power sometimes, not to feel rather dotty and hysterical about it.

Dear Eric, I know you are too kind and decent ever to talk about my problems, mental and physical, to other people; that is why I can tell you. I have to risk putting you <u>completely</u> off me. Perhaps I have already. But there it is. I can't put on an act for you. I know that faint possibility that I just might be well-known one day (if I don't die) doesn't cut any ice at all with you. I would hate it if it did. It's all muck to me, compared with the feeling I have for you.

(Please don't think it vain of me to talk about being well-known in that open way. It doesn't look too good now I've written it down)

I really think that in some ways I am the complement of you and that because of that we can be good for each other, in spite of ourselves. You say that I can bring the best out in you, and you certainly do the same to me. The process may not always be particularly pleasant, it's much more comfortable to have the good in one left quietly alone. I sometimes feel that it would be much easier for me to be faky and glittery and superficial with someone else than sober truthful and ordinary with you. I'd much rather be the last, because it's real, but the other would be much less effort because it's so shallow and means nothing.

I have to make efforts with you and you no doubt have to make efforts with me. But I think that should be <u>very</u> good for both of us. We just haven't got to be too lazy, and sloppy and stuck in our own grooves. And after all this dwelling on our differences, aren't there some things in which we are rather alike, under the surface?

I think the very fact we were both born in the same year, both ran away from school, both had brothers from whom were somehow cut off, should in itself bind us together.[38]

All thro our lives we have been babies, infants, children, boys, youths at the same moment although utterly unknown to each other. And all that time we have been searching for the same thing.

I think we would be <u>crazy</u> and <u>wanton</u> now to reject each other just because some parts of the pattern didn't fit absolutely perfectly. Nothing in the world ever does fit absolutely perfectly.

I wish with all my heart that I could realize all your ideals and be something all sufficing to you, but this would be a tall order for any human being and certainly an impossible one for a person like me.

All I can do is be as true & real with you as I can, and hope that somewhere is a side of my nature which you can respect.

If I fuss you and worry you, it is only that I want you to be as comfortable as possible and I can't believe anything's right. I'm absolutely unused to being with anyone else I like, and so it gives me a sense of responsibility. I also want to look after you, because I think you don't take proper care of yourself. You may think this is all very feminine and unnecessary, but there it is. Just put up with it, or tell me to shut up.

I must too say I'm sorry for trying to thrust money on you in that impulsive, vulgar, offensive way. That too is part of my anxiety neurosis about you. I feel that you may really be needing money, and it seems awful that I should have any here lying idle.

I haven't much money now that my Pa's dead and his estate all un-settled and buggered up by the Japanese,[39] but what I have & what I can earn, I would always want you to make use of, if need arises.

If you ever wanted anything, I'd love to get it for you; if I had the dough.

Yesterday I had another fan letter from a guy who wants to paint a picture of me! Can you beat it! I don't know what to answer. "What would you do chum?"!!

I've been correcting my new story for "Horizon" all this morning. I think it's awfully peculiar and don't know what the great British Public will think. I hope it will shake them and send electric shocks down their spines.[40]

I feel awfully sadistic about the reading public. Don't you think they ought to be woken up? I shall probably get myself locked up for "obscene reference." You will have to come and feed me thro' the bars then. Good-bye Comrade Oliver till Sat. week D.V.

From your friend D.

D.

Wed. March 21st 1944

My dear Eric,

I don't mind if you poke fun at tubes;[41] I can take it—from you. You never worry or offend me as many of the women I know do. This weekend Noël, and Frida Easdale came to see me and made me feel like an addled egg.[42] I wished I could have swopped [*sic*] them for you. I understood absolutely what you mean when you say that you think women are affected and you wish they would stop talking!

Yesterday I sat in the haystack where we picnicked and had my lunch there again.[43] But the sun wasn't shining and so it wasn't so nice.

Did you go about Friday without a shirt? You will soon add to the brown which you have kept from last year. I also want to go out and sit in the fields with no clothes on, as I did last year. I do hope you will be near here in the summer, so that we can go down to the river together. I used to go there and sit on the banks and read & write and eat nearly every day last summer.

I liked your letter so much. Don't let's worry about evening up, or cancelling out our feeling for each other. I think it's a wonder that we like each other at all. I really think that this is a wonder, because I've never before been able to establish so much contact and feel so happy with as different from me as you are.

You are a delightful change for me, and you teach me a lot. I only wish that I'd known you a long time ago. It would have helped it, and I thought I never would. I had begun to think that it was quite impossible—that a person like you could have understanding or feel interest in a person like me. The fact that you can, even a bit, has really made me much less pessimistic.

There have just been two colossal bangs!—bombs, I suppose; which reminds me that I am not really brave, as you suggest. I suppose I have the quality which makes people salvage as much as they can from the wreckage![44] I've certainly had to do that with myself after my accident; but I don't think that's bravery; that's just making the best of a bad job. What is peculiar is that I feel quite brave when I'm with you. I feel much more able to face an unforeseen thing that may happen. I suppose what I really imagine is that you'll be able to cope with the situation, and this gives me a freedom and bravado, because I think you'll do the dirty work!

I am so looking forward to seeing you Saturday. I have just taken the empties back to the Brooms and got some more beer![45]

I hope we will be able to talk again deeply and say exactly what we think. It isn't always easy, but sometimes time and circumstances are just right and things can flow.

You needn't ever be afraid of offending me or hurting me, you know. As I've said before, I really can take an awful lot, and I like more than anything to know the true feelings of another person. Nothing else matters but that.

I'm glad we're quits about telling mild lies. It takes all seriousness away from it and only makes it funny! You must tell me the naked truth about the General story, if you feel like it. I'd love to hear.[46]

Dear Eric, I always write too much to you, because I don't know how to stop. I ought to stop now because it is getting late. The aeroplanes are droning about, the All Clear has gone. I sit here under the wooden angels wings and with the lamp all shaded and draped with newspaper.[47] Miss S. is fumbling in her room going to bed. I wish you were here with me now, when it is utterly quiet and still and peaceful. I want to tell you all my thoughts.

It's fine knowing a person like you. It's made a terrific difference to me.

Good night, sleep tight, (only in the best sense of the word of course) you know how much regard I have for you, so I need not say anymore.

From your friend D.

Ɫ♥

March 29th 1944 Wednesday

Thanks so much, dear Eric, for remembering my birthday and writing to me on it. I was awfully pleased to see your handwriting and to think that you had bothered. But on <u>no account</u> must you spend your money on me, not even a tiny bit. You'll embarrass me and make me feel a skunk if you do. You have already given me <u>so</u> many things, and <u>such</u> nice things, that I'd feel terribly uncomfortable to receive anything more.[48]

You know what you're like when I try to give you anything, so just remember.

Of course, I'd much rather the Demon Drink didn't swallow up your finances, because I think He has often completely messed up your life; but there is no excuse to spend what you save from Him on me! There are so many things, like clothes, etc. to buy for yourself. Anyhow, have you remembered that you gave me [a] complete page of personal points on Sunday? Surely that's present enough. It's more than anyone else has ever done!

I can't repay, too, things like your goodness to me when I'm ill. Instead of sitting down and reading, and then going out for a drink, you stay by me and do all you can to ease my discomfort and pain. This made an enormous difference at the week-end. I wouldn't have been nearly so well on Sunday, if you hadn't behaved as you did.

No one else has ever done this for me, either.

All these last 4 months have been different for me, anyhow,— something quite new. When I look back to the beginning, I see that I must have been getting set and ready for this new phase in my life. Nothing had happened to me for so long and all my interest seemed in my work, but underneath I knew that I was working up to some new thing in my life.

It was funny when I heard you and Francis murmuring lowly to Evie in the kitchen, when I was up here in bed. I thought, "I can't see another bloody person, my head's splitting. Francis would be the last straw. That baby voice! Those unspeakable teeth!" Then I thought "Who's he got with him?" and I knew that something was going to happen. I must always thank Francis for swinging you into my ken. It was a pretty mean thing that we didn't meet; I wouldn't see you for quite a long time. And if I hadn't seen you that day, I doubt if you would ever have come again, because Francis left so soon after that.[49]

I can only be grateful for the something which made me change my mind at the last moment.

Today I am in bed again. Isn't it a curse. My temp. is only 99, but I feel low and rather useless. I am going to take things very quietly for some little time, to see if it makes any difference to my comfort and well being. If it doesn't I shall just go back to doing as much as I can manage. It is really no use my being super careful if no good arises.

————

Now it is night, and Noël has been here all afternoon talking with me. She brought me [a] very pretty little antique watch pinchbeck and blue glass with white enamel face. (The silver one at Christmas I broke the hair spring of) She also had made me a cake and put a large pink 'D' on it.

So I had a very nice birthday in spite of my guts. One aunt sent me a £1 and another her kind regards! And most amazing of all, I had a wire from my brother Bill who has arrived in England and is staying at the Conservative Club!!![50]

Isn't this frightful? He'll be down here any day now, because I've written to say I've not been well. He'll read both my new book and the 'Horizon' article which comes out in April. This worries me far more than it ought to, I suppose. I feel very guilty about maligning him in print. I think that it will hurt his feelings more than it was ever meant to; I felt that he'd be out of the country and that he'd never read anything I wrote.[51]

It is nearly eleven o'clock and the wireless is playing wild Scotch reels that make me want to jig.

Evie has been a terrible bitch all day. I suppose I've insulted and offended her and she wants to get her own back. I hate her like anything when she's like this. It's specially awful when I'm ill.

I've had another amazing fan letter. This is from a girl in Free French Forces, Volontaire Rose-Marie Aubépin!!! What can I do for this poor girl? She's dying to come and see me & my house, but I wouldn't be the slightest good to her. I'm thinking I'll have to ask you here and secret you in the cupboard; then perhaps if you liked the look of her, you could appear at the right moment & I could tactfully withdraw.[52]

If you're going to your mother's, won't you want to take the sheets to her. Or doesn't she need them yet? Do you want me to send them to her? I can, if she's now at the address you gave me.

I wish I could rid my mind of the thought that you come to see me, because you think it pleases me. I wish I thought that you did it purely to please yourself.

I think I talk to you too much about popping oneself off.[53] It's only because I think I'm going to have a very sticky death, and so I want to be able to do myself in as bearably as possible, before I have too much lingering and languishing. Anyhow, perhaps I'll live for years, in spite of all my imaginings & premonitions. Tonight I don't feel as if I would though! I feel as if everything is falling to pieces, and I'm the chief piece of garbage!

I must say good night, Eric. It's nearly midnight and I ought to try to sleep. I wish you were here with me.

———

March 30th. <u>Thursday</u>
I will just finish this letter off now and send it to the post. I've been working all morning on my book decorations,[54] but now I'm a bit ill again and am lying on the bed. I really seem stricken down this time by a much longer bout.

The day before yesterday I found my pass-port,[55] and it has my date of birth & everything marked in it, so I will show it you and you won't think I'm quite crooked as to tell you two lies!! It also has a really horrible picture of me at the age of sixteen, with black-button eyes, awful crimpy hair that's come out much too dark, and a frightful cod fish expression. I have very fat cheeks. I remember thinking at the time that it was taken that it was one of the cruellest caricatures I had ever seen.

Talking about photos, when you go to your Ma's won't you look up some old snaps for me? I'd love to see them; and later I could make a picture out of a good one. Do bring me some to look at, if you can.[56]

That would be an awfully good birthday present for me. I am living in fear and trembling of finding an agrieved [sic] brother standing on the door step. I wonder what he will look like now. I haven't seen him since about 1937.[57]

You're not going to drink a lot this week-end, are you Eric. I sound a bit temperance preacher; I suppose it's my high temperature. I think what stops hundreds of people drinking is that they get the habit of reading a lot. Once you've got it, you feel awfully content and not bored when the day's work is done. It doesn't always work of course, but generally. I know that's what keeps me going when I'm more or less alone for days.

I mustn't drink for a long time. I'm afraid those five gins and byke riding set all this off; but perhaps it would have happened anyway.[58]

Good-bye, be good. You know that I am your devoted friend,

D.

Wednesday April 5th 1944

My dear Eric,

It <u>was</u> good to have another letter from you—especially as I didn't expect it. I had made up my mind that you wouldn't write again and that I'd hear no more until I saw you. It's always nice to be proved wrong in these things!

I've been thinking about you a lot wondering what you were doing and how you were feeling, but I had decided not to write again, knowing what a fag answering is sometimes. I've been thinking over those stories of your past you told me and picturing it all to myself and remembering the sort of things I was doing at the same time not so very far away from where you were. How terribly tame my life was compared with yours![59]

I had a dream the night before last in which someone sprawled on my bed and put his head on my stomach (like you did the other Saturday when I was ill) but it wasn't you, it was an awful sort of negro with frizzy hair but a <u>white</u> face! It really was rather a nightmare.

One of my fly buttons has also come off now and I've been too lazy to sow [sic] it on. But no one can see, at least I imagine they can't.

You don't have to feel sad about my precarious health, nor do you have to come to see me when I'm ill. It must be very boring for you to watch me lying in bed. I must admit it cheers me up a lot, but it can't exactly be your idea of pleasure! Did you know you left a letter from your mother here? I'm afraid I read it, but I think you were going to show it to me anyhow, weren't you? She doesn't sound very light hearted in the letter, so I expect she'll be very happy to have you with her. You will be several days away, won't you? Will you see other old friends as well?

My brother hasn't turned up yet, but I'm waiting for it at any moment.

A review has appeared in the "Spectator" mentioning my story in "New Writing" It says "Mr Welch has produced another tremulous and sexy story in the manner of 'Maiden Voyage,' all about a fat woman in stays, and the contrasted beauty of a tramp who comes to sleep in the barn."[60] Pretty steep this, isn't it! What will they say about the new book![61]

I think I will not post this letter now, but finish it and send it to Endsleigh Mansions.[62] I hope this is all right by you & that you'll get it safely. If I send it to Appledore you may have already left.

Yesterday I went out for first ride for a fortnight. I went down to the river. The sun was shining beautifully but I felt very low for some reason. I wished you'd been there, so that we could picnic and sunbathe, and you perhaps even bathe in the water. It was lovely there; no one about, only me, the weeping willows and an old ruined boathouse. You must come down with me one day soon. I think you'd like it. All round only the fields. We could spend all day there in the sun with some food and drinks.

I never hear a word from Francis now. My rudeness has driven him away, perhaps for good. I can't say I'm altogether sorry, as I don't think he liked me very much but only liked making use of me a bit, when he had nothing better to do. One has a lot of acquaintances like that, I think; and I suppose I've often done it myself too.[63]

I wonder if you'll have raids when you're in London. Perhaps not, because I hear it's a full moon.

———

It's now late in the evening and I've been out again for a short ride to Hartlake Bridge (where I first showed [you] the river at Christmas).

I went under the bridge and saw where I'd written my name on the 25th March two years ago. I also walked down to the lock and sat on the grass and remembered how I'd bathed there when I was 22 and how the curate of Tonbridge had chased across the fields after me to borrow my Austin 7![64]

These are silly things to remember, but they all came back as I sat on the lock gate.

I'm better now and will try to be all right when you come next. With care and sense, I should be. A bit thick if I was in bed three times running!

Your letter was so nice that I can't say much. Perhaps I'll just say how fond I am of you, and that I feel I would do a lot for you.

I suppose you were born kind, for you've certainly been very good to me.

Jack was good to me, but then it all ended in the most frightful mess, and that made me think that all friendships go down the drain in the end. I never thought that I'd have anything but the most passing acquaintanceship with anyone again.[65]

I'm so glad I know you. Happy Easter! Eric. I wish I could send you a large pink egg with a face on it. The Russians, I'm told kiss one another on both cheeks and say "Christ is risen." Have a good time with your mother. I think of you and look forward so much to seeing you again.

Denton.

✍♥

April 11th 1944, Tuesday

My dear Eric,

Your lovely long letter has just arrived, and I want to say such a lot in return, but I don't know where to begin.

Over Easter I have been thinking of you with your mother, wondering what you were doing, whether you were enjoying yourself, and whether you were going off on your own or staying with her all the time.

I had a feeling (which I didn't encourage) that you just might write. Perhaps it was telepathy. But telepathy or no telepathy I never expected to get so much.

Let me just say, to get it over, that I wish all from all sorts of points of view (both yours and mine) that I had met you when I was eighteen; but as I didn't that's <u>that</u>, and you <u>must</u> (if you're going to take me at all) take me for what I am now.

I know that your type of temperament is nearly always drawn to someone several years younger, and this makes me think that it's probably <u>quite</u> impossible to get up any real interest in anyone so near your own age as I am. But granted all this, I still think that you make rather too much of your own age and other people's. It should be relatively unimportant, and if you dwell on it too much it will spoil and distort things more than they need to be.[66]

I am glad that it makes very little difference to me whether a person is 19 or 29. Most of the time they seem more or less the same age as me, with the same thoughts & feelings and the same behaviour. I know you can't share this indifference to age, but I think you go too much the other way and make too many distinctions.

You may say that I make too few. I suppose this is one of the big differences in our temperaments.

I certainly often think that it can't be in your nature to care particularly for a person like me, and I wonder how you can show as much friendliness as you do. I must admit this fuddles me and muddles me a bit, and probably makes me act towards you sometimes in a rather strange and changeable way. I have the feeling that you're just doing or saying things because you think I expect it of you, and the next moment, by some look or gesture, you'll show me <u>just</u> where I get off! I suppose this all makes me feel a bit insulted sometimes as if I was shinning up the wrong tree; but honestly Eric, I can put up with all that, if I can only feel that some part of you really and truly cares for some part of me and enjoys being with me.

It's easy for me to like you and accept you at once, whole, with all your virtues and vices! But it can't be so easy for you to swallow me whole, and I don't suppose you ever will. This makes me think it's all hopeless sometimes. I feel terribly lonely then, as if it's stupid of me to make human contacts and much better only to stick to my work and think of my career, such as it is.

I don't suppose I'll ever quite know what you think of me, unless you say it or write it it baldly one day. You're pretty truthful about your emotions, and that suits me, because the one thing I can't bear is being bamboozled; but on some points you keep me guessing.

I'll now shut up about human relationships and our attitude towards each other. It's really a miracle to me that we manage to hit it off at all.

Oh, just one thing more. I have often done things to please you, but you must also remember that they've been to please myself as well. No one could like bicycling miles more than myself, and I hate the fact that I have to be so careful now. And no one enjoys having a few gins and getting gay more than I do. That I do these things when I'm with you, is because you bring that side out in me. I shouldn't do them really, because I have to pay for it afterwards too much; but sometimes it's more or less worth it, and I have to let prudence go hang.

I <u>know</u> you won't like me any better for trying to please you or adapt myself to you. I understand enough from my own experience to know that this vain attempt to please often completely puts one off a person. It is simply that you bring another side out in me that hasn't had free expression because of this invalidism and having to take great care, on account of that damned accident.[67]

I suppose sometimes I feel that it must be terribly slow for you, and I must try to make it enjoyable for you, but that's only the feeling that anyone has when someone's come to visit them.

O Eric you'll find I lack so many things, if you go on looking. Try not to concentrate on them too much. I can't be a different person to what I am; and if you want me to be it's just no good; the whole thing's a phoney set-up and may as well be abandoned at once, in that case.

I don't expect <u>anything</u> from you. Don't feel any responsibility in connection with me, for God's sake. Just tell me exactly what you think.

It's awful if you try to be considerate. Much better to be absolutely frank. And I will be too.

Strange that you should mention cycling on and leaving me behind. I thought at the time that you didn't notice what you'd done, & at first I felt a bit annoyed with you (and myself because I couldn't keep up and had to pant along behind). I don't know whether I looked sulky, but I quickly saw it was nothing to do with me whether you went on ahead or kept with me. We must be allowed the freedom of our actions. And usually you are extraordinarily thoughtful about my limitations.

I must tell you, my French girl fan suddenly turned up on Sunday evening, out of the blue![68] I was horribly taken aback and didn't know what to do, but at last told Evie to show her up. She was small, rather pretty and young with fair hair and was all dressed in Free French uniform. I wondered at once if she would be your type at all or not. She had hitchhiked all the way from London and had taken about 5 hours coming! She was quite self-assured and seemed to take me for granted at once. We were quickly talking in a very friendly way and she had some late tea with me; then we went into the wood & picked primroses. She told me her parents lived in Scotland. She's half English & her father is naturalised, so she is quite at home in the language. I rather liked her, as she was fairly natural and tried no tricks or wiles.

She seemed to like me too and I only hope I didn't appear too sympathetic for fear she gets a wrong impression. She brought a copy of my book with her and I wrote in it for her. Of course when she came to go we missed the bus, but she was lucky and got a car to stop almost at once.

I want to talk to you and tell you all about her and ask you what I should do, as I think she's going to come down here a lot! She talked of hiring a bike! May was awful and said she was such an attractive girl that she hoped it was love at first sight and I would settle down with her for life!![69]

Seeing her onto the bus we ran into all the Slomans,[70] so I think they imagine she is my new girlfriend. And I suppose they are right as far as it goes.

I hope she won't persecute me though.

In your letter you mention all the things I think of too, the things I'm often remembering. I'm so glad you note them down too in your mind. I wish one day you would write a book or something all about yourself.

I was very interested to have the photograph.[71] It <u>is</u> like an aspect of you, but not the "you" I think of most. Evie thinks it very like. I never think of you with smooth hair! You don't look in a very good mood either. Were you brooding? I'm looking forward to seeing the others too.

Noël was here yesterday and we sat on the river bank drinking tea in the sun and she said suddenly, "Does Evie know how much I love you"!! I didn't know what to say and felt terribly embarrassed. This sort of thing is a bit confusing isn't it. I suppose I'll get used to it soon. Nothing ever quite works out as it should does it?[72]

What a bore your ex-schoolmate sounds![73] No wonder you tried to horrify his prejudices with some surprising talk. I loathe people like that. I want to jump on their faces with running-shoes on.

Did your mother mind you going to the pub without her? What was she like? Very pleased to see you & not too fussy?

Your Nazi yearnings are too dotty Eric. You're much too sensible to be anybody's sucker, much less the Fuehrer's! All you feel you need is a sort of discipline of life, and you're quite right too, you need it <u>badly</u>; but not some cock-eyed ideology all about master-races and such stupid muck. It's not good enough for you, it's only supposed to be for fools and slaves.[74]

It's easy in war to hate the stupid patriotism we smear over everything. It's enough to make one hate one's own nation's history for ever. I despise all the silly warlike muck; but that doesn't make me love something else equally contemptible. Nothing is worth anything except the goodness of individual people. To glorify the state is a mug's game. It's there to do our bidding, not to rule and interfere with us. If I give the state all that power, it'll do things to you that you certainly won't like. You'd be the first to object, because you have a love of freedom which amounts almost to licence!

I must be boring with all this amateur political talk.

It all leaves me cold anyhow. I want to be left alone. And so would you, if you could only find something you longed to do.[75]

Talking about longing makes me think of Saturday. Come soon won't you. I get impatient. I want to be as happy as I can while I can.

In spite of being a "Storm Trooper" in "Jack Boots" you have a pretty good slice of your friend Denton's love!!![76]

𝒟♥

27/4/44

Dear Eric,

Yes, do come on Sat., if you feel like it. I didn't pressure you the other Sunday when we were at the 'bus stop, as I thought you might want all your week-ends free, now that you have someone who likes to go about with you.[77]

I had the hell of a time, battling with my body in the early part of last week but am now feeling much better, thank God. I hope this will last over the week-end. It certainly should do.

I am going to see Mrs. Easton on Friday evening to see if she can suggest anything to bring about an improvement.[78] I expect she'll tell me that I must go up to London to be poked and prodded by some horrid specialists. If she tell me to do this, I have decided that I will because life, on and off lately has been pretty unendurable!

I'm afraid this trouble with my body may have made me go rather dead for the moment; (This letter, as I read it thro' sounds stilted and starched) but perhaps you will understand.

I have been out in the sun too, a lot—lying on top of a haystack by the river. It has been wonderful there these last few days, when I've been feeling all right. I discovered a little wood with a stream & miniature bridges and the most wonderful large king-cups. I wandered about in it, with only my trousers on, and picked a huge bunch. Now my chest is beet-root red! It will be brown soon I expect.

I have been writing in bed all morning, but now I must get up and take my picnic lunch to Oxenhoath lake, where I am meeting Noël. Good-bye till later.

————

Now I am back and it is evening. I'm afraid I upset her just before we parted. I felt very uncomfortable and pedalled away quickly down the hill. Human relationships are difficult, aren't they?[79]

I'm afraid Eric I've made a fool of myself with you several times. Please forget it, if you can. It is this that has stopped me writing to you. I seem to have had a complete hold-up.

Thank you so much for amusing letter.—All the news on Saturday.

Always your friend, Denton.

℘❤

Tuesday May 2nd 1944

Dear Eric,

I do hope you got back safely and that you weren't too tired. I hate to think of you walking all that way at night.

I have just heard that I have got to go and see the specialist tomorrow in London. I'm afraid I am dreading it. I wish you could come too, to give me moral support.

I saw Mrs. Easton yesterday and she pumped out some blood & put it in a bottle to be tested. As you say, it hardly hurt at all. She also wanted to examine me; so my trousers remained at half mast for several minutes. I didn't mind this. I don't know whether you would. You seemed to have a prejudice against woman doctors. I think she is very good & understanding and she seems now quite to like me and trust me. She said, "Well, and how have you been?" as if she were really interested and wanted to know.[80]

I enjoyed Sunday so much. I was really very happy with you in the sun, eating the delicious plovers eggs, watching you bathing, and then walking along the bank with you. I wished I was well and we could have gone camping. I'd like that more than anything. But I'll never be able to do it now.

I didn't like Saturday. It all seemed rather unsatisfactory to me; and I couldn't go to sleep. I felt that you didn't understand my character and that you never would, because you thought you knew all about me and so would be too lazy to probe any deeper. I began to wonder why we were friends at all. You seemed like all the other people I'd known, and I thought how very materialistic and hum-drum you'd made every-thing by explaining to me <u>so</u> carefully the small extent of your feeling. This seemed to make the whole situation unworthwhile and stupid.

But I suppose I must be really fond of you, or I would have said Good-bye a long time ago.

I hope your hair looks all right. I will trim it again for you, if you like, to get it into better shape.

When I go to London I'll see what I can do about those trousers for you. I'll tell you what the specialist says.

Love D

⚘

10:35 p.m. May 3rd 1944 Wednesday

Dear Eric,

I'm writing this just before I go to bed, now I'm back from London.

I went to see the specialist at 3.30; and as I expected, he had nothing new to suggest. I am going to be x-rayed in Tunbridge-Wells, just to see if anything more can be discovered; but I suppose I'll have to go on stewing in my own juice.

They don't seem to take any interest at all. Perhaps they do when you're actually on the point of death. I feel it is all rather a waste of time and money my bothering with them at all. It's made me angry and frus-trated, as you can see. I suppose I had a sneaking idea that he might be of some use and make helpful suggestions; in spite of all I've said against doctors. However I'm going to try and give up all bothering about it now.[81]

After the doctor, I went to see Guy at Glebe Place.[82] He came to the door and ushered me into a large very high studio with huge skylights. There were stacks of his & his boyfriend's pictures all round the room and the most arty & ugly hangings and furnishings, all rather dirty! After I had admired everything I was taken into his little cubby-hole under the stairs where he slept. I confess I began to get rather uneasy. I talked very brightly about the photo's on the walls. There was his boy friend, Derek, very nice looking, like the ballet dancer Nijinsky; then there was a signed one of Prince Youssoupoff who killed Rasputin. He was all dressed up in his great-grandfather's Russian clothes; fur hat boots, dagger, and embroidered coat.

With all these photos was a picture of me he had done from the "Vogue" photo! Opposite the bed was a horrible sort of throne made of wood, ivory, leather, and trimmed with lyre birds feathers; really hideous.

Guy next took me & showed me the little room up a flight of stairs (with a window looking down into the studio). This was the one he has offered to me. Whenever I like to use it; so, Eric come one night and christen Guy's upper chamber bed. He'd probably be furious if I went chaperoned but still I think I'd rather. Just before tea the front door bell rang and a woman who used to be a model of Augustus John's came to fit Guy for a coat she is making him.[83] She stayed to tea, which we drank out of dark earthenware bowls! I ate a large Jewish current bun, but left the rounds of herring paste dressed with radish.

There is no bath in the studio, only a shower. So you wouldn't be able to pee in the bath.

After tea God was kind to me for he sent two other visitors, both male. I was saved from being left alone with Guy. One of the males was an artist called, I think, Roger Descombes, (Belgian)[84] He looked rather like a tougher swarthier more negroid me. He wore a yellow pullover. He talked to the other visitor, while Guy & I sat on the bed and looked at snaps Guy had taken [of] his friend Derek in all possible positions. One rather good one in nothing but a tin hat sprawling in the long grass. I imagine that you would like Derek. He must be about 20 years younger than Guy. They looked very happy together in their cottage in Cornwall.[85]

Guy pressed me to stay for supper and spend the night, but I said I had to get back. He asked if he could come here next Wednesday.

I'm afraid he may have fallen in love with me, although it sounds conceited to say it, but he seemed so very protective, and he has bought a Chinese earthenware teapot for me. He had it already wrapped up when I arrived. I think he has a very nice nature; but—

Talking of tea-pots reminds me [of] that awful catastrophe happened this morning. I moved a little table and while my back was turned one of the panels of the red screen fell down and smashed to smithereens the lovely glass you gave me for my birthday. Of course this <u>would</u> happen to the newest thing I have & which I like so much and which you gave me. It was smashed in bits, almost to dust. Miss Sinclair gnashed her teeth too like anything. I keep on remembering it and feeling exasperated and upset.

The first thing I did when I went to London was to ask about trousers for you. I was advised to go to Austin Reed's to see good ready-made ones. I went and have got a nice looking dark pair, which is smart. It may be too long in the leg. If so I can send it back, or have it shortened.

Don't be annoyed, but I also used some of your coupons and got a rough tweed sports jacket (deep & light brown check), which I hope will fit. I think it ought to. It is quite nice tho' not in any way exciting. I want to give it to you, because I think you would look nice in it and it will be useful.

You would look very dashing in new grey flannels, sports jacket, decent shirt, your new shoes and one of my many ties.

Please give me the pleasure of allowing me to dress you next time you come! Come fairly soon, (if you're coming) because I don't want to have these clothes hanging round for ages, if they have to go back and be changed.

I hope you're not furious about my using the coupons. If you were saving them for anything else special, I will let you have 13 of mine in July when I get more.

I was told that I haven't got enough accurate measurements to get you a pair of bags made properly, and I rather agree with this. I ought to take them better another time.

When you come here next you can leave your grey suit to be cleaned; as your mother wanted you to. You ought to have let her do it. You treat your clothes too rough. Anything looks like hell in five minutes if you don't take care of it & keep it as clean as possible. I seem to be giving you a lesson in grooming, but you need it, I expect; being with toughs all the week, who don't even wash, according to you!! You would look awfully nice if you took a little trouble; really handsome as Brenda said!

I seem to be becoming very impertinent, but cutting your hair has given me a complex and I now feel responsible for your appearance, like a valet or a stage-dresser or something!

I have asked my tailor to send me some leather buttons (which you can't get now.) If the coat fits you I will put the leather buttons on, if you like, as they will look nicer than the ordinary ones.

I seem to be full of ideas for your beautification![86] I must stop now as it is nearly midnight and the nightingale is screaming its head off.

The world seems a very odd place to me tonight. I can't tell whether I think it was a good thing that I met you or not.

Ever yours D.[87]

≈

<u>Monday May 15th 1944. 9.p.m.</u>

I am just back, dear Eric, from Tunbridge Wells where I have been x-rayed. It lasted for over an hour and was more of a business than I imagined it would be. First I had to strip to the waist and then lie down on a table; then the doctor wanted to pull my tube out and my trousers down. I was glad my body was brown for I felt it looked better that way. The nurse shifted me into the right position, then off the blue blanket (everything was arty farty blue in the room) and then the doctor told me to hold my breath and there was a peculiar whirring & clanging and a large light went on and off. This happened two or three times, then I was left alone for some time, while they were developing the plates.

When they came back, the nurse twisted rubber tubing round my arm to stop the circulation. She hurt but I didn't say anything. Then the doctor injected a whole lot of stuff into my arm. He hurt too and went on hurting, until I felt my head swimming and going round & round as if I was tight. I thought I was going to pass out, as things were going dark and hot, so I called out. "This stuff makes you feel rather peculiar." He seemed rather surprised and asked what was wrong; I was just wondering how I was going to bicycle all the way home, when I began to feel better.[88]

They were ages taking shots of my back and lower down.

I <u>was</u> relieved to get away and to feel more or less allright again. I had hardly drunk any liquid since the night before as I was supposed not to, also no green vegetables and very little food.

I was so delighted to get away that I bicycled double quick and although there was a freezing wind I stopped on Bidborough Ridge with the wonderful view laid out before me and drank a thermos full of lovely brown coffee and ate some raisins.

I looked towards the river and towards Penshurst and I thought of you there a few years ago. I went on thinking of you. I wanted to tell you how much you help me when you see I'm low and try to pull me round. No one's ever done it before. I've always felt absolutely left.

Late in the night last Monday after you had gone, I wrote to you to thank you for [a] very good time when I felt rather awful by the river; but it was a bad letter in other ways, so, I didn't send it.

When I go all to bits like that it's because I'm ill, and that makes me think that everything has been spoilt for me forever.

You help me to get over the bad time as no one else ever has.

This morning I sent the sheets to your mother. I hope she gets them safely. I've also sent the coat back to Austin Reed's and told them to send a smaller one & one with green in it on approval, if they had one. I may have it tomorrow.

I have shortened your trousers myself, quite well, I think. Noël showed me what to do and I have sewed them well and strong. I burnt my thumb while ironing them and cursed; then I remembered what you said and rubbed it in my hair. I've only taken off about ⅔ of an inch.

It has just struck me that you would really like to know the price of the trousers although I'd love to give them to you. It is rather a coincidence but they were exactly £3, which is just what you left for them. I think they are good ones and worth it, don't you? Although it seems quite a lot for ready made ones. My utility boy's ones were 13/6!

Talking of boys reminds me that yesterday I was by the river, & when I left my haystack, I saw two poor small boys trying to push an enormous cart up an incline. One of them made me think of you, battle-dress like yours. I was afraid my puny strength wouldn't be much help, but I offered to push, and at last we got it moving. The boys had taken off their football boots to get a better grip & then padded along the tarmac in their socks. I told them they'd wear them out, but they just grinned and went on thanking me for helping. They were very polite, which made them rather charming. I thought they'd grow up and be rude & boorish like most people seem to be.

I have had two more fan letters about my "Horizon" story[89] and third from Allen & Unwin to submit a book to them. In all this now makes 4 publishers who've approached me! I have told Routledge and said that I expect a larger royalty & more for my decorations. This is pretty good cheek isn't it! But I begin to feel mildly in demand.[90]

One of the writers of the fan letters is an artist called Keith Vaughan who has a show on now in Bond Street.[91] Several people know of him and Guy has told me that he is about 27. He says my writing leaves him extravagant with admiration and he wants to meet me soon. I wonder what he'll be like. The other chap writes from Sheffield & is called Frank Fenton.[92] I have no dope about Frank at all, so he remains an enigma. I imagine him as a sort of mechanic with a culture mania. I have a feeling he wouldn't like me.

I saw Noël on Friday & it was terrible, because she began to cry. I really felt hot and horrified and helpless. I am wondering what I should do now. I have nearly decided to write and suggest that we don't meet for some time. I do seem to have a frustrating painful effect on her and her scenes shock me, because one sees how much upset and distress each person unwittingly inflicts on another. It's all a perplexing muddle. I wish very much Noël wasn't fond of me. It puts a burden on me, and I want to throw it back on to her. I suppose this is because I have no love or affection for her. I've never had this problem quite like this to deal with before. It isn't "me" a bit. I feel it's quite alien to me. Goodnight my dear Eric.

With love from Denton.[93]

P.S. Mrs. Easton says biking over bumpy ground is what made me ill on Monday, by the river.[94]

☙

May 17th, 1944 Wednesday 9:15 p.m.

My dear Eric,

I've run out of paper, so have had to tear this out of my notebook.

I shall expect you on Saturday. If you come earlyish and I have gone out, I will be by the river, just by the bridge. You can't miss it. You will remember how we went together with the French girl.[95] But I may anyhow be in.

Your letter came just when I had posted mine to you.

It is strange, but I too had had two of those dreams one after the other! I wonder if they were on the same nights! They don't often follow each other like that with me.

I have washed your satchel and have been using it ever since you left. I like it better than mine to use, as it is softer and not so bulky, if I want to put it in my bike basket. I usually wear it and feel very workmanlike. Don't you need it at Appledore? Do you only use your tin? I like it very much.

It is <u>awful</u> but I have written to Noël suggesting that we don't meet for <u>some</u> <u>time</u>! I really felt I couldn't deal with any more difficulties. It simply isn't "me" to have these peculiar entanglements or to "come between husband & wife"! I know Bernhard must hate me like poison; and all for no reason.

Noël's passion for me is <u>really</u> amazing, don't you think! It has been going on now for over a year. And she wanted me to go to Middle Orchard to live with her, and to drive Bernhard out onto the streets!!⁹⁶ I suppose I respect it, like I respect anyone else's passion, but I can't understand how she ever <u>allowed</u> herself to get into that condition of loving, or obsession, or whatever it is. For we are really quite a lot responsible ourselves for these conditions don't you think? As you yourself said, you wouldn't <u>allow</u> yourself to get too fond of Peter or whoever your particular fancy of the moment is.⁹⁷

I suppose I'm not one to talk, when I think of how I behaved with Jack; but I was <u>young</u> & also very ill, which makes <u>tremendous</u> difference to your behaviour.

Now that I have written all this about Noël, I feel rather ashamed and mean; for after all, it is <u>very</u> rare to have people to love one in that intense way, — it has certainly never happened to me with someone I could have loved in return — But I can't understand how my coldness, my frank explanations, have had <u>no</u> effect. All along she has known how utterly alien all this sort of stuff is to me. I feel this ought to have put her off quite a lot, but I [*sic*] doesn't seem to have; it seems to have goaded her on!

All this atmosphere stifles me so. I want to get away from it, and have nobody to love if it entails that sort of thing.

I hope you never thought that I wanted to stifle you in that way, because I never did. I just had an affection for you which I wanted to show quite frankly. I hate possessive people more than anything on earth. I wish I had been more reserved.

Of course you fly to the other extreme and try to kick people off before there is any need.

I often wonder if it is quite dotty for us to go on seeing each other after you have told me so frankly how little feeling you can have for me.

It all seems rather queer and cold and mechanical. I don't want to be anyone's stop-gap.

D.

ℒ♥

Monday evening May 22nd 1944

Dear Eric.

Better call it all off. Now that you've gone and I can think all round the subject and say what I like on paper without thinking of your feelings, I see how mad and weak-minded of me it is not to have stopped seeing you some time ago.

My only excuse for ever beginning anything so stupid is that I was utterly bamboozled by you.

You have forgotten, or are too mean to admit that you have ever been attracted to me, yet you spoke about me in such glowing terms to Francis, that he <u>had</u> to repeat it all to me, saying that you had called me a "smasher" and adding that he thought you would like to meet me again.[98]

This was the beginning of the mischief. It is petty to mention it, but I <u>do</u> want to point out that after this it has not been easy to grasp the fact that you are completely indifferent to me.

I realise it now, only too well—and of course much too late.

In spite of making all this clear at last, you suggest that we should still go on seeing each other and that you should come here for weekends which as you know necessitates our sleeping in the same bed! This I suppose is just about as near as two people can get in this world, and yet from all you say, you have no feeling for me and never have had.

This is the most amazing thing to me of all, that you should still seem willing and even anxious to spend long hours alone with someone, and even to sleep uncomfortably with them in the same bed, when you find that person <u>quite</u> uninspiring.

I shall <u>never</u> be able to understand this, and can only conclude that there is something peculiar about you or that you are too mean & ungenerous to admit freely that you gain <u>anything</u> from my companionship & friendship. There is something so horribly grudging about you; it makes me feel rather sick, sometimes. You so obviously have done many things entirely to please your own whim & fancy (however fleeting & shallow) and then you turn around afterwards & tell me in all seriousness that you only did those same things because you thought I expected it of you. I have sometimes been able to tell, (because of the mechanical quality) that you have done something to please me; but I am also able to tell when [you] have done things spontaneously, and it seems <u>outrageous</u> to me that you should pretend afterwards that everything has been artifice.

To spoil <u>everything</u>, not to give me even the faint satisfaction of knowing that some genuine enjoyment has been experienced, seems extraordinarily miserly, and rather pointless.

If you set out with [the] express idea of being beastly, you could not have treated anyone more cruelly than you have treated me. You have hood-winked and cheated me and then tried to explain your past behaviour away by saying that you did it because you were hyper-sensitive & did not want to hurt my feelings. This would be disgusting enough if it were true; but because it is not entirely true it becomes even more disgusting.

I would warn you against ever being "kind" to anyone again in the same way, as they will not thank you for it. The whole stupid situation arises from ignorance & wishful thinking on my part, and a crooked insincerity and selfishness on yours.

Given the most <u>ideal</u> circumstances, it seems to me that you would never be able to sustain for any length of time a deep relationship with anyone else, simply because you seem to have no solidity or sureness in your nature at all.

You tell me that you are capable of deep feeling, but all you mean by that really is that your lust is capable of being strongly and temporarily aroused by something it thinks particularly desirable at that moment.

You have hurt me, insulted me and made use of me (I don't mean materially, but spiritually & mentally) and then you turn round &

crown all by telling me that the whole painful process has been a disinterested effort on your part to 'please' me!

This is the thing I hate to think of most of all and the thing I can't forgive you for, that you will not admit your own quite substantial part in the silly affair.

I have been utterly idiotic over the whole thing, in fact my foolishness has been quite indecent; therefore I deserve to be bamboozled and made to look a fool; but to be told that there has never been anything but cheating on your part, no real feeling at all, only fatuous pretence is too much. It is enough to make me hate you for the rest of my life. And it is obvious of course that I can never trust another word that comes from your mouth.

I am quite aware that this is the sort of letter that should <u>never</u> be sent, even if one has been goaded to write it. The waste-paper basket the next morning is really the place for it; but I am going to send it tonight, as I think you need it as a warning against ever behaving so horribly and unkindly again.

I have learnt many things from knowing you and the chief ones are, never to trust another human being, to believe nothing you are told, and to keep other people as far away from you as possible.

When I think of all the barriers I have taken down, of all the things I have told you, I am ashamed. To have made myself quite simple and obvious, with no defences up, when all the time you were playing with me is one of those things that are not very pleasant to dwell on.

––––––––

On reading thro this letter, I dislike the tone of almost every single sentence. But however excitable & lacking in good sense it may be, you shall get it, as you deserve it. Whether you realize it or not, you have behaved abominably to me; and I should like somehow to convey this to you, even if it's by a silly unwise letter like this, which is <u>such</u> a giveaway of the weaknesses of my own character.

Please don't show it to Peter, or to any other lout; at least I must trust you that far.[99] I hope you will tear it up or burn it, which is really the right fate for it.

Let me know where to send your ring, snuff-box & other things you've left here—either to the Hostel or your mother's. You must not think me double-faced in parting from you pleasantly & then writing like this; it is simply that I can't speak when you are here. I know now that if I try to talk to you, you will only go dumb & stupid, unless you're drunk. So I have to write it instead.

Goodbye. It will certainly not be my fault if we meet again.

D.

𝓛♥

May 27th 1944
midnight

Dear Eric,

Forgive tonight, but I was tight. You have made me <u>so</u> unhappy. I feel beside myself just at the moment, to think that you can never again even give me the mildest tenderness, because for some reason you have decided that I am utterly unattractive to you. Heaven knows, I probably am; but how in God's name have you given me any tenderness in the past, if that is the case, and how <u>can</u> you stop it in such an utterly callous way if you have <u>any</u> love or gentleness or human feeling in your heart at all? It is too mean.[100]

Have I meant <u>nothing</u> to you since you knew me? Have you got nothing from the deep feeling which I've had for you and which I've never tried to cloak? I have tried to be so generous with you, so utterly without barriers or pretensions and carefulness. I've really wanted like <u>anything</u> to give you what happiness I could; and all I've done, it seems, is to repel you & make you want to get away from me. This is so frightful to me that it goes thro' me like a saw each time I think of it.

I don't expect you to love me like Cleopatra! I feel my demands on you have been almost <u>nil</u>; but when you seem to find even kissing me repugnant, I suppose things are indeed pretty hopeless.[101]

This is much the worst thing of all that even the tiniest demonstration of feeling, you say, does not come naturally to you.

It all makes me see how fatuous I am to go on living. What utter folly to work to strive to do anything when one's whole being or soul can simply be looked at, sampled, and then considered unworthy of further attention.

If I don't die soon, I shall certainly try to do myself in properly. It is always cheap to talk about suicide, but I simply can't go on coping with everything and this added horrible frustration, upset and humiliation. I certainly have no vanity now. You have knocked every scrap out of me. You have knocked everything out of me but bitterness. And I can't understand <u>why</u> you have done it: Curiosity? Amusement? just to pass the time?

Violent passion changes, passionate love changes, but ordinary human tenderness if it is ever given, surely should be constant.

How can you turn round and kick me off, unless you're just devilish.

✐

Pitt's Folly Cottage
Nr Tonbridge
Kent

May 30th, 1944

Dear Eric

Please forgive my behavior, and going off like that. I suddenly saw how unbearable it was of me to thrust myself on you after what you'd told me. I'm not usually as unpleasant as that, but as you say, I'm a bad loser.[102] I simply can't get used to the idea of someone I've become really fond of, no longer finds anything to love in me. You will understand that this is a <u>terribly</u> hurting experience. It seems to undermine all of one's confidence, to make one despise and hate oneself and to feel that there must be something seriously wrong with one's whole make-up.

You have been in many ways the friend that I have longed for, that I can't bear to think that I have come to mean absolutely nothing to you.

This all makes for <u>very</u> unequal behaviour. I have shown the very worst and weakest sides of my nature to you.

Thank you for the week-end and for really, under the uncomfortable circumstances, being as charming to me a[s] possible.

From your true friend, Denton.

✍♥

June 1st 1944 Thursday

Dear Eric

Thank you for your note. I am writing this quickly, before I am muddled by any further letter from you.

I <u>absolutely</u> refuse to quarrel with you, so don't try. Life is too short and too sad to make everything worse by our own perversity.

Just at the moment you will be thinking that it is best if we never meet again, and I certainly think that we should not bother with each other for some time—for a long time perhaps.[103] But ultimately I think it would be just wicked and stupid if we cut ourselves completely off from each other, because of exhaustion and strain on your side, and pique and hurt pride on mine.

You would be silly to harden your heart against me, as a troublesome highbrow fairy with nothing whatever in common with you. And I should be silly if I hardened my heart against you, as a rather dumb near-hearty who just drifted through life aimlessly and couldn't be expected even to begin to understand me.[104] (I <u>don't</u> think this about you and never shall, but I am just saying that I could tell myself to make myself turn away from you and despise you.) As you have been doing to me.

There is a bond of sympathy and understanding which, however much we may tend to disregard and ignore it, will always be there. I think you have spoken to me and told me things as you have done to few others, and I certainly have done the same to you.

I have been wrong in refusing to recognize your desire to be left alone. I have worried and badgered you, and I am sorry—<u>really</u> sorry. It is terribly difficult, as you know, to stifle one's own desire in these cases, especially if one is boozy, as I was on Sunday night![105]

I have been wrong too, in being pettily rude about someone you are very fond of.[106] This is contemptible, but again I can only say that it is terribly difficult not to resent the greater attention paid to another.

You have made it all <u>extra</u>-difficult by shutting yourself off and turning against me abruptly or, seemingly abruptly. (In case you don't know the way to make someone <u>vitally</u> interested in you is to tell them suddenly that you really feel nothing for them any longer. They can't bear the withdrawal of all warmth and affection, and it makes them feel rather mad.)

I am <u>not</u> going to be mad in regard to you any longer, but I am also certainly not going to chuck you off and dismiss you as of no importance. I have <u>loved</u> knowing you and I hope you have got something from knowing me.

I shall not write to you again—unless of course I hear from you & the letter needs an answer—but I hope that if, in the future, you suddenly feel that you would like to see me again, you will just turn up and not let any <u>silly</u> and <u>unreal</u> obstacles stand in the way. In spite of our relationship lacking <u>many</u> things & misfitting in <u>many</u> others, I feel that in some ways it has enriched both our lives ad [*sic*] therefore should not be despised. Let me know whether you want me to send back the things you have left here or keep them for you. I can do either.

Your very sincere friend, Denton.

<u>morning</u>
Friday 2 June 1944

My dear Eric,

Your other letter has just come & I am so glad that I wrote you what I thought yesterday, or I might have been tempted to be much more acid in my reply.

Just let me say at the beginning that I have gradually been led into being <u>terribly</u> unwise with you. As you say it means death when one trys [*sic*] to make someone love one. No one knows this better than myself and I am ashamed of being guilty of this weakness with you. But if I may say so, without putting all the blame on you, you have rather brought this about by your own behaviour, which has been in many ways what would probably be called uncertain & bad.

It does not help to draw a parallel between our relationship, and yours with Peter, and to ask why I have not been able to behave as you do with Peter, because the simple answer is, that you haven't behaved to <u>me</u> as Peter behaves to <u>you</u>.[107]

Although I may have to rub your nose in it before you'll admit it now, you have until quite recently shown me an apparently quite real affection, however superficial and light. This has led me on to <u>great</u> indiscretions. I really was intoxicated that so different a person could ~~really~~ understand me a <u>little</u>, and I wanted to give you everything I could—my love and devotion and any peace or security or happiness that it was in my power to hand out. Because I'm emotional, and in a precarious state of health, and because I have lived so utterly just for myself and my work for some time past, my feelings brimmed up and slopped around all over the place. It must have been a disturbing sight to you, whose affection was so much less, but it would not have been nearly so disturbing if you hadn't tried to thwart me rather cruelly. You gradually shut every door in my face with a very school-masterish air.

(Even you will realize how disastrously our week-end began to deteriorate the moment you made yourself out of sympathy with me. I think we were quite happy, I certainly was, when we were resting on Sunday afternoon; but by the time we got to the "greyhound" you had turned against me, I suppose because you thought I was going to get tight and troublesome. I wasn't; I really wanted to behave as well as possible, but I sensed that you were criticising and warding me off and <u>not</u> trying to be generous and this made me feel quite distracted. It seems intolerable to me that you could make yourself so hard and cruel instead of trying to help me. I never really recovered from this resentment. I knew you felt ill and wanted to be left alone, but I could not swallow the feeling that you had been unjust to me and extremely selfish at a most inopportune moment.[108]

Please let me say here that I have <u>never</u> tried any psychological tricks on you. No one could have been more open, transparent and generally simple with you than I have been. In fact I think I have been much too simple. I have more or less given myself to you on a plate—a thing I've done to hardly any one else in my life. If I have appeared to cross-examine you, it is only that I <u>love</u> to talk. What is a human relationship if there is no communication? And you talk so well and simply if only you can get going. I love to know what you or anyone else is <u>really</u> thinking— sometimes even if it hurts—and I feel that it is such a terrible waste of time simply to sit about like farm labourers, just grunting and chewing our pipes![109]

You agree with me really in this, although you are more inhibited.

I have known that you are a slower & more silent person than I am, and I have often tried <u>not</u> to be a gad-fly, but at others I've felt that you really needed to be bitten into life. It was impertinent, and you probably didn't like the process; but why the hell should you sleep all your life away? You won't get another.

There is no need to make excuses about "overtime" and not being able to come here so often in the future.[110] You have of course never been under <u>any</u> obligation to come here, and you need never come here again if you don't wish it. It is nothing whatever to do with me and has always been a matter which rested entirely with yourself.

I imagined, perhaps wrongly, that you enjoyed coming here and that the change & respite from the hostel were really rather refreshing and welcome.

For this reason, although you might not think it, I have put myself out quite a lot. I have never before had anyone coming to stay with me regularly and it has needed some readjustment. I am generally a person who does not find it easy to share his personal life & belongings with another. I've always hated the very thought of someone else getting into my bed, using my flannel, comb, all those little domestic things. I will not say that I have hated you using them because I have not, I have enjoyed it; but the idea took some getting used to.

It would be wrong and wasteful of you to set your face against me, because you have found me a strain and difficult. I have said that I am <u>truly</u> sorry for that, and if you will be generous and admit it, you will say that you have sometimes rather enjoyed knowing me.

You have given me a most unpleasant time, but I don't really regret knowing you. I still like you very much indeed. I know your limitations, and I know that you can not share many of my innermost thoughts; but I still think that we could be very good friends if you will open your mind and allow it, instead of putting up artificial barriers.

I suppose, in some ways, in spite of ill health, I have more to look forward to in life than you have. And I certainly have no feeling of loneliness when I am not upset & thrown into a flap; rather a delight that I am left to my own devices. I could have many, many friends if I wanted them, as you know. I should dislike it very much and think it very stupid of you if you came to see me in the future because you thought I was lonely. You are not cut out to be a Christian martyr, because you can't sustain the role. To make up for it, you have to turn round and be a devil the next moment.[111]

———

<u>Evening</u>. June 2nd, 1944 Friday.

O my dear don't make excuses about overtime. You have of course never been under <u>any</u> obligation to come here and you need never come anywhere near me again if you don't want to. The matter rests, and always has rested, <u>entirely</u> with you. It's nothing to do with me.

I really believed that you enjoyed knowing me & coming into a different atmosphere. And if you did, it is mean & ungenerous not to admit it. If you didn't, all I can say is that I am terribly sorry you have spent so many uncomfortable week-ends. I thought you liked the change.

You seem to have made me nothing but sorry. I am sorry I've pestered you, sorry I've bored you, sorry I've been too fond of you. Can anyone say more? I have written you another page-long letter this morning, but what is the good of sending it? You are so obviously <u>insisting</u> on being out of sympathy with me. There is no need; I shan't worry again.

D.

I've <u>never</u> tried any psychological tricks with you. Nobody could have been more transparent & simple—too simple. I don't give way either to illness or loneliness. You ought to know that.[112]

✐

June 27th Tuesday 1944

My dear Eric,

Just a line to ask if you're still alive! I hope no Doodle-bugs have been shot down or landed too near you. It has really been quite exciting here. One went off at Hadlow Stair & shattered lots of glass and tore off some tiles; then a worse one messed up the top end of Tonbridge for quite a distance, but killed nobody. And Noël at Crouch had almost the first one of all which went off in a nearby mulberry field and twisted all the catches of her windows. The nights, as I expect you know yourself, are hellishly noisy & I hear shrapnel pattering down amongst the trees. One was also shot down near Golden Green (where we go down to the river) so you see there has been quite a plague of bugs. No doubt you've had just the same sort of thing where you are.[113]

————

<u>Later</u>

I've just come in from Oxenhoath Park and while was having my tea
one was shot down just about 300 yards away—appalling bang!

I have been able to buy a green battledress for a guinea and have
worn it an awful lot. I like it so much because it has so many and such
big pockets. I am able when I go out to carry everything I want with me.
Maurice Hughes,[114] who came again the other Friday, showed me that
inside, there was even a pocket for a French letter. They think of everything, don't they?

I have just heard from Marcus—your namesake[115]—to say that he
may shortly [be] going to be moved very near here, & I was to write to
him care of the Tonbridge P.O. I wonder when he will turn up.

Peter Cromwell, the new fan, came to lunch a few weeks ago. He is
thirty two, slight, with little moustache and rather nice mild face. His
real name is Neville, but he writes under Cromwell. I quite liked him,
but I found him a little languid. I think he would depress me if I saw a
lot of him. He wants me to go in and have lunch with him in Berkeley
Square or rather, Mount Street where he has a flat. He seems to have
some sort of war job attached to the Foreign Office.[116]

Guy has been down again too—and later in the summer he wants to
camp at the end of Mary's garden with his nineteen year old German
friend called Vernon Foy. Vernon apparently likes "Maiden Voyage"
very much and wants to see the author. From what Guy tells me of him
he sounds nice.[117] It is pelting with rain now and I am so pleased to be
in my little room warm & snug. I have been wearing shorts whenever
it has been warm so my legs are quite brown. I had a free bath today,
because I only had shorts on when the storm broke in Oxenhoath. The
rain is lovely on your body isn't it?

On Saturday I had rather a nice time, because I made a new friend. I
went down close to the river at East Peckham and on walking round a
bush close to where the children bathe I came upon a youth lying on his
stomach with no clothes on at all. He looked up, startled, and we both
laughed; then I sat down and began my picnic, we were soon talking a

lot, and I shared my food with him as otherwise he would have had to go back to his grandmother's. His name is John James Bloom, he has rather a nice face and gold hair and because he works in London during the week his skin is quite white. I think you would like him, although you might think him rather mild. What was so amusing was that he had been a patient of Dr. Easton's, and liked him better than any other doctor he'd known! As you can guess, we discussed Jack's good points for a long time and the unpleasantness of some doctors as a contrast.[118]

About tea time, I asked him if he'd like to come back to the cottage, so we pedalled back and I showed him my things & the picture of Julian which I am now nearly finishing.[119] Afterwards we walked in the wood and then had some beer which made my head buzz. I was just feeling rather tight—a thing which has never happened to me before on beer— when Evie brought up hot soup which sobered me.

About ten thirty John left taking "Maiden Voyage" with him. He glanced at the first page then shut it and said "I know I'm going to like this" I hope he will!! We are going to meet again D.V. this Saturday for lunch. If he's not there I'm to know that he has been kept in London. He says his grandmother can remember the time when she & her husband would go into the pub. on a cold day and order whiskey, lemon, crushed sugar, boiling water—price 2d each!! John's mother is dead and he was the only one with her when she died at the beginning of the war. He was very fond of her, as I was of mine.

He now works at a music publishers in the Charing Cross Road. I imagine, like myself he is out of the war because of health, although he looks pretty well.

I have been busy correcting proofs of the new book which have begun to arrive in small batches.[120] I don't like it much on rereading, but perhaps this is partly because it is stale to me. I hope so.

A poem has come out in this month's "Life and Letters." It was written about you when I had once seen you off at the station, but I don't know what you'll think of it.[121]

I am sorry about Whitsun, Eric.[122] I have never consciously wanted to force myself on anyone, but I was terribly unhappy then; and I felt so deserted and exhausted and ill. The drinks at the "Greyhound" took away my last shreds of good sense and consideration. I could think of nothing but myself. I have such a terrible sense of the urgency of life when I am like that. It makes me quite desperate. Please understand.

Anyway it is all finished and done with now, and I did not want even to bring it up again, except that—I felt perhaps I ought to try to explain.

I knew how stupidly I was behaving, but I could not stop myself.

Affectionately, Denton.

Just heard from Noël that she's flitted from Middle Orchard to Harrow on the Hill, because of the Spook-Buggy (as John heard a doughboy call it.)[123] The ex-fighter pilot who lives next door has also gone! People don't seem to like them, do they! D.

♥

July 4th 1944
Tuesday

My dear Eric,

What has happened? Are you dead? If not, do drop a line just to let me know how you are; otherwise I shall be worrying so much, thinking that the doodle-bugs have got you!

They really are getting frantic now. They've been bursting all round here. Hadlow, Golden Green, East Peckham, Tonbridge, etc. Each one seems to burst nearer. I'm wondering when one will be brought down on the house! I shan't move tho' till I'm blown out.[124]

On Saturday night I felt rather dismal because I had been working hard all morning and then found that John Bloom whom I was to have met at the river, couldn't get away that weekend. So after having my lunch alone in a light drizzle of rain, I came home and did some more writing and then jumped on my bicycle and pedalled into the King's Arms in Tonbridge.

I sat there drinking gin & lime all alone, listening to other people's amusing, dotty conversation; then I had no more money left, and it was supper time, so I decided to go home, have supper & then return with more money.

I gobbled my supper quickly and was back there about 9. It was terribly full now and boiling hot. The woman of the house said, "I remember you dear, you were in a few months ago." (That was when we went in together, on your first visit to me from Appledore.)[125]

There was only beer left now, so I had half a pint and sat in a corner, watching. Soon I got restive and went into the back room. Pandemonium was raging there. It was full of young boys and girls and soldiers. I felt suddenly that it was just the place for me. There were four soldiers with their heads close together and there [sic] arms round each others [sic] shoulders, crooning, really very well, into each others [sic] faces. They sang "I think that I shall never see a lovelier poem than a tree" and when they came to the verse "A nest for robins in his hair" one of the soldiers turned to me and lifted up his hands to his head. I laughed and another of them (who later I learnt was called Al) pulled me into the circle, calling me kid and telling me to cheer up! I had not realized that I was looking glum. Soon we're [sic] were all singing together in the most idiotic way, making faces and grimaces and gesticulations. It was lovely. The climax came when an absurd, dumpy, middle-aged hop-picking-looking woman insisted on dancing with the handsomest of us—a young soldier with rather flashing eyes, curved nose, bristling with life. He had somewhere a slight look of you, but I could not pin it down.

They danced a mad Lambeth Walk & bumped bottoms in Boomps a Daisy, then they turned each other round in a crazy minuet. Al & I screamed with laughter and bought each other drinks; for I was now getting to know him the best of the quartet.

Suddenly the Salvation Army lass burst into the room rattling her wooden box and selling the "War Cry!" She gave me a sharp look and I began to feel guilty, as if I'd been the most revolting drunkard on earth. Isn't this ridiculous! I suppose it was the power of her professional look.

I hurriedly put pennies in her box and bought her paper.

At last of course all this reveling had to come to an end; but we went on singing in the lavatory for some time; then we kipped out into the yard and it was almost dark.

Al and I began to walk home together. Suddenly it began to rain again in earnest. After we had passed the school, we decided to take shelter in a shed full of hay in a lane. We stayed there some time, talking and resting, while the rain beat down outside. I realized that I had been quite drunk, and Al was <u>very</u> nice to me, because he saw I was not quite my own master!

He wants me to go again tomorrow & sing properly with the others, and a mate of his who plays the piano—also on Sat. evening, which of course is <u>the</u> evening.[126]

I don't know whether to go or not. I should like to, but I feel that I might romp like that once too often! But on the other hand it is perhaps a good thing to have a little gaiety & friendship before you're dead, isn't it? I felt terribly like that on Saturday night; as if nothing mattered except having friendship and sympathy for other people, <u>whoever</u> they are. Surely the terrible mistake is the isolation we place ourselves in, thro' hate, fear, laziness, greed, pride, stupidity. It leads to nothing but emptiness and the terrible "left," utterly deserted feeling which inevitably overtakes us when we realize that we have lived and behaved in such a way that not a creature cares whether we're alive or dead.

I have only just begun to see that human relationships are the <u>only</u> really important thing on earth. Nothing else means anything without them.

I have so often turned away from them, thinking that it was a grand thing to live in isolation; always criticising, despising, seeing thro' people, thinking nobody good enough for me. But I know now suddenly what all that egoism leads to. It leads to death, negation, nothing. It is as if one were still alive and yet had committed suicide. If one does <u>no</u> good, gives <u>no</u> happiness, goes out to <u>no</u> one, what is the point of living at all?

Dear Eric, I must stop this philosophizing, else shall bore you and make you think that I am "getting at you! I am not; I am getting at my-self, because I have tried to live up till now, shut in my own little private box, and it's burst upon me that this is the wickedest, stupidest thing that anyone could try to do.

I expect John Bloom will turn up this Saturday or Sunday with my book; if you'd like to meet him, do come along too. You know how much I should like to see you, and I feel you might enjoy it too.

On Saturday evening we could go to the King's Arms to sing with Al and the others, or we could stay here quietly if you preferred it. The cellar is well stocked![127]

I feel the summer is melting away, and I should so love to go down to the river again with you & picnic and sunbathe. Heaven knows where we'll all be next year! Nothing but good can come really from our knowing each other, if only you will just accept me quite simply & not kick against me because I'm fond of you. In no possible way can I interfere with your life; all you owe me is the ordinary decency of human kindness. Don't feel so weighed-down by any human tie, however slight. You need them as much as anyone else, you will realize that one day if you don't already. It can be nothing but an advantage for you to know me. I really can help you in some ways, just let me know whenever I can do anything for you.

D.

July 5th 1944 Wednesday.[128]

My dear Eric,

I was so delighted and relieved to get your good letter! It has just arrived.

I waited till yesterday to get a reply from you; then I got really worried, feeling that you must have been bombed. I wrote a long letter, but felt that was no good, so I waited till the evening; then phoned the hostel twice, before and after supper. It took ages and both times no answer, not a squeak; and the bell ringing everlastingly in the emptiness.

This so got me down that I telephoned your mother; & of course she was out.

You can guess I was rather worked up by that time.

Then I began to think that you were not bothering to answer my letter and I should never hear from you. I'm afraid I had a bad time. Dearest, I want to say something quite simply to you, and yet I am afraid of appearing excessive. Anyhow—here goes: It is quite obvious that I am really devoted to you, else I never would have stood some of the things you've said and done to me. I will not deny that you've hurt and wounded me till I felt almost mad. And lately I have been so unhappy that everything has appeared utterly worthless and I only wanted to die.

But in spite of all this I <u>know</u> that it is right for us to be friends and I <u>know</u> that I can help you and comfort you in your unhappiness over Peter or any of the other things that life does to one. Just as Noël with her devotion and <u>real</u> <u>love</u> has helped me when I felt deserted, kicked off, despised. In a way I have learnt an awful lot, thro' having such a painful, agonized time with you. And the chief thing I've learnt is that the love and friendship of other people, whoever they are, is <u>all</u> <u>important</u> and ought <u>never</u> to cut oneself away from it, as one is tempted to do, when things go wrong.

I know that you have not a tenth of the feeling for me that I have for you, and I <u>do</u> <u>not</u> <u>expect it</u>; but I think that you have a kind and <u>deeply</u> <u>understanding</u> heart, that you wish me well, even believe in me a little as a writer; and I think from all this comes a wish that I should have a little happiness before I pop off, which you also know might happen rather suddenly. I think deep in your heart you have a real sympathy for me, because in some ways I've had quite a bad time.

You know that you can give me a sense of security, by allowing me to think that you are my <u>trusted</u> <u>& reliable</u> friend, and you know that it gives me the greatest delight to see you sometimes—yet you feel that in committing yourself like this, you are burdening yourself with a responsibility and that I will make demands on you which you cannot fulfil. Let me here promise faithfully that <u>I</u> <u>will</u> <u>not</u>; and that you stand only to gain by continuing to be my friend. I really feel that I am sent to help you in some way, and that something in our natures—no matter what—is complementary.

The very fact that by being ordinarily humanly kind to me you give me the greatest pleasure, should in itself be a satisfaction to you. It should give you the feeling that at least you have done that amount of good in the world. Does all this sound terribly extravagant and sentimental to you? I hope not, because I <u>really</u> mean it, & I have not written like this to anyone else before in my life.

I know that because of my love, I have been unwise & troublesome once or twice, but surely you can understand that and forgive it. I think you know that I have tried very hard to do things properly. Does my behaviour since Whitsun prove that? I think it ought to.

I could go on still writing letters on the surface of things, but because I trust you, I think best to mention these deeper things this once.

I trust you so much that I am even going to risk annoying you by asking you to come and see me again soon and by sending you your train fare. <u>Surely</u> friends should be allowed to do this for each other! I have taken so much from you & given so little in return, and I have felt always that you spent so much on trains in coming to see me.

You mentioned overtime; & I know you have often lost money by staying on here. I can't bear to think that in any way, I've been a drag on you.

Please take it Eric without fuss. I really can afford it at the moment, and I know you would do the same for me in the future if need be! Besides I have no right to ask you like this to come and see me, but I <u>hope</u> you will. I think we could have a perfectly happy natural time without worrying about the past and you need have no fear that I will cross-examine & force, because I won't. I am not as stupid as that, & I really mean you well & <u>always have</u>.

If you can come this week-end, do, because I expect John Bloom will come along too, and you might like to meet him.

I am enclosing yesterday's letter just in case you'd like to plough thro' it. It might amuse you. As I have suggested, we could go singing with Al Saturday night, or stay here quietly, or go somewhere else. Anything you like.

Dear Eric, I will never make the mistake of worrying you, when I know you want to be left alone, that was only my extreme unhappiness. I really am getting to know your nature, just as you are getting to know mine, — and if we're intelligent at all we <u>must</u> make allowances.

————

I've just opened my other letter this morning and it's a poem from the Sheffield School boy, Frank Fenton! He wants me to judge it really stiffly! I can't think what he's like. He pays me a lot of compliments and says that time always separates the wheat from the chaff. I hope he considers me wheat![129]

I shall <u>so</u> look forward to seeing you if you can get away.[130]

I know you will think I'm quite right being quite frank & open with you & not pretending. We need not talk about it at all after this, if you do not want [*illegible*] you're coming. Just turn up.

D.

ℒ♥

Pitt's Folly Cottage
Sept. 28th 1944 11 p.m.[131]

Dear Hero,[132]

I was amused today with your letter, and the photos.[133] Thank [*obliterated by ink stains*]

Now it is late and I must try to go to sleep, but I thought I'd just try to write a scrap.

Noël has been here all afternoon and I have had a slight temp. and have been doing nothing, only lying on the bed in my cassock talking.[134] Noël has brought a pump for the bike and says she thinks a middle-aged writer friend of hers might like John for his house boy!![135] She is going to sound him tactfully. It sounds ideal, I think for John.

May also has been in and suggests that you might like to [*ink obliteration*] something-a-week" job which may still be going begging. I said I'd tell you; but I expect it is snapped up by now because it is cushy.[136]

Good-night. I have been busy sending two stories out & some poems, also writing in the mornings.[137]

I haven't gone out because I feel slightly queer.

Don't the two pictures make you look different [*ink obliteration*] And a different cat[138] [*ink obliteration*]

I have dyed Richard's shirt[139] dull mustard colour for you & washed your grey flannel bags! Also Eve's taken your other shoes. All these parental duties!

Thank you for spreading the Gospel of Welch with the dentist. Perhaps he'll extract my teeth extra painlessly on 10th.[140]

———

Friday.

May has just been in again. She seems job-mad, for she now suggests that you [*ink obliteration*] to Redlands [*illegible*] and help Commander Wheelright make his special rubber dingies or collapsible boats of some sort. (Simple work, quite light, nice airy rooms, banging in nails with other men & girls) He wants anyone he can get to help, full time, part time, take the work home if you like. May is going herself to help some mornings. Does it sound awful or good? She says she will take you along herself (I don't know if that [*ink obliteration*] you or not!!)[141]

But perhaps by now you have hatched some quite different ideas.

You know Eric, you must do so exactly what you want to do yourself. I never know what you're turning over in your mind so I can only make suggestions blindly!

Perhaps you're already thinking that life with me has been terribly dull & you'd rather stay at home for the time being. I don't know— You say so little at [*ink obliteration*] of times that all I can do is to guess!

You know you can come here <u>whenever</u> you want to, and I suppose I must leave it at that till you make up your own mind.[142]

Jean faces herself up again pretty quickly, doesn't she. I <u>shall</u> be interested to hear more about new Johnny.[143]

Best wishes to your mother. Always your friend, Denton.

☞

Pitt's Folly Cottage
Oct. 2nd 1944

My dear Eric,

Thank you so much for the letter. I wanted to write quite a lot back, but Noël is here and so I can't think & this must go to the post. (I've just read this to Noël & she sends her best wishes & hopes to see you soon.)

Come back when your mother can spare you. I'll write again perhaps tonight.

Always
D

☞

Pitt's Folly Cottage
Oct. 2nd 1944
9:15 p.m.

Dearest E,

I couldn't write to you properly just now because Noël was with me & had been talking solidly for hours. I wanted to say quite a lot. I hope it hasn't all gone out of my head. It may have, because she exhausted me a bit, although I suppose I like it really.

I pictured you, walking about the ruins of your father's factory; and I saw it all as if it had happened to me.

It is so often what I have felt in my own life—the extraordinary sadness of everything. Sometimes, when I think of all the things that will never happen again, the feeling seems to quite swallow me up. And at those moments, as you pointed out, there is usually nobody one can communicate one's feelings to, and one almost expects to burst.[144]

I felt like this rather last night, under the huge hunter's moon by the river, looking for mushrooms.

It was one of the first times I had gone out since I was ill and I was all alone there, and I kept on thinking of myself as a child and my <u>mother</u>.

———

This is tomorrow morning now, as I had to stop thro' nearly falling asleep last night.

I've got your other letter to answer now too. You are quite right I shall <u>have</u> to work or turn to making boats or <u>something</u>.

All this week I have been writing every day, but it is such a plaguing and worrying job. I begin to feel quite addled but I hope something will emerge. Do you think I'll be able to write properly and not be too moody & peculiar when you are here! I hope so. Let's try anyhow & see how it works—that is if you want to too, <u>really</u>.[145]

I think <u>you</u> sometimes know more or less how I feel about the general situation, but <u>I</u> am never quite sure what surprise you will have for me up your sleeve! And so I get the idea that it is hopeless to plan anything.

It would of course be quite crazy for us to live together for any length of time, if you were continually champing & chafing & feeling a fish out of water.

Although you say I will never face facts, I can see as well as anyone that it would be murder for me as well as for you.

Selfish or not—you <u>must</u> believe me when I say that I would like you to be happy, quite apart from any considerations of my own.

Now I must stop all this to catch the post. Will your mother let you come back before Friday? I hope so, as I think Eve has got a chicken which will need eating.

Dear Eric, I really am so fond of you; but I don't think I'll ever drive you crazy again—unless my fussiness does this time! You can always pack up and fly. The only thing you can't do is to bring a buck-negress home. It would make the "Ladies" jealous.

Gina pines for you, I think.[146] See you soon. Thursday?

Smacks & munches, D

Pitt's Folly Cottage
Monday 6th 1944

My dear Ike,[147]

Thank you so much for letter. <u>Don't</u> bother to the shop in Promley now, because the parcel has arrived.[148] I hope this gets to you on time.

I have been going mad this afternoon, trying to do the decorations for my ghost article.[149] I suppose something will come of it soon. The writing, I've told myself, is finished.

I've had to write to a guy in India about my paintings. He wrote to the Redfern Gallery. I wonder if he intends to buy one & have it sent out there or what. He's in the Air Force! It sounds crazy to me.[150]

May's tea party yesterday was what Frankie would call Bloody Awful.[151] I felt quite uncomfortable. Mrs. Littleton & her son Rob were there,[152] & Bob (Air Force) started talking about one of his friends who wouldn't sit in a railway carriage with an Italian prisoner and so kicked him out. Other stupid things were said & May told everyone that I was going to stop behind afterwards & wash the tea things up! I wouldn't have minded doing that a bit, but to insolently show off in that way is just what she shouldn't do, if she doesn't want me to avoid her. I said, "Oh, am I?" in a loud innocent voice and people tittered.

I made my escape, & sent biographical particulars and photos. to Routledge.

It must have been gloomy going over Jimmy's things.[153] It is strange to think of a person being dead when you see and touch their clothes.

May's new kettle caught fire at the tea party.

Noël brought a little picture of you—rather nice—and I have hung it by the bed.[154] John was such a bore that I could have yelled. I'm praying that he's going to London today to his old job.[155]

Fay Compton's secretary went off with my book which May gave her, so some eyes will be opened at Redlands.[156] Myrtle has been all right except for today when she fed one of the cats out of my oldest & best saucer! She said, when your letter arrived & I asked her if there was [*ink obliteration*] "Isn't that enough for you? I thought a letter from Eric would last you for five days."[157]

She is a monster.

I am glad you had a nice ride. I thought about you, and hoped you weren't hanging on to the back of the lorry.

My work is becoming an obsession. I wish I could be like a good machine & work without any hitches.

Not too many bangs near you, I hope. [*ink obliteration*] & some pillow slips won't you, if you can.[158]

If your mother wants you there & you want to stay, you won't come back for me, will you? I'm quite content flogging my brains (not what you thought) I go to dentist on the 9th, and don't forget Syphilis Pete for week-end.[159] Life is indeed a rich pageant, isn't it! What a silly letter from your very peculiar friend D. who sends an enormous slice of l'amour.[160]

℘

Pitt's Folly Cottage, Nr Tonbridge
Nov. 25th 1944 Saturday

What a thoughtful Monster, to pinch that lavender water & pack it off to me at once! I wondered what the parcel was. Thank you.

Weren't you rather glad that your Aunt Rose was going with your mother to the American party?—but what a turn you must have had when you heard that she was coming back to stay! I shall want to hear all about it. Although it must have been rather an ordeal, I think it's a good thing it happened, don't you?[161]

One evening after you left, Bernard appeared with the milk & your picture! I suppose Noël had driven him over, poor thing.[162] She had a very successful tooth pulling & is coming on Sunday, I think. She has spoilt the little picture hasn't she—with the varnish and some changes to the face. It's a pity.

Robin Cornell's naval friend wrote, asking to meet me sometime. I said he'd have to come down here.[163]

May came in and told me more about the drunken christening party. Quite disgusting!

I'm glad your mother liked the book.[164]

I'm still in bed,[165] but doing things—writing my book & writing letters—really very contented and busy, so you won't hurry back on my account, will you? There is so much for me to do.

I thought for a moment that the parcel was Moseley's ring. Do you think he'll get it done in time? If he doesn't I don't know what I can give Noël.[166]

There have been quite a few bangs here. I hope none near you.[167]

You never took any rations to your mother. Do you want cheese, fat etc? Tell me.

Eve's been reading the new English Story book to me, but not my own piece.[168] May tried to read it while she was here, but I stopped her by interrupting all the time. I am enjoying the bed very much & imagining all the other places I would like to live in.[169]

I wonder if I will have a beard when you see me again? I have quite a good one even now.

Of course I didn't mind you going to your mother's. It was quite the right thing to do. These temperatures just have to go off of their own accord—and anyhow it's good for me to be on my own.

Let me know if you want any rations.

This is a dull letter, but I'm not quite in the mood. Perhaps I'll write again.

From the Bearded-Queen-Bee-D![170]

✐

Pitt's Folly Cottage
January 22nd Monday 1945[171]

Dear Tunyer,[172]

(Which is my new way of spelling it) I nearly didn't get your letter this morning. The Harlot swore that she had looked & there was nothing for me; then a little later she came my way with your letters, saying it must have gone in to the Ladies.

No Lady, thank the Lord had yet come in here. I'm hoping she's about as frightened as I am.[173]

Mrs. Adeney also has not appeared. She has a cold & sent Bernard with the milk and a note. He said "How are you? You look rotten" People ought to be gagged, if they say these things.

The snow is thick everywhere. I went for a walk last night & my feet were so cold that it hurt to put them on the ground. I am now wearing four sweaters.

I've been trying to work quite a lot, but my brain goes dead in the evening & I wish some very nice interesting people lived next door so that I could go and talk to them.

I've written to Guy,[174] thanking him for all that food. I said it was quite different to anything we ever get here! I had Turkish coffee in bed today after my lunch.

If you can make inquiries in the trade about Geo. III teapot, about (1780 to 1800) won't you.[175]

Fine about the strainer. It's rather queer without you here. No one else has been, so I'm the perfect hermit.

I've sent article and pictures to "Vogue" though I'm not satisfied with them.[176]

I don't suppose you had time to go to the Leicester to see if my pictures were sold.[177] I have a feeling they aren't.

I've got to totter to the post box now. My beard's coming off on the first spring day. I think Francis is quite right—my line is to try to look boyish, not dignified.[178] It's almost dark now—I've been reading a book by J. B. Priestly, who sounds an awful man.

It's all about the industrial North & the Potteries. Not exactly me, but it has a perverse fascination. I keep thinking about all the dirt and factories and the brass people used to make hand over fist. I can almost understand what fires business men.[179]

See you soon
Love D.

ℒ♥

Pitt's Folly Cottage
Sunday. March 18th 1945

Dear Tunia,

I'm in bed because last night I began a temperature, not too bad tho,' and today it's been scarcely up at all, so I'm hoping I've nipped it in the bud.

Noël appeared yesterday while I was putting the fanlight into the doll's house.[180] I hadn't shaved and looked frowsty, but she sat & watched me working and it went fairly well to begin with; but after a bit I seemed to dry up and I rather wished she'd go. I bicycled with her to Stallion's Green & then she would insist on sitting on the side of the road for hours. I became surlier and surlier & she asked me why I had "gone far away"[181]

It was awful. At last I got up to go and when I arrived home I knew

I was ill. Eve read to me & afterwards I tried to go to sleep, but it was rather a bad night.

Early this morning there was the biggest rocket noise of all. I thought windows or beams were going to crack. It seemed to go on for some time, like an earthquake. I'm wondering if it was in the Crouch direction.[182]

I've been doing nothing all day, for fear of bad results. It's disappointing that I've had an attack, as I thought I'd beaten them down.[183]

The ladies came home last night & had forgotten their key, so they called up to me to let them in! I ran down & all was very smooth and affable. I hope there'll be no more difficulty.[184]

Have you had any thing near you? I really thought that something awful was going to happen last night.

The "John of London's" review is quite long & with a photograph of me. Rather good on the whole.[185]

The door of the doll's house looks awfully good now with the fanlight. Have a good time & give your mother my best wishes.

From your Dublin Prawn[186]

June 21st 1945 Thursday.
4. p.m.[187]

Dear Tu,

I'm afraid you must have got v. wet; but the sun came out afterwards, so perhaps you got dry again. I suppose I was rather like a quacking duck, while you were going off, but comings & goings always make me feel as if I had to do a hundred little things all at once. An anxiety feeling. I'm wondering if you've been to Julian's yet, and if you have, what the visit was like.[188] I am expecting the silver-gilt snuff box by any post now! Cigarettes just fit into it.[189]

Eve has just got up from her siesta to make tea, and I hope to do a little work this evening, as I have done nothing so far.

I hope the little Mrs. A won't come crashing down on me tonight.[190]

Let me know if you need any more £-s-d, as you didn't take much. I'll send on anything that comes for you. Have a good time.

Always D.

ℒ♥

Friday June 22nd 1945
9:25 p.m.

Dear Lobster,

How quick you've been! Did you just turn up at Julian's on spec.? I'm so glad you caught her in, even if she had only just got up. I hoped she would give you a little drink of champagne. She has some—as those two boys who broke into her house, when the doodle-bugs were bursting, drank a bottle. I wonder what she will write and say to me.[191]

I'm glad Brown liked the pictures too.[192] I'm getting the others ready for him. With your letter arrived one from that Tricksy Bloom, who wants to come & bring some rasberries [*sic*]. Isn't it awful! I don't know what to do. I don't want to encourage & don't want to be like an animal. I'm going to think it all over before I answer.[193]

It is good about your mother letting the flat to the Americans—guys or dames?—but what is she going to do. Is she going to stay with them, or going to Torquay? How do you fit in? Do you sleep with the Americans or do they sleep in the sitting-room?[194]

Phil[195] turned up last night with Iron Jelloide[196] for Miss E.! She wouldn't be paid for them, & first of all she couldn't come upstairs. Then she came and sat on the edge of a chair for a minute before she went down to the river. She was half-hoping, I think, that you were still here to go with her. She kept saying that you looked just like a nice seal in water![197] I didn't go out—except into the ward, where I found a very unusual flowering shrub in that forgotten garden part.—Huffy pink flowers.

Today is going to be boiling, I think—and I'm just about to drop this & begin work—more later. . . .

I have just finished lunch of Welsh rarebit & tomato, & I am going to give this to Eve, as she is going out to search for lettuce & fruit. I am expecting Noëlly to appear like a whirlwind tonight. There is an electric guitar on the wireless, which reminds me of Michael! Is it really his favorite?[198]

I wrote rather well this morning and didn't feel agitated, but I'm afraid the book may sound awfully peculiar and I expect nobody will like it. I must finish it though, as I myself like it the best of all.[199]

The Ladies[200] are out so when Eve goes, I shall be in solitary possession.

Look after yourself, and give your mother my best wishes.

Love from D.

Ɛ♥

Pitt's Folly Cottage
Nr Tonbridge
Kent

Sunday June 24 1945

My dear Tu,[201]

I can't write much as I am ill again. Isn't it a curse. It began this morning, but I haven't been sick or anything so it may go quickly. I went down to the river yesterday. That may have started it. I can't <u>tell</u> you how morbid it makes me feel—sort of death in life! But it's only passing, I suppose.[202]

Thank you for letter yesterday. Eve has been reading to me, to while away the time. Wish my head would stop aching. I always have the feeling that it never will again.

You be <u>very</u> careful of yourself, won't you.

Love D.

✿❤

Pitt's Folly Cottage
Nr Tonbridge
Kent

June 26th 1945

Dear Piece of Fruit,

What a present from the U.S.A.!![203] I only hope that everything is quite in order and that no handsome G. men arrive in a racing car to transport you to Sing Sing or somewhere. The lavender water too is just what I am needing to feel less frowsty after bed.

I must have been recovering even as I wrote to you the other day, for yesterday I was much better, & today better still. Noël suddenly appeared yesterday & stayed from lunch time till 10 o'clock. But she was fairly good on the whole, and I smoothed her down as much as possible. Once, I <u>think</u>, she tried to make trouble between you & me, but I took no notice, so nothing came of it.

She thinks now, and I agreed with her, that if we go getting the milk from her, it would be better if you just collected it and went off, as if it were a shop. She thinks that if she asks you in and trys to get you to talk, she will get into more difficulties. This is really <u>much</u> best, isn't it? as she can't get the hang of you properly.[204]

As mildly as possible, I tried to point out what made her difficult to get on with, but it is not much good; only a bald statement would get this and then she would make too much of it and dwell on it for days. She wants to know if you & I would like to go there for a week on about July the 7th.

I said did they <u>really</u> not mind lending the house & she seemed to want to, very much.[205] I can't really tell what I ought to do, for I hate to be churlish & I hate to appear to get involved in an unsuitable way.

All this we can rake over later! And you can say what you'd like to do.

I seem just to remember the name Glinn-Jones, but he wasn't in my house & I think I couldn't really have known him, except as a name in another house. I can't put the body to the name at all! unless I'm told more. Also the girl can't be placed, though I expect it is all as she said. I expect her parents bought the chest when my father was selling up things he had in store.[206]

It does sound rather a tight fit with the Yanks, your sister <u>and</u> your brother. Don't let them get you to do too much "fatigue duty" as you put it. Make them share the chores & say you want to be treated as the invalid.

It must be good to go motoring again, and if you go to Merstham, I hope you get a swim in that millionaireish pool![207]

When you say my junk shop article—do you mean the thing I sent to "Vogue" which they pretend they haven't used yet? It is mystifying. Have you seen it with your own eyes? Or has someone made a mistake, confusing my picture & the little bit written under it. You must tell me.[208] Bolitho sent all the cuttings on virgin pieces of paper this morning. They look too good to be true. He hopes we'll meet again soon but hasn't sent his article yet.[209]

Julian wrote too thanking me prettily. She said "I thought Eric charming"!! So you see, you should have seen her next Tuesday after all, shouldn't you?

I'm sending this dough just in case you feel short with so much going on around you. All the tit-bits of news on Thursday, but don't miss the chance of doing anything nice by coming back then will you?

I'm quite all right now & am going to be very wise. As you say, my scouting days are over.[210]

Always Denont[211]

✍❤

Pitt's Folly Cottage
Nr Tonbridge
Kent

Monday evening
Oct. 22nd 1945

Dear Dump,[212]

I have just come in from a long day out in the car,—first picnicking where we did with Peggy in front of Peckham Old Church,[213] then walking into the grounds of Mereworth Castle (where they pumped out the sewage.)[214]

Further down the road I found a little ruined cottage or summer house, octagonal with a very pretty doorway. On the door soldiers had painted in bright red a skull & crossbones & Danger. High Explosives; & other ruder things too. But it was all deserted now & the roof would soon fall in. As usual I imagined it all repaired & me living in it with a fire in the grate & some nice food on the table. It would be a fine little retreat as it's in the middle of some magnificent old beeches & chestnuts. At this particular moment I began to rumble inside so I retreated into the bushes to do my duty, as the matron used to say. Judge of my foolish feeling when I looked up in the middle of the process & saw a lance corporal only a few yards away picking up chestnuts! I quickly dragged myself together & I am glad to say that he was too engrossed in his foraging to notice me. I went up to him & asked if I was trespassing, thinking it best to take the bull by the horns. He said "Naw yer nawt trespassing" I can't write it but he came from the North & seemed to think that it was quite all right for me to wander anywhere I liked in the Castle grounds. He said that further down was a prisoner of war camp & that there were only a few servants in the castle. I would like to have gone right through but I felt too tired, so after going a little further I turned back.[215]

When I looked over my shoulder I saw three Germans behind me in a line. I got the absurd notion that they were following me to knock me on the head in the woods, & take my clothes & money to escape with! The feeling was so strong that I got very hot & bothered & walked much too fast & began to feel very peculiar.[216] I was looking everywhere for the lance corporal so that I could make towards him, but he'd completely disappeared & when I looked round again, the Germans in their gray peaked caps had also disappeared mysteriously. I imagined them lurking behind the huge gnarled trunks. It was rather a moment & I wished you were there as moral support.

After these gruesome imaginings, I got out of the wood as soon as possible & went in the car to West Yalding to look in the junk shop (where I bought the shell back chain for 4/6) but he hadn't got anything,[217] so after looking again at the old houses and the unusual-looking, sinister Italian prisoners waiting for girls on all the street corners, I came back via Swanton Pool.[218] I don't know why I went that rather unusual way—perhaps it was suggested to me by something in the air, for just before I got to Harmston's Oast House I saw something black dangling out of one of the windows. Almost at once I knew there'd been a fire, & the next moment I saw that the place had been completely gutted!!

Two small boys were in the garden & I went up to them & asked them all about it. They said that it had happened last night, while Harmston was out. He banked up the fire much too high, as he always does (he burnt the mantelpiece at M. O.) & then went to Trot's.

Absolutely everything is gone,—all his clothes, furniture, papers. Only the walls are standing!—no floors roof or window frames. The bath and water pipes are dangling in mid air. He spent last night with Peggy at Gage Farm!

I stopped at Trot's to ask about it all. They are just off to Cornwall—tomorrow morning at 7. I think Peg & Harmston are very cozy now. They are collaborating on a book.[219]

I feel exhausted after my energetic walking day so am resting on the bed till Eve brings supper.

How has the family reunion gone off? I hope your brother looks well.[220]

May wants to know if you can fetch some Mates from her sister's in Roland Gardens when you return.[221] I'll give you the details later. If you can, snaffle the <u>thermos</u> <u>won't</u> you.

———

Tuesday. A letter today from Peggy, saying that she has to go into a nursing home for a little as she has a patch on one of her lungs—that is why she has felt so bad.[222] I haven't read all the letter yet, because it is so long. Noël also wrote, saying nothing really. It would be funny if you ran into her!

Yours always,
D.

✍♥

Oct 26th 1945. Friday

Dear Tuna,

The parcel only arrived this morning. Doesn't the post take an age! Thank you so much for the fine food. The grated cheese had unfortunately burst a little into the cocao [sic], so that there was a curious colored dust, when I opened the parcel, but only a very little is wasted.

Can you possibly hold out till, say Monday? If it's at all awkward or you are feeling dead from your aunt's and mother's attentions come straight back tomorrow; but if it's all going well, I shouldn't mind another couple of days of brooding solitude, for I am battling with a short story for Harper's Bazaar in America. (They wired Routledge, to see if I could do something for them) I am in rather a state about it and trying my hardest to get it done, so feel afraid of being distracted from it.[223]

But if you've fixed up for certain to come tomorrow, do come and I can just shut myself up even if you are here.

I should very much like to see the picture of brickwall, so I hope you'll bring it back with you—also your riding breeches and the thermos, if possible. (I feel like Fagan, training the boy pickpockets)[224]

Yehudi Menuhin is doing his stuff on the wireless so my thoughts are disintegrating.[225]

Two catastrophes have happened since you've been away. First one of my tooth stoppings[226] has come adrift and next, the car got a puncture just as I came home on Wednesday! I haven't even attempted to change the wheel, thinking of my weak and dithering state. So will have to try & do it together next week. How I wished you'd been there to cope. I had just come from seeing that house Little Hawkwell. They want over £4000 for it and the rain was thru the roof. It was very gruesome all alone in it. I sort of enjoyed my own horrors. At one moment I thought I saw a ghost out of the corner of my eye. It was only of course one of those huge stairs in the darkness. The ball on the tap looked like a misshapen head looming up at me.[227]

We would indeed need some of Bolter's £30,000 if we were going to live there.[228]

<u>So</u> glad you have seen your aunt, I knew she would be delighted. Hope your ma doesn't feel eaten out of house & home. Don't give Alethea a child.[229]

Miss D. Morgan 15 Roland Gardens S.W.Y. is the address for May's platts [flat], near S. Ken. or Glos. Road tube.[230] But don't worry if you can't manage it; she says she sends love.

See you soon.

D.

Pitt's Folly Cottage
Nr Tonbridge
Kent

M.O. [*The printed Pitt's Folly address is crossed out and "M.O."—for Middle Orchard—is written in to the left.*]
Aug 9th 1946[231]

Dear Dump.

Just a hurried note, as Noël is about to set out for Pearson's. She won't go back to London, although Rich & she are going to be there for the week-end. She says she doesn't like to leave me alone—and all the time I am so longing to be left alone![232]

All my good flow of writing in my journal was broken up this morning, but I shall have to bear it, as I can't be any plainer than I have already been. I've more or less said I crave for solitude. I am much better today, & I think I will get better with careful treatment.

The New Yorker asks for a story as they like "When I was Thirteen" in the American edition of Horizon Short Stories so it does look like the story has been reprinted,[233] though again, I suppose by the owners of "Horizon" so perhaps I don't get paid again.[234] The naval man has written too, but I can't read it,[235] also John [of the] Pearsons saying they like the drawing for "Vogue" v. much.[236] Love to Eve. Tell me of all your doings. Hop.[237]

Thank you for rude postcard.[238] I'm glad you met someone you knew. I don't remember that name though. Everything going well here—ducks thriving, Eve busying about.[239] Your room has been gutted. I would have done more but have maddeningly had slight temperature. We've been having lovely rasberry [*sic*] & strawberry shortcake. Nobody has called. No Adeneys have appeared. Henry came to cut the grass on Sat. but since then it has rained. I hope he comes again on Monday.[240] Have you seen things you wanted to buy? I haven't been out in the car because of my "indisposition." The garden is still looking very good. No one in the Reffold's yet.[241] Jo at the village hall yesterday in the rain to enter her bottled gooseberries, I suppose.[242] I haven't asked if I've sold a picture.[243] Remember me to your mother.

D.

2.

Pitt's Folly Cottage
Nr Tonbridge
Kent

M.O. [*The printed Pitt's Folly address is crossed out and "M.O."—for Middle Orchard—is written in to the left.*]
August 13th 1946

Dear Dump,

A quick note to thank you for your two good letters. I have left it late because I have been trying to begin my illustrations for Katherine Mansfield's story this morning.[244] I must run out in a minute with this & with Bills' [*sic*] airmail letter.[245]

The Adeneys were coming yesterday, but didn't because Noël had bellyache or something. So I have been quite a hermit since Saturday. I wish I had been as good as I sometimes am, then I could have got a lot done, but all the same I have done a "certain" amount, and have managed my meals v. easily. The only thing is this new treatment doesn't agree with me too well, I don't seem to want to eat, only drink quantities, hot or cold—just what I mustn't do![246]

I have discovered a fine way to do plums—bottle them with no water at all—they stew in their own juice & are very rich and dark. I had a letter from Michael Ayrton this morning—the guy sometimes on the Brain's Trust.[247] He wants me to exhibit with others at Heals in a show of small pictures priced below £40.[248] He said he hoped we'd meet, as he is an admirer of my work! I was pleased to have his letter, but I didn't like him at all on the wireless—a sort of smug conceited tone. But the wireless must be a terrible ordeal to face.

My naval comdr. has written too a lot about "In Youth is Pleasure." Very sensible really. He sounds intelligent in a naval officer way. He treats me a little like a difficult school boy or, perhaps it would be a midshipman.[249]

Of course at night the wireless often turns to gruesome subjects and I have to listen in a very matter-of-fact way and keep my imagination from dwelling on any horrors! But I enjoy it here too very much.

If only I had more time I would pack up some more food for you. Cheese and fat, because I don't need it, perhaps I can tomorrow.

Have a good time & don't hurry back. I can send more oof,[250] if needed. Love to Eve, & thank her for her note. Did you get the two letters I forwarded. Mildred has just appeared!![251]

D.

.✐

Thursday July 4th 1947[252]

Dear E.

Just a tiny note, in case you want more dough; I went to the bank yesterday.

What do you make of this letter from the Adeney? Doesn't it take the biscuit, after all the repressiveness? I've been frightened of even mentioning the house. I've written now to say that I shall be only to [sic] pleased to know exactly what they decide to do.[253]

Do you think there is a nasty tone in the letter?—I think so a little.

Bosanquet has written a nice letter from the Scilly Isles.[254] She liked my poem in Orion.[255] Henry has been here one day collecting hay.[256] Someone called Charlie is coming in three weeks to see the house before painting it. <u>Rene</u> rang up and offered some black currents! The whore answered.[257] D.

Have a good time.

D.

ℒ❤

July 7th 1947

Dear Dump.

Thank you so much for amusing letter; it took the taste away of this silly enclosure. I suppose the lady[258] feels neglected and uncossetted [*sic*]. How awful to want interest and attention so much.

Don't steam roller your poor Ma too much; perhaps we can buy a thermos ourselves now. Ask her where she got it. She will be afraid to have you stay, if you are so eager to part her from her useful possessions.

I don't like the sound of Auntie's Bank Manager. I should be inclined to poison her mind against him, if he's too unwholesome; but I expect she believes in him heart and soul and wouldn't hear a word against him.[259]

I have been wasting all morning writing an answer to the Lady's nonsense. If she writes again I shall just reply, "Wait till we meet to talk it over."[260]

Of course come back any day you like. We're all set for you. The whore picked three sweet-peas before I could tell her that they were sacred; however she says it will only make the others grow all the more flowers. I think she's right really, but I've told her not to pick any more.[261]

Yesterday I painted a new picture, from after breakfast till the evening. I think it will be quite good.[262] Braxton came with Mil, but I stayed closeted in my room.[263]

When I went to the bank I gave a lift to a pleasant P. of W. who was going down to the river to bathe. I nearly asked him back to tea, but felt awkward & remembered their five mile limit. I do think it is difficult to be matey. One feels that they resent one in some ways—only too understandable, of course.[264] When N. talks in her letter of your misreporting, I suppose she means that I said you were vague about the time of her train. Had she really settled for you to go and meet her? I don't think she had; she seemed to murmur something about not waiting if the car wasn't there. Isn't she insanely petty?[265]

I really think we are all as nice to her as can be expected, taking our different natures into account. I hope no upsets get too unmanageable. I've told her we must have a more business-like arrangement in March. I wish they'd sell.[266] Now I must stop and bath [*sic*]; it's 2:30 p.m. See you Wednesday,

Love D.[267]

Notes

1. Francis Streeten. A homosexual literary friend of Denton's, whom he met in 1937 in Tonbridge while he was living at 54 Hadlow Road. Streeten had learned of a "mysterious artist who was said to roam the countryside making ambiguous approaches to young rustics" (Making of a Writer, 122). Streeten figures, in rather unflattering terms, in Welch's short stories "A Fragment of a Life Story" and "A Picture in the Snow." In early November 1943 Streeten brought Eric Oliver to visit Denton at Pitt's Folly Cottage in Hadlow. He is described by Welch in his journal and in a postcard to Noël Adeney as a "new hearty land-boy friend." A more complete description of this first meeting is included in the introduction to the letters. The journal entry commemorating this meeting is for January 25, 1944 (Journals, 125). Both Francis Streeten and Eric Oliver were then living in a hostel in Maidstone where they were working for the Kent Agricultural Executive Committee doing alternative service, Francis as a conscientious objector and Eric because of high blood pressure.

2. Denton's invitation for Eric to return to Pitt's Folly Cottage is accompanied by directions from Hadlow Road. Welch had moved from his former accommodation at Tonbridge (Pond Farm) sometime in June 1943. The cottage was owned by Mary Sloman, the estranged wife of Harold Sloman (former headmaster of Tonbridge School). De-la-Noy notes that Denton had probably met the Slomans through Francis Streeten, whose stockbroker father had been a governor of Tonbridge School. Denton and his housekeeper/caretaker Evie Sinclair moved into rooms over a garage located adjacent to Mrs. Sloman's cottage.

3. This "scolding" about Eric's leaving Denton's letters around the Maidstone hostel probably originates with revelations by Francis Streeten that this was occurring. The "cold and dull" letter "about Christmas day" was never sent and was probably destroyed by Welch.

4. The manuscript for *Maiden Voyage*. A letter from Edith Sitwell of December 22 reveals that Roger Senhouse of Secker & Warburg had written her "enthusiastically" about the manuscript. Welch dedicated the novel to Sitwell, his first literary champion (see introduction). *Maiden Voyage* was accepted for publication by Herbert Read of Routledge. Edith Sitwell wrote a fulsome introduction to the novel in which she refers to Welch as "a born writer."

5. Denton met Noël Adeney in late 1942. She and her husband, Bernard Adeney, were painters, the latter of whom had founded the London School. Upon Welch's relocation to Pitt's Folly, he became involved in a problematic friendship with Noël, whose holiday home at Middle Orchard was located six miles from Pitt's Folly Cottage. She was his confidante during the early stages of his relationship with Eric Oliver, but this connection turned sour when Welch realized that Noël was becoming progressively more infatuated with him and jealous of Eric. She would write a scathing—and for the most part fabricated—fictionalized account of their relationships in her 1956 novel, *No Coward Soul*.

6. Eric had arrived late and drunk to Christmas lunch at Pitt's Folly. Eric's shyness and discomfort at meeting strangers had resulted in his getting up "a little Dutch courage on the way." Denton notes in his journal entry of January 25, 1944 (*Journals*, 127) that Eric accused him of writing an invitation that was "cold and unsatisfactory," that Denton was not a "true friend . . . cold and ungenerous." The quarrelsome attitude assumed by Oliver while in "the cups" accounts for Denton's concern over the former's drinking. The evening ended with a crying spell, and both felt "frightfully muddled and stupid and sad, and utterly hopeless." The muddled part, as will be seen, related to the confusion that both were experiencing about the sincerity of their developing relationship.

7. See note 3.

8. A reference to his continuing tubercular fevers. He had contracted a bone infection as a result of his accident in June 1935 (see introduction). He would not actually visit the specialist in London until May 3 (a description of this visit is found in the letter to Eric of the same date).

9. Eric's mother, Amy Oliver, was then living in London. As the letter reveals, Denton is concerned about the effects of the blitz, and concerned for Eric's safety if indeed he did visit his mother.

10. The "new book" would eventually be published as *In Youth Is Pleasure*.

11. Welch refers to Rosemary Mundy Castle, the daughter of one of Welch's patrons. Her mother, Peggy Mundy Castle, had purchased a painting, *By the Sea*, from him. According to Methuen-Campbell, Denton experienced his first air raid while on a visit to the Mundy Castles at Tonbridge. After hearing an explosion in the direction of Platt, Welch breezily said, "I expect it's the Hop Garden." After his visit at the Mundy Castles, Denton "spent the rest of the evening in the congenial company of three cadets." Upon arriving home, "there was the most almighty explosion. A time-bomb had landed in the garden only eight yards or so from the house. . . . Apart from broken windows, the damage was slight. None of his treasures had suffered" (*Writer and Artist*, 100).

Although Welch refers rather cavalierly to Rosemary's discomfiture at hearing of Eric, it was a brief tryst between Eric and Rosemary following the group's trip to the Rose and Crown pub on Christmas evening that had resulted in the emotional exchange between Welch and Oliver referred to in note 6. It also underscores Eric's bisexuality. Welch's journal entry for January 25, 1944 (*Journals*, 128–29), presents a lengthier description of these events.

12. Eric was in fact still at Mereworth but would move to a hostel at Appledore in Kent on February 7, 1944. This was thirty-five miles from Denton's cottage.

13. The reference to "wretched bombers circling overhead" and "peculiar lights which flash from the hillside" are to Luftwaffe bombing raids and to anti-aircraft activity. By 1944 the German aerial attack had begun to include unmanned V-2 rockets.

14. Evelyn "Evie" Sinclair was originally Welch's landlady in London (34 Croom's Hill) while he was attending Goldsmiths School of Art, 1934–35. She visited Denton while he was convalescing from his accident at Southcourt Nursing Home, Broadstairs, at which time she informed him that her brother, who owned the house at Croom's Hill, had "sacked" her. Welch was struck with the possibility of hiring her as his housekeeper once he was dismissed from the hospital. This in fact was negotiated and she accompanied him—and ultimately Eric Oliver—through successive households at Hadlow Road, the Hop Garden, Pond Farm, Pitt's Folly, and finally Middle Orchard. The relationship, as may be seen from his letters and journal entries, was not always the happiest or most salutary.

At times it seems that only an uneasy truce existed between them throughout. However, she figures significantly in his fiction, particularly as Miss Hellier in *A Voice through a Cloud*, and she, along with Eric, provided a degree of comfort and care for the ailing author through the entirety of his creative career.

15. Welch made the understandable error of notating this date as "1943" rather than "1944."

16. Here Denton is referring to an occasion noted in his journal entry of January 24, 1943, when he took Eric to visit Noël Adeney at Middle Orchard. He characterizes Eric's attitude to middle-aged women as one of "horror," as he thinks that "he appears nothing but a dull oaf to them" (*Journals*, 122). Welch describes the meeting as follows: "His nervousness was funny and tragic. . . . Conversation was difficult. I wished and wished that Eric could communicate his thoughts more easily. I could see the tenseness and nervousness in him. I felt alarmed. He really looked so caged and frightened, and you can almost see the panic of thoughts in his head" (123). The gathering he refers to in his letter was one arranged by his landlady, Mary Sloman, and Brenda Cobb (then living with her) to introduce Welch to a young actor friend and what they believed to be a romantic "prospect" for him. As is evident, Welch much preferred the "hearty" athletic type to what he describes here as one of "those egoistic buggers."

17. As De-la-Noy relates, Eric was the fifth of six children and the youngest of four boys (*Making of a Writer*, 181). His three older brothers had attended Dulwich College, but Eric had failed the common entrance exam. He was thereafter sent to the Ongar Grammar School and then to the cathedral school at Salisbury. His period of schooling was extremely troubled, characterized by his running away and threatening one his masters with a table knife (referred to in *Journals*, 131 [February 2, 1944]).

18. The poems were evidently never published during Welch's lifetime. Welch's poetry was collected in 1976—along with the decorations for them— by Jean-Louis Chevalier from manuscript notebooks at the Ransom Center for the Humanities, University of Texas at Austin (*Dumb Instrument: Poems and Fragments* London: Enitharmon Press, 1976). The manuscript-notation dates given by Chevalier indicate that the poems "Crater of Love," "O Keep the Sugared Pill," "Understanding and Fighting," and "Hold On to Happiness," are most likely those which Welch wished to dedicate to Eric. Such lines as "Yet here I lie / Deep buried in your cave / Burnt into by your fire / And slashed through with your knife" ("Crater of Love"); "My friend and I / Are close and blind and warm, / —Sometimes. / And then we find / All happiness in being still / And knowing the dark earth . . . / But other times / Our hearts are far apart . . . Only the cruel words are said / And ancient wounds remembered" ("Understanding and Fighting"); and "Hold on to happiness /

With all your heart / And make it yours / As long as you can breathe" ("Hold
On to Happiness"). The poems clearly reflect Denton's developing love for
Eric, and the doubts that plagued the writer during the early stages of their
acquaintance.

19.   Here Welch is referring to the prospective dedication of his first novel,
Maiden Voyage, to Edith Sitwell ("some highly respectable and emminent [*sic*]
woman.!").

20.   "Your letter is *good*." As De-la-Noy relates in his biography of Welch,
only one letter from Eric to Denton survives (*Journals*, 183 n10). Oliver told
De-la-Noy that he had destroyed all of the others because he believed them to
be badly written. Obviously, Welch felt differently.

21.   Dr. Jack Easton was one of the physicians who attended Welch during
his convalescence at Broadstairs in 1936. Easton befriended the young invalid,
taking him on excursions outside the nursing home and even inviting Welch to
his own home. He encouraged Denton to begin painting again and to locate an
independent life for himself as a writer and artist. However, Welch developed an
embarrassing infatuation ("quite an overpowering obsession") for Easton and
felt betrayed when his friend and confidant revealed that he was going to establish a practice in Tonbridge. One of the reasons for Welch's decision to locate
near Tonbridge himself following his hospitalization was so he could be near
this man on whom he had developed a degree of dependence. Easton figures
significantly in Welch's autobiographical novel, *A Voice through a Cloud*, as
Doctor Farley. Just how advanced Denton's infatuation had become is demonstrated not only in the novel but also in the short story "Alex Fairburn."

22.   J. E. refers to Dr. Jack Easton; see note 21.

23.   Rosemary Mundy Castle; see note 11.

24.   On February 7 Eric moved to a new hostel in Appledore. He left his
signet ring and snuffbox with Welch for safekeeping. Welch's journal entry of
February 6, describing a picnic they had in the woods near Pitt's Folly on the
day before Eric left for his new assignment, reveals the developing affection
between the two men and the pervasive sense of doom connected with Denton's
continuing illness and physical debility:

> It seems unbearably sad now to think of that picnic, so unsuitable for
> the time of year, so lost in the wood and in time and with only two tiny
> points of humanity to remember it. . . .
>
> I knew I would remember it afterwards and always. It was too sad
> to forget. . . .

> Eric saw how sad I was and he kissed me and lay down on the
> ground and shut his eyes. We both felt then, I think, how doomed we
> were, how doomed everyone was. We saw very clearly the plain tragedy
> of our lives and of everybody's. A year after a year after a year passes,
> and then you look back and your sadness pierces you. (*Journals*, 133)

With this episode in mind, there should be little wonder at the vehemence of
Denton's response to Eric's apparent "doubt," or lukewarm attitude toward
their friendship, expressed in the latter's letter of February 9.

Methuen-Campbell incisively describes Eric's state of mind at this juncture:
"Denton needless to say was still besotted with Eric, but the relationship was
very one-sided. Whilst having an appreciation of the difficulties Denton was
suffering, Eric, lacking in self-confidence, could not really understand why he
had been befriended in the first place, especially when he had made it plain to
Denton that he was 'not his type.' . . . Eric, totally inexperienced in close relationships, read these letters with incomprehension and a certain amount of
unease. Looking back, he admitted that his behaviour to Denton *had* been
pretty appalling" (*Writer and Artist*, 150).

In the above journal entry, Denton describes the letter as "a good one,
which at the end hurt me so that I wrote a ten-page answer, probably very silly
and bad-tempered and unwise" (*Journals*, 134). As De-la-Noy points out, "The
combined effect of his ill-health (did anyone realize just how unwell he was, or
take account of it?), the emotional strain of his feelings for Eric, and now, it
seems, an absurd confusion in his friendship with Noël Adeney, must account
for much of what Denton dashed down in his 'very unwise' letter to Eric that
day" (*Making of a Writer*, 200).

25. Welch writes at length of Eric Oliver's time as a farm laborer near
Penshurst in his journal entry of February 11, 8:30 p.m. His letter parallels the
notebook description in some respects, but the journal goes on to describe
events in Eric's life in an imaginative, literary mode: "as I passed the pub [at
Penshurst], I thought of Eric who lived near here, on a farm, when he was
twenty-one. He told me that once he won a race in the village sports and Lord
De L'Isle gave him a money order for ten shillings which he spent on cigarettes.
I can imagine him running, running in Penshurst Park with the ancient trees
round him and the people in white and colours. I can see it; the heat of the day
and Eric younger, chubbier as he puts it, with his dark hair stuck on his forehead with sweat, and the Adam's apple swelling up and down in his throat. I
can imagine him afterwards with the village youths and girls and I long so

much to have been there too so that afterwards we could have had a lovely
night talking and drinking and singing." He goes on to say that, as he passed
the "Fleur de Lys" at Leigh (near Penshurst), "again I thought of Eric, for he
told me he used often to get tight there. . . . Curious to think that all this time
while Eric worked on the farm, hated it, was utterly lonely, got tight as often as
possible just for something to do, I was only a few miles away at Tonbridge,
walking streets in my restlessness, trying to make myself iller and iller by foolishness, wanting to die. And we never met and all the years in between, seven, eight,
we knew nothing of each other, they all melted away and were wasted" (*Journals*,
134–35). Denton refers to the period just after his dismissal from the nursing
home at Broadstairs (1936), when he lived in Tonbridge with Evie Sinclair.

Both the letter and the journal entry express Welch's deep sense of a life
wasted by the impact of his accident and subsequent illnesses; "Nothing can
make up for the fact that my very early youth was so clouded with illness and
unhappiness. I feel cheated as if I had never had that fiercely thrilling time
when the fears of childhood have left one and no other thing has swamped
one" (*Journals*, 134).

26. This apparent concern of Eric's about his problem of "mixing well"
with Denton's "circle" has previously been noted in his obvious discomfort in
dealing with Welch's middle-class female friends, including Noël Adeney,
May Walbrand-Evans, Peggy Mundy Castle, and so forth. It also has to do
with Eric's feeling that a social divide existed between Welch and him. Note
that earlier in the letter, Denton tries to allay Eric's concerns by his comment
that "I am *not* tight and smug and prim. I judge *nobody*. You don't have to put
a 'proper' act on with me, because I'm not 'proper'! I need no living up to *at
all*."

27. By the time of this writing, Eric had decided to come on a visit in response to Denton's invitation of February 18. Welch's letter of the eighteenth
had done much to reconcile the two and to allay Eric's fears of his emotional
and social inadequacy.

28. Obviously meant ironically, judging from Welch's concern about Eric's
drinking habits.

29. Decorations for *In Youth Is Pleasure*, accepted for publication by Routledge on January 17, 1944 (*Journals*, 135 n8). Welch did the frontispiece and
chapter designs for all of his novels and articles.

30. After the publication of *Maiden Voyage* (1943) and a print of his painting
Portrait of Lord Berners as a Child, Dressed Up as Robinson Crusoe in *Vogue*, Welch
began receiving quantities of fan mail and requests for visits from enthusiastic

readers. Many of these new contacts were from homosexual readers who seem
to have found a refreshing freedom and comfort of identity in Denton's autobiographical fiction. As De-la-Noy meticulously points out in his note to
Welch's journal entry of July 21, 1942, the Lord Berners painting had been
done from a photograph of Berners as a child, included in his autobiography,
First Childhood. Welch attempted unsuccessfully to sell the painting to Berners,
after which he displayed it at Leicester Galleries. It was eventually given to
Helen Roeder, a painter friend met during Welch's time at Goldsmiths School
of Art.

31.   John was one of Eric's fellow agricultural workers at Appledore. While
Eric and Denton were waiting for Eric's train back to Appledore on Sunday,
February 27, they met this young man, whom Welch describes in his journal as
having a face "quite cracked . . . and a great tone of culture with a capital K."
Welch goes on to relate the story of John's "girl" and the "doughboy": "he told
us how a woman friend of his was walking home with an American doughboy,
who, when she reached her door, suddenly gave her a great biff for no reason
and then disappeared. This story seemed horrible to me, but John didn't seem
in the least perturbed. 'My friend thinks he must have had a brainstorm' was
all he said" (*Journals*, 137).

32.   The mutual caretaking roles adopted by Denton and Eric at this juncture is made clear by Welch's repairing Eric's frayed shirt. Welch re-creates this
incident of the weekend of February 26 in a poignant journal entry of April 2:

> After three weeks of letter-writing and keeping away, Eric at last came
> from Appledore to see me. I went to Tonbridge to meet his train on the
> Saturday morning. I was late and so I looked in all the pubs round the
> station for him. At last I ran him to earth in the one near the public
> library. It was warm and dark and dismal in there; and there was Eric
> looking lost, distraught, restless, unhappy, his shirt all frayed, a large
> black pint in front of him. . . .
>
> At home Evie had kept the lunch hot, so we ate it after three o'clock.
> Then we rested and tried to sleep off the gin.
>
> The rest of the day we spent talking very little, just happy to be
> together again.
>
> I took the frayed shirt off Eric and gave him one of mine, which
> luckily fitted. I said I would get his mended. (*Journals*, 135–36)

33.   Part of the text of the letter at this point is blotted out.

34.   Welch refers to the March 1944 *Vogue* article referred to in note 30.

35. The complexity of Denton's relationship with his eldest brother, William "Bill" Welch, has been discussed in detail by Michael De-la-Noy in his biography *Denton Welch: The Making of a Writer*. Bill (b. 1908) was seven years older than Denton and—due to his extended absences in boarding school and university—had little contact with his younger brother except during holidays at the family residences in Oxfordshire or Shanghai. Welch re-creates the nature of this relationship in his short story "When I Was Thirteen" (pub. *Horizon*, April 1944; collected in *Brave and Cruel*) and in the novels *In Youth Is Pleasure* and *A Voice through a Cloud*. The nature of their respective interests and personalities was truly disparate. Bill completed his term at Repton and then went on to Hertford College Oxford, where he was a member of the college ski team. He later went into business with their father in Shanghai. Denton, on the other hand, ran away from Repton School, and after a long visit with his father and brother in Shanghai, he entered Goldsmiths School of Art. Bill lived extravagantly, flying airplanes and driving expensive cars. He was truly the middle-class "hearty" and the favorite of the boys' father, Arthur. Denton, on the other hand, was small of stature, introspective, not given to games and team athletics. Welch believed his brother Bill viewed him as "petty, spinsterishly careful, really rather contemptible in my concern for pennies and shillings." Orvil (Denton's persona in *In Youth Is Pleasure*) was "very much afraid of his eldest brother. Charles [Bill in the novel] was always able to make him feel small, young, effeminate, inferior, cowardly, and disgraceful. . . . [H]is rages were so terrible. For no apparent reason he would suddenly pour out a stream of shaming words which seemed to shrivel up Orvil's soul for days afterwards. The uncertainty of his temper was the most terrifying thing about him" (quoted in *Making of a Writer*, 38).

Further evidence of Bill's temper can be seen in an episode related autobiographically in Welch's story "When I Was Thirteen." Based on a Christmas holiday trip to Switzerland taken with Bill when Denton was thirteen, the story describes the physical abuse Bill inflicted on his younger brother when he discovered that when he left Denton alone at the lodge to go skiing with his college friends, the adolescent boy had spent time with another of Bill's fellow undergraduates who was suspected of being homosexual. Significantly, two of the epithets used by Bill as he is beating Denton with a hairbrush and forcing his head into a basin of cold water are "harlot, sod."

In Welch's description of the relationship between the autobiographical personae of Orvil Pym and his older brother Charles in *In Youth Is Pleasure*, he hints at Charles's repressed homosexual tendencies and self-loathing: "Charles would lavish a curious love on him [Orvil] sometimes—in the privacy of a bedroom in the early morning, or in a car at night—but by the light of day, and with other people present, he was mocking and contemptuous" (quoted in *Making of a Writer*, 38). The publication of "When I Was Thirteen" in *Horizon*, April 1944, was heralded by Welch in a letter of April 19, 1944, to his friend Marcus Oliver: "A frightfully chi-chi story of mine has just come out in 'Horizon.' Read it if you ever see that mag. I think it will make some people's hair stand on end, as it's not a bit cloaked really" (39). One of the individuals whose hair Denton suspected might "stand on end" was obviously his brother Bill. However, as De-la-Noy has pointed out, Bill evidently took these fictional references to his relationship with his brother in perfect stride. In fact, Bill was very solicitous of Denton's welfare throughout the remainder of the writer's life.

36. The "talk in the woods" occurred on March 11 (*Journals*, 137–38 [April 2, 1944]). Eric and Denton had had "double gins" in the Volunteers pub in Tonbridge, among a group of soldiers and Italian POWs. Afterward, they bicycled into a nearby wood to have a picnic lunch. Welch relates: "I was much drunker this time [than on the previous episode in the wood; see note 24] after five gins and when we sat down at the foot of a tree in the delicate warm sun I suddenly burst into tears. Frightful, but true. And this flood set us talking, talking, talking about friendship, love, hate, fear of death, on, on, on."

37. The "painful," "humiliating" details about his accident would certainly have included the fact that his spinal and pelvis injuries had rendered him partially impotent. De-la-Noy, in his interviews with Eric Oliver for Welch's biography, discovered that Denton could "achieve an erection but not an orgasm" (*Making of a Writer*, 97 n1). This perceived failure of "manliness" on Welch's part must certainly be at the heart of his remark that "I'm so conscious of the quality that I lack—you've no need to tell me—it hits me in the eye everyday when I wake up. And this knowledge makes it difficult for me to believe that you care anything for me at all." See also references to the difficulties in sexual relations between Denton and Eric in the introduction.

38. Both had been born in 1915. Denton ran away from Repton in 1931. He and his brother Paul—two years his elder (born 1913) and with whom Welch had a much closer and healthier relationship than with Bill—were returning to Repton from their summer holidays. While at the train station in London, Denton "gave his brother the slip" and made his way to Salisbury (where he visited his first cathedral) and Exeter. Having run out of money he turned to a cousin, May Beeman, who was then living in London. While in London and

waiting for his brother Bill and aunt Dorothy (Lady Fox) to retrieve him, he was shown around various London art schools (he had shown a particular aptitude for drawing and painting while in grammar and public school). Once his older brother and father had been alerted to Denton's unhappiness at Repton, and for that matter, with the prospect of a conventional public school and university education for him, it was decided that the boy would go—at the end of the Repton school term—to Shanghai to visit his father and thereafter be enrolled in an art school in London. Denton seems at times to have been too cruel in his characterizations of his brother Bill and of his father (particularly of the latter's remarriage to Ada Henderson, whom he accused of "gold digging" and cheating him out of his inheritance), as both tacitly accepted his sexual difference and fostered his artistic education. All of these incidents are autobiographically portrayed in Welch's novel *Maiden Voyage*.

Eric Oliver had not the same advantages as the upper-middle-class Welch. He had been sent to Ongar Grammar School, from which he had run away, and later to Salisbury cathedral school. He was allowed to leave this boarding school at the age of thirteen after complaining to his father about the "other boys getting into bed with one another" (*Making of a Writer*, 181). Thereafter he went to work at his father's London business of manufacturing jewel cases. He didn't stay long here either, drifting from one job to another, often taking "land jobs" (agricultural labor). He maintained little contact with his older brothers, who had matriculated from Dulwich College.

39. Denton's "pa," Arthur Welch, died in a Japanese internment camp near Shanghai. He had been a director in Wattie & Company, a firm of rubber estate managers based in Shanghai. In later journal entries (September 9 and October 18, 1945), Welch complains that either his father squandered much of his estate or that his stepmother, Ada Henderson Welch, had deprived him and his brothers of their inheritance. Interestingly, it was Denton's brother Bill who championed the family's cause in regard to Arthur's will.

40. "When I Was Thirteen," published in *Horizon*, April 1944; see note 35. The "great British Public" would, Welch feared, be shocked by the frankly homoerotic theme of the story, as well as by its indictment of public school hypocrisy on the subject of homosexuality.

41. "Tubes" is probably slang for a catheter Welch was forced to wear as a consequence of his injuries. Methuen-Campbell provides the following information concerning the necessity of Denton's using catheters in order to urinate: "[A] catheter had to be passed into his bladder through the urethra. This process, when performed regularly, nearly always led to the patient getting an

inflammation of the kidneys and a symptom of this was the blinding headaches from which Denton suffered for the rest of his life. Also there would be high temperatures" (*Writer and Artist*, 68). From the journals of this period it is evident that Denton and Eric were by this time sleeping together. Clearly, this is a reference to an earlier, more intimate discussion. Note also Welch's concern with sexual dysfunction caused by his accident.

42. Frida Easdale had been Welch's neighbor when he lived at the Hop Garden in St. Mary's Platt. On December 3, 1943, he had been with Frida and his brother Paul on an outing to discuss the possibility of buying the cottage. While they were away a fire destroyed much of the house, taking with it one of Welch's most precious mementoes, his mother's silver. While Easdale and Adeney were in fact not only friends but at times patrons, it seems the height of "bitchiness" that he would repeatedly show a tendency toward misogyny and back biting.

43. In his April 2, 1944, journal entry, Welch recounts this incident, which resonates with Denton's concern with the passing moment: "In the morning we took out our lunch again and climbed through Oxon Hoath to Gover Hill. We lay in the charming haystack beside the avenue. It began to sleet and we hid in the warm hay. I saw Eric's eyes glinting at me through the mass of hay. And I wished I could always sit in haystacks with Eric, feeling the sun on us and eating pilchards" (*Journals*, 138).

44. The atmosphere of wartime England is reflected in this letter. The threat of bombings and V-1 rockets was very real for Welch. The Hop Garden had been slightly damaged by bomb explosions shortly before its destruction by fire in 1943.

45. The Brooms was a Tonbridge pub frequented by Denton and Eric.

46. Though several of Eric's stories concerning his bouts of drinking and an attempted suicide when he was eighteen are included in the journal entry of April 2, no reference can be found to the "General story" either here or elsewhere in the journals or letters. With the military buildup in anticipation of the Allied invasion of Europe of June 1944, any number of scenarios involving officers at the rank of general—American or British—could be involved here.

47. The "wooden angel" refers to a large baroque angel that, along with a lacquered Chinese screen, a Louis XV secretaire, a harpsichord, and an extensive porcelain collection, was one of his most prized possessions. As noted in the introduction, Welch had an artistic fascination with minutiae and antiques.

48. Denton's twenty-ninth birthday was on March 29, 1944. In the journal entry of April 2, Denton does refer to his birthday celebration:

On my birthday on Thursday Noël brought me, as I lay in bed, a charming little eighteenth-century watch. Rich gold pinchbeck with a lovely disc of gorgeous blue glass at the back. The face wonderfully smooth and white with spidery Roman numerals. The hands two delicate gold antennae, beautifully, thoughtfully and strangely shaped.

The original old label is in the back of the outer case.

I played with it all afternoon, but it had then to go back to the maker to be made to go. I am waiting impatiently for it.

Noël has also made me a birthday cake with a pink "D" on it. It was nice suddenly to have a birthday recognized. And strangest of all, my brother Bill sent me a wire from the Conservative Club where he had just arrived from Africa. (*Journals*, 140)

49. This premonition that Denton "knew something was going to happen," refers to the first meeting between Denton and Eric, when Francis Streeten brought him by Pitt's Folly in November 1943; see note 1. He describes this first meeting with Eric in his journal entry of January 25, 1944:

Evie answered [the door], telling me that Francis had arrived with a friend and could they both just come up for a minute. I consented, and saw, walking into the room after fat Francis, someone in battle-dress trousers [fatigues], Wellingtons, and a jersey and white shirt, open, also white tops of pants showing above the trousers, large leather belt, face red-brown, with a very good throat. . . .

They had been drinking in a pub and had come on to me later. They were mildly redolent of the pub and beer. They talked a little wildly.

When they left, Eric turned at the door and gave me a long sharp look. "Why don't you get up and come and have a drink with us?" he had asked the moment before. Now he knew I was ill and he was sorry and he liked me. (*Journals*, 125)

50. See note 48.

51. As referred to in note 48, William Welch had returned from Africa. His concern about literary characterizations of his brother is discussed in detail in note 35.

52. Rose-Marie Aubépin had "discovered" Welch through the publication of *Maiden Voyage*; see note 30. As Welch mentions, she was a volunteer in the Free French Forces under the command of General Charles de Gaulle. She in fact paid Welch a visit on Sunday, April 9. He recounts this visit in his journal

entry of April 10 and in the letter to Eric of April 11, 1944. His suggestion that
Eric hide in the "cupboard" and that he "tactfully withdraw" if Eric "liked the
look of her," is a playful reference to Eric's bisexuality.

53. Denton's concern over Eric's suicidal tendencies may have their origins
in the latter's drunken "funks." Welch's journal of April 2, 1944, includes an
account of Eric's attempted suicide at the age of eighteen:

> [Eric] had taken 12 £ from his mother's suitcase with which to buy
> drink and did not know how to face her.
>
> He was at an older friend's house, the chap with whom he had
> been drinking. He locked himself in the bathroom and began to take
> two hundred Aspirin tablets. He said the taste was awful and the
> amount of water he had to drink was enormous. And as he took them
> he thought of all the other people in the world who did not have to die
> and he envied them with all his heart, and longed and longed not to
> have to kill himself. But at last he swallowed them all, and then the
> friend, Jack, came battering on the door, shouting for him to open it. . . .
>
> [T]he friend, although tight, immediately regained some wits and
> telephoned the ambulance and hospital at once.
>
> Eric was taken off in the white van, pretending to be more uncon-
> scious than he was. He had lost the use of his limbs, but he knew what
> was happening. At the hospital the young doctor used the stomach
> pump on him which was awful. . . .
>
> Then the doctor turned to Eric and asked kindly why he did it.
> And Eric was at such a loss to know what to do that he said, insolently,
> "Oh, I just had a fat head." The doctor turned away and said, "You'll
> hear more of this." (*Journals*, 138–39)

After an attempt by the authorities to charge Eric with the criminal offense of
attempted suicide, he was forced to undergo psychological testing.

Welch relates his love and concern for Eric at this juncture of his journal
entry: "When Eric tells me things like this, life seems so terrifying that I want
to die. And I long wildly to have known him all my life. I know it would have
been different if I had. Perhaps not better, but different, less mad" (*Journals*,
139).

Welch himself—if his accounts in *Voice through a Cloud* and his short story
"Alex Fairburn" are to be trusted—attempted suicide by taking a number pills
from one of his medications. It had been done in order to engage the attention

of Dr. Jack Easton, the physician for whom Welch had developed an infatuation during and after his convalescence at Broadstairs. See introduction.

54. For *In Youth Is Pleasure.*

55. The passport contains Welch's actual birth date of March 29, 1915. He had previously lied to Eric about his age, maintaining that he was two years younger than Eric. According to De-la-Noy, Eric Oliver was only six months Denton's senior. In his letter of March 14, Welch told Oliver the partial truth about his age: "It seems that I have to be *quite* truthful with you. I even have to admit it when I have told you that I am nearly 27 when I am nearly 28. And for me to have to confess that I've told you a silly, petty; pointless, vain lie like that is *very* difficult."

56. To this editor's knowledge, Welch never made a portrait of Eric. Noël Adeney, however, did make one of Oliver in November 1944, when he was twenty-nine years old (*Making of a Writer*, 236, 238–39). Eric did bring Welch several photographs as he requested. This is mentioned in the journal entry for April 17, 1944: "We looked at some old photographs he [Eric] had brought, of himself and family. (This is always such a curious mix of sadness and ribaldry)" (*Journals*, 142).

57. Welch had last seen his brother Bill and his wife, Anne, in February 1937, before the couple left for business in Shanghai (*Making of a Writer*, 213).

58. Denton describes their visit to the pub and bicycling on Oxon Hoath in the journal entry for April 2, 1944; see note 36. The journal attests to the role Eric had already adopted as part of his relationship with Denton, that of caretaker during the writer's frequent illnesses: "I was in bed with a temperature of 104 and Eric came up to me and put a towel under my head and a flannel soaked in cold water over my temples and eyes. He did this many times, soothing me. He told me he had learnt it when he had all the terrible hangovers of his early youth" (138).

59. See note 53. Welch possessed a real fascination for Eric's raucous youth, accompanied by a sense that his own life had been wasted by having not found Eric earlier in his youth. He recounts a story of an alcoholic "black out" Oliver experienced when he was seventeen or eighteen:

He was drinking in a pub and had been for days on end, waiting for them to open. And suddenly the publican saw him plucking at his shirt and knew that something would happen.

Then all went black and Eric rushed out into the yard, and the next thing he knew was that he was lying on the ground in a horse box in the stable, kicking and screaming, and people trying to calm him and hold him and hold him down.

Then he was taken to hospital and stayed there three weeks. And he saw the sides of the building fall down and windows crash and doors dissolve, and animals unreal and terrifying. (*Journals*, 140)

Note that in the previous letter of March 30, Welch attempts to convince Oliver that there are other—less destructive—ways to allay boredom than alcoholic binges: "You're not going to drink a lot this week-end, are you Eric. I sound a bit of temperance preacher; I suppose it's my high temperature. I think what stops hundreds of people drinking is that they get the habit of reading a lot. Once you've got it, you feel awfully content and not bored when the day's work is done. It doesn't always work of course, but generally. I know that's what keeps me going when I'm more or less alone for days."

He goes on to express his regret at not having been able to help Eric at this juncture in his life: "Surely this is enough to make anyone cry, especially as it happened to one naturally sweet and kind, terribly young, foolish, generous, utterly without guidance and judgement. . . . *Again I say how I long to have known him then, to have seen what was gnawing at him all the time*" (*Journals*, 140; emphasis mine). Welch is here expressing the lover's quandary of wishing to remake the beloved's past and to ease the pain that shared recollection brought to them both.

60. The story in *New Writing and Daylight* was "The Barn." This "tremulous and sexy story" involves an adolescent boy's attraction to a young vagrant who stays the night in the family stable. Welch's homoerotic description of the boy's sneaking into the barn to lie down beside the sleeping man is both tantalizing and repellant, speaking to Welch's impish desire to shock the "great British Public."

61. The new book is *In Youth Is Pleasure*.

62. Endsleigh Mansions was the residence of Eric's mother, Amy, in London.

63. Francis Streeten; see note 1. Streeten was included in Welch's short fiction as Danny Touchett in "A Fragment of a Life Story" and in an untitled story appearing in *Chance* (1953), and as Danny Whittome in "A Picture in the Snow." (The titled stories were first published posthumously in *A Last Sheaf* (*Journals*, 26). Streeten had last shown up at Pitt's Folly in December 1943. According to Welch's letter to Noël Adeney of December 7, Francis was in a

"maddeningly babyish mood." He had not eaten, so they "all devoured toast and talked at cross purposes. It was terrible" (*Making of a Writer*, 183). Welch's "rudeness" to Streeten seems to be at odds with the gratitude repeatedly expressed in the letters and journal entries for Francis's role in introducing Denton to Eric in November 1943. The journal entry of March 23, 1946, shows how Streeten had been the instrument of his "destiny" in locating his companion: "Francis brought Eric quite unexpectedly, and because I was so ill and exhausted that evening I nearly did not see them. What would have happened if I hadn't suddenly changed my mind? Another door was opened on to a landscape that I thought would always be quite foreign to me. All those crags and pools and frowning storm-clouds; a degree of sharing quite outrageous if it had been prophesied to me; unhappiness and feeling of waste that I thought I had done with for ever; cosy snugness of friendship that I only remember very early with my brother [Paul]" (*Journals*, 259).

For earlier references to Paul Welch, see note 38. Paul was serving in Tunisia and Italy with the North Irish Horse. He won the Military Cross for meritorious service (*Journals*, 21 n31).

64. The Austin 7 automobile had been given to Denton in 1937 by his father. There is no journal entry referring to the incident with the curate of Tonbridge or to his graffiti on Hartlake Bridge. As he notes later in this letter, "These are silly things to remember, but they all came back as I sat on the lock gate."

65. The "frightful mess" about Dr. Jack Easton relates to the infatuation that Welch developed for him while the former was his attending physician at the South Court Nursing Home (Broadstairs). Denton's decision to move to Tonbridge in 1937 was in large part based on the fact that Easton had relocated his practice to that town. As De-la-Noy points out, Welch made "a considerable nuisance of himself." The following description of Welch's behavior after moving to Tonbridge amply illustrates the situation: "When Denton moved into his flat in Hadlow Road he would visit Dr. Easton's house at all hours of the day and night. If Easton was not at home he would even hide in the house until his return, sometimes being discovered by Mrs. Easton, to whom Denton's behaviour was profoundly annoying. Finding no response to his passion, Denton took to throwing tantrums, clinging to the banisters when told to go, trying to force a confrontation with the object of his love, and finally succeeding in making the doctor lose his temper. Eventually Easton was compelled to pass Denton over to one of his new partners, Dr Tuckett, which must have left Denton feeling more rejected than ever" (*Making of a Writer*, 125). Fictional

renderings of these confrontations are found in the short story "A Fragment of a Life Story" and in the novel *A Voice through a Cloud*.

Methuen-Campbell notes that "despite this broadening in the range of his [Denton's] interests, it would seem that Denton's obsession with Jack Easton had lost very little of its intensity; on 19th December 1938, the doctor felt compelled to send him a letter aimed at terminating the unbalanced relationship once and for all. 'I do very definitely say,' Easton wrote, 'that I must see no more of you and that this business of seeing you occasionally is no good'" (*Writer and Artist*, 87).

Methuen-Campbell also points out that a more accurate version of the story is contained in Welch's journal entry of December 2, 1942. Welch relates one particularly violent episode concerning his relationship with Jack Easton, which ultimately led to a not-very-convincing attempt at suicide by the twenty-two-year-old convalescent. This would provide Welch with a sense of affinity with Eric Oliver whose own feelings of hopelessness had led him to take a similar action when he was eighteen (see note 53) and with the seemingly self-destructive binges upon which Eric continued to launch himself during the early stages of his relationship with Welch. Though Welch's reaction to Dr. Easton might be seen as merely the adolescent maunderings of first love, it is particularly important in how it contrasts—and is contrasted with—the developing seriousness and maturity of Welch's relationship with Eric Oliver by April 1944. In his February 9, 1944, letter, Welch tells Eric that "I don't pretend that I would ever have loved you as insanely and unreasoningly as I love J. E.—that sort of thing only happens when one is *very young, very ill, and very inexperienced*" (my emphasis). The December 2, 1942, journal entry is a draft of a section of "A Fragment of a Life Story":

> I passed down the High Street and climbed the hill inevitably to J. E's house [42 Pembury Road]. I spied through the hedge but could see nothing; the curtains were tightly drawn. Then I slunk into the garden and flattened my face against the pane of the living room window. The warm lamp was shining, and through a crack in the living room curtains I could see the corner of a bookshelf and the cream paint of the wainscot. Once the little black Aberdeen ran across my line of vision, then there was nothing.
>
> I took my face away in despair and utter hopelessness. It was then that I had the idea to kill myself. "These things are cumulative," I remembered reading. "If you go on trying, you'll one day succeed."

Alertly, and with more vigour, I threaded my way back through town. I knew now that there was something I could try. When I got back to the flat Francis [Streeten] was waiting for me. . . .

I was in a sort of drunken state with a hard stone in my heart and stomach. I went into my bedroom "to change my shoes," as I told Francis. I sat down on the bed and looked out [*sic*] the little black-and-white box of Prontosil tablets. I looked at them long, nestling in the puce lining of the box. I counted them. There were sixteen. I had been ordered three or four a day and was always asked rather anxiously if they made me feel depressed. I thought from this that they must be poisonous.

Sixteen, I felt, would be decisive, or at least enough to make me extremely ill.

Getting some water in a glass, I sat with the water and tablets before me; then I began systematically to swallow the tablets until they were all gone.

I stood up desperate and happy, wondering when I should feel the effects. I ran back into the other room where the soup was already steaming in two bowls [Streeten had come by in time for dinner]. I felt that I must enjoy my last moments to the full. I laughed and shouted. . . .

Suddenly I burst out with what I had done. I became terrified and ecstatic because I felt a creeping tingling and swimming in my head.

"I've just swallowed sixteen Prontosil tablets," I shrieked. . . .

I seized the sherry bottle again and poured more out, slopping it on the tray and feeling sorry at the mess and the waste. I suddenly realized that it would not matter how much I spoilt and degraded the things I loved, for I was going to die. I almost knew it, yet I could not quite believe it. . . . I wanted to cry and laugh and smack myself and wake up to find that I was still a small boy of nine or ten whose mother loved him and had a warm place by the library fire at night where his father would sit reading some old, leathery, upholstered, comforting fustian. Something about Maria who lived in Genoa which was the great and wicked rival of Venice where the winged lion, so wonderful and fierce, swam against the sky in the square of St. Mark's. (*Journals*, 26–28)

Welch's housekeeper, Evie Sinclair, called Dr. Easton, who after attempting to induce vomiting, left Welch to sleep off the effects (*not serious, except for a burning stomach and severe headache*). Welch's entry ends with this commentary

on the radical difference between the perceptions of those who are healthy and
those of the chronically ill:

> I lay back in the dark room, thankful to him [Easton] and grateful but
> just a little resentful about his seeming unconcern about the effects
> of prontosil. . . . If only there had been more tablets I would have
> swallowed them all. I am fond of him for being nice. *He is young and
> lusty and quite different from me and those people are only nice when
> everything else is stripped away, and they see someone else left quite hopeless
> and "dished." In ordinary circumstances they are bound up and encased in
> all their funny little fetishes and taboos.* (*Journals*, 29–30; my emphasis)

Welch's chronic bouts of high fever and confinement due to illness would
intermittently cause him to contemplate suicide, should life become unbearable. His March 29, 1944, letter to Eric Oliver contains this poignant testimony:
"I think I talk too much about popping oneself off. It's only because I think
I'm going to have a very sticky death, and so I want to be able to do myself in as
bearably as possible, before I have too much lingering and languishing. Anyhow,
perhaps I'll live for years, in spite of all my imaginings & premonitions. Tonight
I don't feel as if I would though! I feel as if everything is falling to pieces, and
I'm the chief piece of garbage!"

66. Welch is still concerned about having lied about his age to Eric; see
note 55.

67. "That damned accident": Welch's life-changing bicycle accident of
June 7, 1935. See introduction.

68. Rose-Marie Aubépin; see note 52. In his description of the visit, Welch
rather impishly queries whether she would be Eric's "type," or "not at all." It
seems as if he is teasing Eric about his purported bisexuality. A description of
Aubépin's visit of April 9 is also to be found in Welch's journal entry for the
following day.

69. May Walbrand-Evans was a self-described "Edwardian beauty," the
widow of the vicar of Hawkhurst. Denton and May met in 1937, and thereafter
they became close friends. Welch describes her as being schoolgirlish, prone to
coarseness and ribald behavior. She is most extensively portrayed as the character
Julia Bellingly in his short story "Brave and Cruel." May lived in a converted
eighteenth-century pub called the Brown Jug near Tonbridge, and when Denton
and Evie Sinclair moved from Hadlow Road to the Hop Garden in January
1940, they stayed briefly with her (*Making of a Writer*, 129).

The following description of May Walbrand-Evans, from Methuen-Campbell's *Denton Welch: Writer and Artist*, explains why Denton was drawn to her: "By temperament they may not have been especially compatible—she could be brassy and insensitive—but her iconoclastic sense of humour and her eccentricity in filling her home with mountains of furniture and china all contributed to make her a person whom he found irresistible. . . . Another factor in May's favour was that she had an impeccable artistic pedigree, having studied at the Slade School alongside such distinguished painters as Augustus John and William Orpen. . . . Although he [Denton] used to speak disparagingly of her [artistic] efforts in many ways she was by far the more accomplished draughtsman, particularly in portraiture" (98).

May and her entourage of middle-aged female friends provided Welch with a constant supply of gossip, and more than a little irritation. Walbrand-Evans's seemingly undiminished sexual energies and her teasing concerning his male and female friends or visitors were particularly distasteful to Welch. In this letter he alludes to her intimations about his relationship with Rose-Marie Aubépin. On one occasion, when Welch's friend Marcus Oliver (no relation to Eric) visited the Hop Garden, May inquired as to who the visitor looking like Ivor Novello (a 1930s English screen actor) was. Welch later wrote to Marcus about Walbrand-Evans's tastes in men: "Mrs. Bitch-Brennan told us that she thought you were rather too worldly and sophisticated for her taste—the sexy old thing loves young men that strip to the buff for a bout of fisticuffs, so what *can* you expect!" (quoted in *Making of a Writer*, 129).

70. Mary Sloman and, presumably, her estranged husband Harold; see note 146.

71. The photographs Eric brought from his mother's flat in London; see note 56.

72. Denton's concern about women "shinning up the wrong tree" in showing a romantic interest in him seems to have some legitimacy if his descriptions of Rose-Marie Aubépin's and Noël Adeney's overtures are to be trusted.

73. No information is extant as to who this school friend was.

74. Eric's infatuation with the militaristic trappings of fascism (particularly its appeal to the disaffected *lumpenproletariat*, to which Eric might be temperamentally attracted) is problematic for Welch. He—like E. M. Forster—takes an intellectual tack in defending democracy and liberalism. Note that he fears for a loss of individual freedoms (including sexual liberty) should Eric's ill-considered preference for totalitarianism be realized. One wonders whether

Oliver's attitude wouldn't have quickly changed had he been called to active service.

75. Eric would unfortunately never find something he "longed to do." His finest legacy is his meticulous concern for preserving Welch's reputation as a writer and an artist. He helped to bring out the posthumously published *Voice through a Cloud*, as well as the collected short fiction and poetry. His testimony to his relationship with Welch and his circle of friends was invaluable to the completion of Michael De-la-Noy's biography *Denton Welch: The Making of a Writer*.

Methuen-Campbell elaborates on Eric's unsettled life: "Ill at ease with any kind of authority, Eric hated school and Mr Oliver [his father], who owned a small factory that manufactured jewellery-cases and died three weeks before his youngest son's twenty-first birthday, had been very concerned about his future. Of the different jobs Eric tried, only farming was at all congenial. A career in the Army lasted just eighteen months (Eric was in the Pay Corps), after which he was perhaps tactfully 'excused' on account of high blood pressure; his war work continued with the land army in Kent" (*Writer and Artist*, 139).

76. Ironic references to Eric's ill-considered fascism.

77. This "someone who likes to go about" with Eric was Peter Clements, a fellow "land boy" (alternative service worker). According to Denton's journal entry of April 13, Eric and Peter had missed the last train to Appledore, as they had stopped at Tonbridge for a drink. Eric had then come to Pitt's Folly to ask that Denton put them up for the evening. In a letter to Noël Adeney he described Peter Clements as having "sticky-out ears, large, smooth-faced, rather pug-nosed baby looking." The actual visit is described in the journal as follows:

> After some laughing and smiling and slight confusion I made them both sit down and gave them beer. Eric got biscuits out of his bag and gave them solicitously to Peter. . . .
>
> I kept wondering as I talked to them brightly how I could possibly manage to have them both in my room for the rest of the night. It would be impossible, I knew, for me to sleep with two people in my room.
>
> I wanted to put Peter downstairs on a mattress, but the floor in the kitchen is stone, and I did not feel that even I could be so inhospitable and cruel.
>
> Soon the floor was covered with the spare mattress, blankets, flea-bag, torn pillow cases; and after a lot more talking we began to get undressed.

Both Eric and Peter snored and so there was no sleep for me, and soon the nightingale began to pour out its never ending song . . . until the moon began to shine through the window on to my face.

It shone on Eric's face too, and I saw his curved nose in outline, the hollow of his cheek, and his pushed back hair, like a dead face floating on the water.

In the morning we all had breakfast round my bed, eating porridge from bowls, and reconstituted scrambled egg [wartime rations], coffee and Noël's marmalade. Peter talked about the nice police sergeant he knew who was friendly with Somerset Maugham, E. M. Forster etc. He also talked about his crook friend who likes licking girls all over in Hyde Park and who made £900 out of the Black Market. A curious mixture. Peter was rather alive and enquiring, but at bottom inescapably shallow and rather vain. I listened, amused, and Eric sat quietly smiling and smoking his pipe.

Afterwards we walked through the wood and then I went to lunch with May [Walbrand-Evans], carrying my own roast potatoes with me, and Eric and Peter went off to Maidstone (stopping on the way for four pints, as I learned afterwards). (*Journals*, 141–42)

As will be noted in later correspondence, Denton would in fact become jealous of the time Eric spent with Peter. However, at this first meeting, he seems fascinated with the latter's stories about the homosexual literary subculture of Somerset Maugham, E. M. Forster, and John Lehmann.

Welch had in fact received a "fine letter" from E. M. Forster sometime in the spring of 1943 "full of very *sensible* praise of the book [*Maiden Voyage*]." According to Methuen-Campbell, Denton received five presentation copies from his publisher. One he sent to Margot, Countess of Oxford and Asquith, another to Lord Berners, and a third to E. M. Forster; all responded with letters (*Writer and Artist*, 126). De-la-Noy says that Denton sent a complimentary copy of his first novel to Forster, whom "he admired enormously and with whom he was later to correspond on the subject of homosexuality and the law" (*Making of a Writer*, 164).

However, as De-la-Noy points out, Forster himself would vacillate concerning the quality and nature of Welch's writing. In an undated letter found in the Ransom Center Collection, Forster would write to William Plomer (another member of his homosexual clique) that "Denton Welch is certainly easy to read, and he doesn't in this book tease anyone whom I think ought not to be teased.

Anyhow he is the sort of writer I am always grateful to. They will never do any better, but that is their cul-de-sac, not mine." Forster moves away from this grateful but dismissive position when, in a letter to John Lehmann on July 17, 1951, he commends Welch's courage "not only to bear his disasters but to *see* himself, so far as he can," and praising his "sensitiveness, visual and tactile, and his occasional wisdom" (quoted in *Making of a Writer*, 164).

Yet another journal entry (April 17, 1944) refers to Welch's jealousy of Eric's friendship with Peter Clements, to the increasing intimacy of their relationship, and to Welch's growing need for commitment on Eric's part. The following excerpt speaks for itself:

> Eric was coming for this week-end anyhow, so I saw him again on Saturday. . . .
>
> After supper we were talking of the picnic with Peter on Wednesday, and suddenly Eric and I began to quarrel, or rather I began banging against Eric and he became almost tongue-tied, except when he came out with rather hurting home-truths [the difficulties of sexual relations between them, due to Welch's partial impotency?].
>
> How we quarreled, and how terribly unhappy I grew, and how hopeless.
>
> In desperation, in the long silence when Eric drank bottle after bottle of strong beer and I smoked cigarette after cigarette until my fingers were brown, I took up Rothenstein's *Men and Memories* and opened it at the place where Oscar Wilde wanted to sit near the band because he liked one of the musicians and how this angered the prim Rothenstein.
>
> And then Eric made it up with me and sat on the stool and took my feet (which were already on the stool) on to his knees. So we sat in this curious position and made friends again, and I felt I would forgive him almost anything.
>
> It was after two before we got to bed, but for a wonder we slept well. Only once or twice I woke up to see the moon on Eric's face, making it look like lean, lovely, hollowed sculpture, and with the sound of his breathing was mixed the wonderful nightingale which never stopped. And I felt so much better and less worried by my body that I rejoiced, and I could not resist telling Eric how eased I was.
>
> And it seemed a miraculously pleasant end to our trouble and unhappiness.

All morning we lay about undressed, and all afternoon too, Eric in my priest's cassock looking strange and interesting and historic, his hair all tough, bits of his body showing through the black as he pulled at his neck or tossed his legs about on the bed or in the chair.

I thought that it was always easy to be friends with Eric and difficult, terribly difficult, to keep up a dignity and grievance. I wondered how much like butter I would appear to other people.

I don't know what will happen in the future to our friendship, but now it is good to keep it alive all I can. And I will give all I can.

I have written nothing to him this week for several reasons, some good, some not so good. He shall write to me when he wants to. He knows he can always depend on me, but I think he wants to [*sentence unfinished*]. (*Journals*, 142–43)

78. Dr. Caterina Easton, wife of Denton's physician; see note 65. Jack Easton was then on active duty in North Africa.

79. Welch here alludes to his continuing discomfort with Noël Adeney's affection for him.

80. "She seems now quite to like and trust me" alludes to the embarrassing—and irritating—situation earlier created for Mrs. Easton by Welch's infatuation with her husband; see note 65.

81. Welch's distrust of doctors may in part have derived from his mother's Christian Science background. Rosalind Bassett Welch was an early convert to Mrs. Mary Baker Eddy's revivalist sect. The idea of total dependence upon prayer as a means of healing illness and injury gave solace to Welch's mother, who suffered from chronic nephritis. She died of this kidney ailment in Shanghai on March 3, 1927, at the age of forty-one. Denton continued through much of his life to associate with his mother's Christian Scientist friends. De-lay-Noy remarks that "the most formative years of his [Denton's] childhood were spent in the company of a fervent believer—his mother—struggling with an incurable illness. He was later, through intellectual scepticism, to discard any formal allegiance to the faith, but its influence, perhaps because it was so strongly associated with his mother, never entirely left him; on the whole, while making use of doctors in later life, he disliked and distrusted them" (*Making of a Writer*, 31).

82. Guy Allan was a London artist who became one of Welch's earliest fans, as a result of reading *Maiden Voyage*. He had written to Welch offering to nurse him during his illnesses (*Making of a Writer*, 218). Welch's visit to Allan at Glebe Place, London, is re-created in his journal entry of May 4:

Yesterday I went to London to see the specialist. And as I expected he had nothing new to suggest. . . .

After the specialist I took a taxi and went to Guy Allan's studio in Glebe Place.

He opened the door and ushered me into the large, uneasy atmosphere of a lofty studio with holes in the skylight where shrapnel had come through.

Stacked in great masses were his own and his boyfriend's canvases. They were really a little better than I thought they would be.

While I was in the lavatory a sort of gypsy woman who had been Augustus John's model came, to fit Guy for a coat she was making him. She stayed to tea which we all drank out of thick earthenware bowls. I had a Jewish currant bun, but did not eat the rounds of bread spread with herring and radish slivers.

There was a strange half-Eastern cat, grey and fawn, which wore Guy's naval identity disc round its neck.

After tea we went into the hole under the stairs where Guy had his bed. Opposite the bed was a hideous sort of throne topped with Lyre-bird's feathers, which Guy said had come from the old Duke of Connaught's sale.

On the walls were pictures of Guy's friend Derek, Prince Youssoupoff in his grandfather's Russian clothes and some other people I did not know. Two other people had arrived by this time, a Belgian artist, Roger Descomes, and someone else.

Guy showed me photographs while the others talked. He was not so extraordinarily dressed as he was when he came to see me for the first time last week. Then he wore harlequin socks and open-toed sandals. A Chinese crepe shirt and a jersey with a belt round it. Large Etruscan silver rings on his fingers and a Canadian lumber jack's jacket. His face looked slightly painted but that may have been my imagination.

When I left, he gave me a parcel which he said was a little Chinese earthenware teapot for my early morning tea! He wants to come and see me again this Wednesday.

It is strange meeting people who have written to you out of the blue. Guy must be forty-five. He is now a Christian Scientist. But when he came to see me last Wednesday he told me how about fifteen years ago a very charming Chinaman kept him drugged in a studio in

Paris for some time. At last Guy couldn't work and the studio became indescribably filthy.

Some acquaintances finally came and dragged him away and got him back to England. Guy puts all this down to Christian Science. He also says he was cured of consumption. And now he thinks that God has sent him specially to succour me. I wish he'd begin his work. I should love to be succoured.

Guy also told me that the Duchess of Choiseul's daughter was once very fond of him, and her Belgian husband became so incensed that he nearly killed them both in a car crash by mistake on purpose. (*Journals*, 144–45)

Methuen-Campbell makes additional comments concerning Denton's relationship with Guy Allan: "Guy, Denton discovered, was also a Christian Scientist. Whilst living in Paris he had made a miraculous recovery from anthrax and had joined the church out of a sense of gratitude. . . . Denton and he were to remain in touch for several years and on three occasions or more Guy brought down his young artist friends to visit him in Kent. . . . Guy and Eric did not hit it off. 'I was a fly in the ointment,' Eric recalled. The older man could not understand why his new friend was attracted to someone who appeared to have virtually no interest in art or literature" (*Writer and Artist*, 149).

83. Augustus John was a popular portrait artist and intimate of the Garsington circle of Lady Ottoline Morrell. Welch refers to John's portrait of the famous literary patroness in his journal of October 26, 1943. Welch saw the painting on a visit with Ottoline Morrell's daughter, Mrs. Julian Goodman, in London. According to an earlier journal entry (*Journals*, 91), Goodman had liked *Maiden Voyage* so much that she had purchased Welch's painting *Piebald Cat* from the Leicester Galleries, where a number of his paintings had been placed on consignment. Denton was thereafter commissioned to paint her pug from a photograph she sent him. When Welch delivered the painting to Julian Goodman, she remarked that John's portrait of her mother was "not a caricature," but was "cruel."

84. Actually, Roger Descombes was a Swiss painter and engraver, born in 1915, the same year as Denton.

85. This image of an idyllic homosexual relationship, including a "cottage in Cornwall," has its parallel in Welch's growing perception that he might find domestic happiness and stability with Eric. Much of the remainder of his life

was spent seeking a suitable home for him and Eric to settle down in (Middle Orchard was intended as a temporary residence while Denton sought out a house of his own). Welch's reconstruction of a Georgian-style dollhouse seems to have been a sort of vicarious fulfillment of his desires in this area. See later correspondence and journal notes.

86. Denton's fussiness over Eric's appearance ("I seem to be full of ideas for your beautification") and his solicitous attitude toward dressing him properly, is a touching portrayal of his growing affection for—and an envisioning of partnership with—Eric. In fact, cohabitation seems not far off if one considers that the friends were now sharing war ration coupons. Somewhat less romantic is Denton's unsubtle attempt to remake Eric from a "tough" into a respectable mate.

Methuen-Campbell describes the back-and-forth tension and sense of security experienced by Eric as he grew to understand Denton's motives and desires: Denton's "possessiveness of Eric, and perhaps the wish to 'improve' his friend's personality lay at the heart of their difficulties. Denton told Noël Adeney of his absolute determination to make the relationship work, even if this meant going against his better judgment. Gradually Eric became less suspicious. Although he had never thought of himself as the sort of person who could be close friends with an artist or writer, he liked the idiosyncratic lifestyle at Pitt's Folly Cottage and was flattered that someone so obviously his intellectual superior could have fallen for him. From June 1944 the friendship between them became more stable, with Denton even acknowledging that it was having a constructive effect on his emotional development. No longer did he hanker after the romantic life of a recluse" (*Writer and Artist*, 152).

87. Denton's doubts about the wisdom of his decision to love Eric ("I can't tell whether I think it was a good thing that I met you or not.") is reflected in the journal entry of May 8: "When you long with all your heart for someone to love you, a madness grows there that shakes all sense from the trees and the water and the earth. And nothing lives for you, except a long bitter want. And this is what everyone feels from birth to death" (*Journals*, 145). At this stage in the relationship, Denton was still uncertain as to the extent of Eric's real feelings toward him.

88. Welch's moving narration of yet one more hopeless session of medical examinations, and his escape to a scene of remembered happiness with Eric, is described more completely in the journal entry of May 16, 1944. He doesn't miss an opportunity to make a swipe at the medical profession and at heterosexual fustiness:

All the [examination] room was blue, with baby-blue blankets and horrible little glass fishes and china rabbits and bronze dogs and clay horses and woolly birds on the mantelpiece. Also pictures of darling children and little wife. Why *do* doctors always go in for this sort of thing? It was as if they would obtrude their private life on you against your will. One could not miss so many toys and photographs, however blind. . . .

I stopped on the way back on Bidborough Ridge and drank my scalding coffee, gazing at the wonderful air. There was sleet in the low flying clouds, and I looked across and saw the white puff of a train, and Tonbridge in the valley, and I thought of Eric at Penshurst in 1936 and me in Tonbridge.

And it reminded me of our last week-end together when Eric brought pheasants' eggs which we ate on toast, and how afterwards we went out and spent all day by the river in the sun with only shorts on. We wandered across the fields like this and came to a stream and Eric saw a nest on a tiny islet so he took off his shorts and waded into the freezing water and brought back some moorhens' eggs.

Afterwards we discovered two bomb craters with irises growing at the bottom of them. (*Journals*, 146)

89. "When I Was Thirteen," published in *Horizon*, April 1944; see note 35.

90. The only information available on Welch's publication fortunes is found in the journal entry of May 16: "I have had Allen & Unwin as well as Hamish Hamilton wanting me to submit books to them because of my *Horizon* story. And it has been mentioned by Vita Sackville-West in the *Observer*, and also in *Statesman* and *Time and Tide*, all very favourably. *English Story* paid me £15 this morning" (*Journals*, 146).

91. Keith Vaughan was a member of a circle of painters collectively known as the Neo-Romantics. Vaughan's homosexuality explains his interest in Welch's story about an adolescent's homosexual awakening. Interestingly, paintings by both Welch and Vaughan were included in a 1987 show at the Barbican Art Gallery, London, entitled *A Paradise Lost: The Neo-Romantic Imagination in Britain, 1935–55.*

92. This is the only reference to Frank Fenton. No further identification could be found.

93. Methuen-Campbell notes: "Noël Adeney, much to his [Denton's] alarm, was growing increasingly possessive, and one day, sitting on the banks of the Medway in the April sun, she assailed him with the extraordinary question,

'Does Eric know how much I love you?' Inwardly he must have recoiled in horror" (*Writer and Artist*, 149).

De-la-Noy gives more evidence of the strained relationship between Noël Adeney and Welch. He quotes from Denton's May 16 letter to Noël: "I wonder if you will think it quite wrong-headed and rather peculiar of me if I suggest that we don't meet for a little time? I seem to have become slightly diffused and dissipated lately, what with one thing and another, and I feel that I *must* brood and dwell on my new book in a lean and lonely period. . . . I don't really think that you want to change me, but I think that being such very different types of people we are bound to react rather badly on each other sometimes. But I don't think that matters if one just takes it all in one's stride" (*Making of a Writer*, 220).

De-la-Noy goes on to relate that Noël Adeney's annotations to the letter conjecture that the "lean and lonely period" referred to Denton's continuing doubts about the seriousness of Eric's affection for him.

94. Dr. Caterina Easton; see note 78.

95. Rose-Marie Aubépin; see note 52.

96. Bernard Adeney, Noël's husband. Denton mischievously calls him by the German form of his name.

97. Peter Clements; see note 77.

98. The bitterness of Denton's remarks expressing doubts as to Eric's sincerity is clearly connected with the degree and nature of their intimacy at this juncture.

Almost immediately after sending this letter to Eric, Welch felt regret and fear of loss. In his journal entries of May 23–28, these feelings are clearly demonstrated:

23 May, 9.15 a.m.

The postman has just come to take the appalling letter that I have written to Eric. I hear the slam of the car door and the starting of the engine, and now I know that he will really get it. It is on its way already down the drive, to the road, to the office, to Ashford and at last to Appledore.

The face at the other end, as it reads it—what will it be like?

———

26 May. Five to eleven p.m.

Now I am utterly alone on my bed, on the too-hot velvet eiderdown in the close room. And outside, the moon is showing sharper and clearer every moment although there is light from the sun still.

And I think all the time of Eric at Appledore. And I wonder what he thinks and whether I shall hear in the morning.

———————

28 May, 7.15 a.m.

Every night now comes over me the terrible restlessness just before bed, which I thought would never come again. And I feel that I must tear the walls down. I must go anywhere out of the house to wander in the lanes on my bicycle. I cannot keep still. And the thought of Eric haunts me like a ghost.

Last night, just as I passed the tiny chapel "Fish Hall," I looked up and I saw the text displayed on the "Wayside Pulpit" board, "Let not the sun go down upon your wrath," and I felt madly that I must telephone to Eric.

Of course, when I did, and after I said that I was sorry, I made everything much worse than it was before.

Now I am just waiting to telephone again, and I am going up to London if I can, to try to settle something.

This whole week has been such drab monotonous pain. And nothing to hear or see. No letter.

My work has somehow died to nothing, and I think of nothing but dying or killing myself. I could kill myself so easily with tablets, no other way. The right time and place really only remain to be found now.

How nasty the talk of suicide, yet how inevitable it sometimes seems. (*Journals*, 147–48)

99. Peter Clements or another of Eric's fellow workers at Appledore.

100. Once again, Welch expresses his doubts about Eric's feelings for him. It was part of Eric Oliver's nature as a drifter that he was unable to fully commit to a relationship with Welch. One can discern from the intermittent frustration found in Welch's letters of this period that Oliver was either unable or unwilling to engage in the kind of emotional immersion that his friend expected of him.

The parallel passage in his letter of May 15, 1944, takes an intimate turn, indicating how naturally Eric was falling into the role of caretaker: "Late in the night last Monday after you had gone, I wrote to you to thank you for [a] very good time when I felt rather awful by the river. . . . When I go to bits like that it's because I'm ill, and that makes me think that everything has been spoilt for me forever. *You help me to get over the bad time as no one else ever has*" (my emphases).

101. Denton's perception of repugnance on Eric's part probably had much to do with self-consciousness about the partial sexual impotency resulting from his 1935 accident. He also indirectly alludes to Eric's bisexuality, which seems to demand a feminine object of affection for true passion to be possible ("I don't expect you to love me like Cleopatra").

102. This letter and the following one of June 1 arose out of Welch's visit to Eric at his mother's flat in Streatham, London, on May 29. The tone has now changed to one of self-recrimination and regret for having accused Eric of "devilish" behavior. Denton's plea for forgiveness for having "thrust himself" on Eric is followed though by an obvious attempt to elicit feelings of guilt in his friend: "I simply can't get used to the idea that someone I've become really fond of, no longer finds anything to love in me. You will understand that this is a *terribly* hurting experience."

103. The decision not to see one another for a time, but with the understanding that it would be foolish to break "the bond of sympathy" between them, arose out of the London meeting of May 29. Welch related what happened in his journal entry of June 3:

And I have told Eric that we should not meet for some time but eventually we would be stupid if we turned against each other and quarrelled.

My weekend with him ended disastrously.

On Sunday night we went to the Greyhound at Dulwich. I thought everything would go fine, because that afternoon we had talked for a long time in St. James's Park under a plain tree. . . .

And talking there under the tree, I really thought that we had decided to be friends and not quarrel.

But at the Greyhound I drank eight gin and limes and it was gloomy and tragic and we talked too much and walking home was swaying. . . .

In the bedroom Eric came up to me and said, "Denton we must go straight to sleep." But I lay in my bed restless and buzzing for most of the night. . . .

Afterwards Eric and I made the beds and then walked on Streatham Common. The heat was overpowering. Eric had already had one pint. He lay dissatisfied in the grass, telling me how he had hated the rackety friends of his early youth, and how he had never had any real friends because he had always wanted to be alone sometimes and kick off from them. I saw how out of sympathy he was getting but I could do nothing. . . .

He saw another pub and dragged me into it. I would drink nothing. I looked at the raucous dripping scene, somehow so meaningless and undesigned.

Things were going from bad to worse. We traipsed home almost silently.

Then after lunch we lay down on our beds and tried to rest. I read the *Book of Snobs* until I could bear it no more. I jumped up and said, "I'm going." I packed my satchel. Eric said nothing. I asked him what bus to take. He said, "I'll come to the station." I said, "What for?" as freezingly as possible.

Then I went and said goodbye to Mrs Oliver and flapped out of the house with Eric following me.

I walked fast and he kept up behind. Just as we reached the stop a 59 bus approached. Without looking at Eric I heard him say, "This is the bus."

I didn't turn but marched on to the bus as if I had never known him in my life.

Suddenly as it was moving off I had the longing to see if he was looking after me. I dodged this way and that, and I thought I saw the grey Aertex of his shirt stretched across his broad back, but the conductress stood four-square, worrying for my fare, obliterating. I went right up to the front of the bus upstairs, and then I began crying in total disregard of all the passengers. I had dark glasses on but I suppose no one who looked could fail to see the tears trickling down. I really felt done for in some way.

In Whitehall I jumped into a rare taxi and told him to drive to Helen's in Ladbroke Square. I felt that someone somewhere must give comfort or distraction.

But, of course, no one was in, only some foreign girls gibbering in the gardens; so I wended my way to Charing Cross and sat in the sweltering heat of the bus with a little fair haired boy who had caught a tiny silver fish in the Round Pond and was taking it home in a jar. He said that the last one had died and he hoped this one wouldn't. I was so grateful to have someone uncomplicated to talk to that I quite loved the little boy for a moment or two. He was so amusing and precocious and somehow religious about the little fish.

I came home in the train with a vast woman in pucey red crepe floral dress. The journey was terrible. For two pints I would have poured out all my sadness to her. (*Journals*, 148–50)

104. This self-characterization as a "highbrow fairy" and of Eric as "a rather dumb near-hearty," though made with the obvious purpose of "tweaking" his friend, is at base a recognition of the divide of class and intellect that existed between the two men.

105. Knowing that Denton and Eric often slept in the same bed on their visits to one another, it is understandable that Welch had difficulty stifling his desire, *especially* if he was "boozy."

106. Another reference to Eric's Appledore friend, fellow farmworker Peter Clements.

107. The distinction Welch draws between his relationship with Eric, and Eric's with Peter Clements, seems to have to do with the difference between simple friendship and the *real affection* existing between lovers. This is what Denton refers to as the "superficial and light" feeling which led him to "*great* indiscretions."

108. See note 103 for the journal entry in which Welch recounts the events.

109. A swipe at what Welch perceives as the shallow nature of Oliver's Appledore friendships.

110. Overtime agricultural work at Appledore.

111. In these references to his solitary and introspective existence, Denton is attempting to demonstrate for Eric the sacrifices he is making in continuing their relationship; that the writer's creative existence is somewhat compromised by the association.

112. Welch continues the idea that he is capable of surviving on his own; that Eric should not feel compelled to visit. He also manipulates the idea that *he was deceived* into believing that Eric enjoyed the weekends they spent together. Welch's claim that he has "*never* tried any psychological tricks" with Eric is certainly given the lie here.

113. This letter reveals not only Denton's continuing preoccupation with Eric, but also a more urgent concern with the destruction being visited upon England by German V-2 rockets ("Doodle-bugs"), with news of the Normandy invasion (June 6, 1944), and the RAF and American bombing missions over Germany.

The journal entries for the month of June further emphasize these sources of anxiety, exacerbated by the anniversary of his accident. On June 6, 1944, he writes:

> Just heard that the invasion had begun on Northern France; and the weather is windy and sunny and I have nothing but an aching feeling in my heart, and I wonder if Eric has been made to leave Appledore or whether his idea about the coastal district being cleared for the invasion was incorrect. (*Journals*, 150)

Welch continues, the next day, to voice his concern for the combatants participating in the Normandy invasion, for his own deteriorating health, and for Eric's welfare:

> What a day of aching and giving up! The day nine years ago on which I was run over and my health ruined for ever. And Eric, I think of him all day and hear nothing. Last night I woke up hot and steamy and dulled and peaceful, through the night going to the battle, and the whole world seemed more wicked and mad than seemed bearable. (*Journals*, 151)

After having tea with May Walbrand-Evans and her friend Mrs. Phyl Ford, Welch further ruminates on the war:

> I thought how strange to sit with elderly ladies in such a clean, such a Tudorized house with radiators and frigidaires, while the most un-speakable atrocities were happening in masses only a hundred miles away at least.
>   I have sworn that I will not write to Eric for a whole month; but now I hope that he will write to me before that. (*Journals*, 151)

By June 16 Welch describes his first experience of mechanized warfare:

> All night long, and just now too at breakfast, have been coming strange things, rocket planes, mechanical toys with thousand-pound bombs in them. They make a rude noise and the soldiers shoot off a little gun that sounds like pepper exploding. The rocket planes are radio-controlled, with no one in them, and when they crash they explode.

I wonder what will happen if the soldiers so near by will be hit by one. (*Journals*, 154)

De-La-Noy, in a note to the above journal entry, explains that Welch lived along the German V-2 flight path to London and that the first rocket landed in Kent on June 13, 1944.

The journal entries relate the terrors of the blitz, through the eyes of survivors whom Welch met on his walking or bicycling excursions. On June 20 he encountered two young boys fishing from a stone bridge near Oxon Hoath. They were on a camping trip from London. They told him about their "close call" from the night before, and about conditions in wartime London:

> They went on to tell me how disturbed a night they had had. They said about fifty pilotless planes came over and the tracer bullets were bursting all about them raining down shrapnel. First they dashed to the tent, where they had just made themselves cosy, and hid under the deep overhanging riverbank; then they left that position and fled to the trees.
>
> At last they shut themselves for about half an hour in an old hop-picker's lavatory. They got hardly any sleep at all.
>
> They told me of their memories of the blitz in London. They lived near a railway bridge. This bridge kept recurring in the stories. Two mad boys lived near them, and one of these boys, when a bomb dropped and everyone downstairs was playing cards, rushed up to the top floor and began playing the piano. . . .
>
> The boys knew far more than I did about the pilotless planes and everything else to do with the war.
>
> They said that near Bethnel Green, where they lived now, only the young women went into the shelters. The men wouldn't, and the older women wouldn't, and the children just stayed in the street, playing and singing. They said one little girl put her fingers in her ears, and if a sound penetrated she would scream madly. She seemed to be the only screaming one. (*Journals*, 155)

At the end of this journal entry Welch returns to a more personal description of the impact of the war on him and his friends. Dick Bosanquet was the son of Mrs. Mildred Bosanquet, the woman from whom Welch had acquired an eighteenth-century dollhouse, which he spent many hours restoring (*Journals*, 92):

Poor Dick Bosanquet, at twenty-five, has been killed in Italy. It was in yesterday's paper, and I have written to his mother. He had reddish hair, a high voice and was attractive in some ways, though not easy to talk to, and wrapped in a certain amount of quiet complacency because of Eton scholarships and King's.

He was the first person to talk a lot to me of Housman's poetry. He said, "I'm rather a fan," and he lent me all the three books and Laurence Housman's *Life*. (*Journals*, 155)

Welch experienced some close calls of his own from the V-2 rocket attacks, as related in his journal entry for June 23. As he was investigating a Gothic arch and an adjoining icehouse in Oxon Hoath Park, Welch experienced the first-hand terror of such an attack:

Then as I was staring at this date and at the domed earth, tumulus-top of the old ice house, a most amazing burst of fire sounded from a nearby gun, and I realized that one of the doodle-bug pilotless planes was coming over.

I had got some way from the opening now, but the gun-fire was getting so smashing and loud that I hurried back to the opening and took refuge in the Gothic tunnel.

There seemed to be guns all round, and above them the doodle-bug's droning. Shrapnel came scattering down through the branches of the beech tree. I wondered if the plane would be hit and blown up. If so I wondered what it would be like in the tunnel, whether I should be buried and, if so, how long I would be left undiscovered.

After two doodle-bugs had flown over without being hit, the noise slackened and at last I ventured out.

Already the wood pigeons had begun to coo again and the land girls and men to go on building their haystack.

I had to stop writing because another one came over and the sky was punctured with black puffs and shell bursts.

I ran to a stone bridge. I saw the land girls [*sic*] running to the trees and two children throwing themselves down under a bush.

More shrapnel than ever fell this time. I heard its wicked whine and thud.

Just after I went up to the children, and they showed me evil jagged pieces they'd found, enough to kill one. (*Journals*, 156–57)

114. This acquaintance who showed Denton the convenient storage place for condoms is otherwise unidentified.

115. Welch met Marcus Oliver on November 4, 1937, and thereafter kept up a continuing correspondence with him; see introduction. According to De-la-Noy, though Oliver "liked to parade as a dapper lady's man, his true predilections lay the direction of what Denton would have understood as rough trade. And over the next decade, he and Denton were to exchange scores of letters full of camp gossip, tittle-tattle and scandal" (*Making of a Writer*, 121). Marcus Oliver lived in Earl's Court Road, London, and worked for John Haig, the whisky distillers. He made his way into Welch's fiction as the character Angus in the short story "Memories of a Vanished Period," recounting a drinking bout in London during the war (*Making of a Writer*, 121).

116. Peter Cromwell had learned of Denton through his *Horizon* story, "When I Was Thirteen" (*Making of a Writer*, 222). Clearly another gay reader intrigued by Welch's forthright account of homosexual coming of age.

117. Guy Allan; see note 82. A further reference to Allan's anticipated visit is made in Denton's August 10, 1944, letter to Noël Adeney: "We are expecting Guy to have the most incredible camping outfit, tassels and bells and chiffon flags hanging from the corners of the tent, and inside, incense censers and artificial water-lilies floating in black bowls. I suppose we will be disappointed and he will come down as practical as a boy-scout!" (*Making of a Writer*, 233).

118. Welch gives a more detailed account of his meeting with John James Bloom in his journal entry of June 26:

> On Saturday I went down to the river near East Peckham, and just as I had crossed the wooden bridge where a man was fishing and his woman was watching him, I stood irresolute, wondering which way to go and where to spread my coloured handkerchief for my picnic.
>
> When I turned the corner of the bush I expected to see a bathing party, but instead there was only one youth there lying on his stomach with no clothes on at all, reading the *Reader's Digest*.
>
> He jerked his head up and we confronted each other and smiled spontaneously if rather nervously. With no more ado I plumped down on the ground quite near him and began to unpack my picnic, asking him how warm the water was.
>
> Soon we were talking quite solidly. I learnt he lived at East Peckham, or rather stayed there at week-ends with his grandmother. In the week he worked at a music publisher's in Charing Cross Road.

I began to take him in more carefully physically, as he looked rather interesting, quite naked except for a wisp of a towel, against the vivid green grass in the violent sunlight. There were no clouds at all. For once a pure azure sky. His skin was very white, not yet sun burnt, his hair very full with blond streaks on top, rounded limbs, not very strongly built but what is known as "shapely." He sat up with cross-legs, rather like the Buddha, and I offered him some of my picnic lunch to save him from going back to his grandmother's. He gladly accepted so we had cheese and toast there together and treacle and coffee and raisins and cherries (provided by him) and chocolate.

After, we smoked his cigarettes and still went on talking. The sun was burning us now, and my head was beginning to throb, so we went under some trees further down and I took out my proofs [*In Youth Is Pleasure*] and said I ought to try to do some corrections. This led to talking about books, and from books somehow we got to talking about hospitals, and it all came out that we both knew Dr Easton and liked him.

We talked about him a lot and our various troubles and times in hospital. . . .

At last I suggested that we might go back to my place and have some tea.

We put on our clothes and pumped up our bicycles and set off. John James told me his grandmother's maiden name was Soult, and he said that it sounded as if it was French.

When we got in he seemed to like my place and stared at things appreciatively. I lay on the bed and watched him as he sat in the arm-chair. He told me how when he was having his tonsils out in the Cottage Hospital, his mother brought him a cold fried plaice to eat.

He also told me that he bled for a week and they had at last to get a specialist from London to deal with him, as he was about to die. This was the time when Jack Easton was good to him.

After tea we walked in the wood and then we came back and had some beer which was quite strong and rather made my head ache. I was getting ever so slightly tight until Evie brought me hot soup and supper which sobered me.

We went on talking until about ten-fifteen. Then John James said that they would be worrying at home and thinking that he would be struck down by a doodle-bug bomb, so he'd better be going.

I lent him *Maiden Voyage* and bicycled a little way back with him. We agreed to meet again next Saturday by the river in the same place, if nothing prevented either of us.

I wonder if he will be there? (*Journals*, 158–59)

The homoerotic theme of this encounter is common fare in both the journals and the autobiographical fiction. Welch also clearly found Bloom of interest due to his health problems and their mutual friendship with Jack Easton, the object of Denton's infatuation at Broadstairs convalescent hospital.

119. Julian Goodman; see note 83.

120. Proofs for *In Youth Is Pleasure*.

121. The poem referred to is probably "Evil Lives in Men's Hearts," later published as number 24 in *Dumb Instrument: Poems and Fragments* (ed. Jean-Louis Chevalier).

122. Welch refers to his "disastrous" stay with Oliver in Streatham Common on June 29; see notes 103–5.

123. Another name for the German V-2 rocket.

124. As Denton mentioned in his letter of June 27, Noël and Bernard Adeney had left their home at Middle Orchard due to the frequent "doodle-bug" attacks. Noël had in fact told Welch that he could move into Middle Orchard should he be "blown out of Pitt's Folly Cottage" (*Making of a Writer*, 225).

125. A reference to the first Christmas Eric and Denton spent together (1943), in which Rosemary Mundy Castle played such a significant and disastrous part; see note 11.

126. Denton's visit to the King's Arms, and his "romp" with the soldiers there, seems to bring an epiphany. Welch comes to the realization that it is better to make an emotional accommodation with Eric than to lose him: "I have only just begun to see that human relationships are the *only* really important thing on earth. Nothing else means anything without them." Separation from Eric, his new acquaintance with John James Bloom, the continuing threat of V-2 rocket attacks, and the exuberance of physical contact with the young men in the pub, take Denton away from the stubbornly isolationist attitude expressed in his letters of late June. He is awakened to the urgency of life as a universal experience in a war-torn world. Welch's journal elaborates on the sentiments expressed in his letter to Eric:

Back now late at this twelve-thirty moment from the King's Arms, Tonbridge, where I have drunk and sung all night; "Trees," "I can't give you anything but love," and oh so many others. And afterwards I walked back with one of my close singers, a soldier called Alwyn, who sleeps in a lorry and has been three years in Gibraltar. We lay in some hay recuperating out of the pelting rain, and we talked, and then a doodle-bug buzzed and guns banged and we got up to go. He was nice and mild and sane, and I was so tight, feeling it was a comfort to have him there like that. He called me "Kid" and wants me to go and sing there again on Wednesday, "really organized," as he says.

I wonder if I shall go? And no sign, no tiniest sign from Eric at Appledore. I thought tonight that it should really have been he who was drinking and singing there.

To see the fat old tipsy woman, dancing the Lambeth Walk, with the young gay soldier, who had a look of Eric, not facial somehow, but in the glisten of the eye. So good, so bright, so bristling with life, swamping one into this drink and din, and after years of decay, no joy, no daring, and no glory, only the old [*illegible*].

And in the drink and the closeness of so many other people, my love for Eric seems to have died away. So real a love to die away into love for everyone, for the whole world. (*Journals*, 160 [July 1, 1944])

127. Denton coaxes Eric back with assurances that he is willing to ease his emotional demands on him, with nostalgic remembrances, and *not insignificantly* with promises of drinking ("the cellar is well stocked") and new young men to look at (John James Bloom and Alwyn). Obviously, this easing of tension between the two friends worked. Eric would come for a visit to Pitt's Folly on July 7, 1944. From this point on, Denton and Eric would rarely be separated until Welch's death on December 30, 1948.

128. This letter continues the sentiment Denton expressed on July 4 that he will not continue to make emotional demands on Eric, to force him to express a love he supposedly does not feel. However, the new tack is for them to trust and depend on one another; to develop a partnership that will see Eric through his financial strain and Denton through the stresses of illness and creative effort. He doesn't stint from recognizing that his time for happiness may be short, before he "pops off."

129. An August 8, 1944, letter to Noël Adeney elaborates on this new epistolary acquaintance: Fenton, a "Sheffield schoolboy," had read Welch's "When I Was Thirteen" and had sent him a poem on Pompey the Great, which he asked the author to "'criticize stiffly,' together with some rather inept criticism of his own of the *Horizon* story" (*Making of a Writer*, 233). This note provides

further evidence of Denton's growing literary popularity, especially among homosexual readers.

130. Eric did in fact take Denton up on his invitation, arriving at Pitt's Folly Cottage on July 7. As the journal entry from July 11 shows, things had changed radically for Eric at Appledore:

> Eric is here and with me now and has been since Saturday. All has gone swimmingly and he is staying for a week. The hostel at Appledore was bombed and ruined—one person killed, one badly injured. They were moved to a nearby mansion, and now his friend Peter [Clements] has left and he feels that he doesn't want to go back to the strange place with no friend, so he wants to stay a week. I was surprised and delighted when he suggested it to me. On Sunday we went over to Chiddingstone Causeway and visited three pubs that Eric used to frequent when he was twenty-one. Many people recognized him at once and welcomed him. He said he used to spend £5 or £6 a night, that he was hardly ever sober.
> We ate our lunch in a Dutch barn because of the pouring rain. (*Journals*, 161)

131. No correspondence exists for the period July 5 to September 28, 1944, attributable to Eric's extended stay with Denton. In fact, Denton had wheedled out of his friend Noël Adeney permission for them to stay at Middle Orchard. As De-la-Noy points out, she had never intended for Welch to move into her home with Eric (*Making of a Writer*, 230). It will be remembered that Noël had earlier embarrassed Denton with her expressions of love for him; Denton's letters to her demonstrating a successful "turn in the road" in his relationship with Eric could only have been excruciating for Noël.

By July 18 Eric and Denton had indeed moved into Middle Orchard, and Denton wrote unabashedly to Noël about their "menage":

> He was writing again to Noël on 18 July, "Just to tell you how much we're loving it at M.O.," and to confess to having broken the handle of a soup cup. So ingenuous was he that admitting to her what a fool he had made of himself with Eric [a confrontation about his friend's seeming overattentiveness to John James Bloom on the latter's visit of July 13] came no less naturally to him than confessing to the breakage, or, indeed, to something she need never have known, that John Bloom had moved in to her house too. John turned up he told her, just as he was cooking supper. "After supper, if you please, he said, 'Do you think

your friend would care if I curled up in one of her chairs? I don't fancy the ride back to East Peckham tonight.' I was hoping and hoping he would go, because I wanted to be alone at Middle Orchard with Eric, but what was I to do after this direct question? . . . Of course he stayed, and did nearly all the housework (very well and efficiently) on Sunday . . . Before he left he said longingly, 'I *do* hope your friend loans you her house again.' He seemed quite entranced. He slept in the living-room on the bed you'd put there." (*Making of a Writer*, 231)

Denton's exuberance in Eric's decision to stay with him clearly did not take into account Noël Adeney's feelings, as evidenced in his continuing correspondence with her:

Unsparing of Noël's feelings, Denton went on [in a letter of July 18], "Eric and I quite shamelessly use your bed, which is lovely. *Do you mind?* I wondered and wondered before deciding, but all the other beds are far away from each other and narrower, and now we feel wonderfully safe with the doodles whistling overhead and the balloon barrage pimpling the sky all above Middle Orchard. (Did you know it was here now?) All the crews are camping in the fields about.

"Do you feel, Noël, that we have turned M.O. into a bear garden and that I should have driven John Bloom away? I hope not, but I have slight qualms about making such complete use of your place. I can't remember enjoying myself so well before. Now I am going to stop as I want this to get to the post and Eric wants to put a tiny note at the end.

"We are having all our meals in the garden and only going in to sleep at night. Eric wears no clothes at all."

Eric's tiny note read: "Dear Noël, Thank you for letting me stay at your house with Denton. We are having a really good time. I hope you are enjoying the change just as much. My best wishes, Eric." (*Making of a Writer*, 231–32)

By August 8 Denton was writing to Noël about his and Eric's growing realization that they could live together successfully: "Isn't it extraordinary that Eric and I can live together for five weeks in spite of peculiar moments. I can't get over it. What will happen next?" (*Making of a Writer*, 233).

Denton's journal entry of September 13, 1944, written at Eric's mother's in Streatham (the first since July 11, after which he and Eric had moved into

Middle Orchard), emphasizes the fact that the relationship was going extremely well, and that the two were beginning to play essential roles in each other's existences:

> Today I am ill in bed, but yesterday Eric took me to Dulwich Village to see the picture gallery hit by a flying bomb. And we walked down a road by green fields which was the way to his first school, now with all the windows blown out and derelict. . . .
>
> We sat on a seat looking on to the grounds of Dulwich College and we both smoked the same pipe and then walked down the road where Eric's house of his childhood used to be. Now utterly destroyed by 1941 land mine. . . .
>
> How tired I was trudging back, thinking of myself and him and childhood and age and everything decaying.
>
> The whole city [London] falling to bits, gradually obtruding its skeleton. The war has made the city and everything grow older with a rush. . . .
>
> Eric and I have lived together now since July at Pitt's Folly, at Middle Orchard (Crouch) and now at Streatham. And in some ways it is the strangest thing in my life—to share almost my entire existence like this. I have not even written in my journal, let alone at my book. (*Journals*, 161–62)

Denton had told Noël Adeney (letter of August 10, 1944) that, "What I want to do is look after him [Eric] and to make his life as pleasant as possible. This may be considered domination of the worst kind, but I can't help that. It is so obvious that in all ways he looks miles better thro' staying with me. You've said it; May's [Walbrand-Evans] said it; Evie [Sinclair] has. Three *very* different persons!" (*Making of a Writer*, 233).

132. Eric had gone to London for a one-week stay with his mother. As De-la-Noy points out, this letter is the first in which Welch addresses his friend as "Hero." Eric's roles as caretaker and nurse to Denton, as well as companion, are reflected in this moniker.

133. The reference to "photos" is unclear, perhaps models for a portrait that Noël Adeney was planning to make of Eric. In fact, by the next day (October 1) Denton was discussing the prospect with Noël: "If it comes off, I shall be interested to see what you make of him. He should be good to do, don't you think? If he flattens his hair out, you must push it up on his forehead; but I

have told him about this, so perhaps he will have it wild" (quoted in *Making of a Writer*, 235). Denton might also be referring to newspaper photographs of Eric shown to him on an earlier visit to London. Welch's September 13, 1944, journal entry includes this description: "And now today Eric showed me a 1933 Sunday paper with his picture in it holding a black-and-white cat and underneath the headline: 'Boy risks his life to save cat.' He ran up the stairs of his father's burning factory and saw the cat lying there and brought it down" (*Journals*, 162). The next sentence of the letter, beginning with "Thank" is obliterated by ink stains.

134. The increasing intensity of Denton's illness is clearly underplayed in this letter. He may be putting on a brave face for his absent companion. His journal entry for September 24 is more candid:

Yesterday I was sick and ill all day. So ill that I couldn't eat or think, only lie in pain, waiting for the next wave of sickness to come over me. And Eric looked after me wonderfully, staying with me all day, watching me, making the bed, and putting cold towels on my face. I thought it would never pass; all life seemed an agony of sickness. But even when it was wonderful to have a friend near you, to help you all he could. The desolation of sickness was lessened somehow. (*Journals*, 164)

135. Although the identity of Noël Adeney's "middle-aged writer friend" is unclear, Denton seems to want to find his friend John James Bloom (see note 118) a homosexual connection in London ("house boy" is a euphemism for being kept or supported by an older man). As earlier noted, Bloom seems to have been in need of financial backing.

136. Welch seems here to be masking his own desire to keep Eric busy behind May Wallbrand-Evans's ostensible preoccupation with Oliver's employment. The "cushy" job she had in mind was probably at a Commander Wheelright's factory for the production of "special rubber dingies or collapsible boats" referred to later in this letter. The demands of writing under the cloud of Eric's listlessness and boredom prompted Denton to confess to Noël:

So I am rather enjoying the queer feeling of having all the day to myself. Life seems more luxurious for some peculiar reason. Is it the absence of the necessity to adapt oneself at all? Perhaps I like the feeling because I know I shall be glad to see Eric at the end of the week. I hope to do quite a lot of writing. So far I have only washed Eric's trousers and sent off some awful poems! (quoted in *Making of a Writer*, 235)

137. The stories probably were "The Coffin on the Hill," first published in *Life and Letters*, June 1946 (reprinted in *Brave and Cruel*), and "At Sea," published in *English Story*, 1944. The "awful poems" haven't been identified and were perhaps never published.

138. See note 133.

139. A hand-me-down from Richard Adeney (Noël and Bernard's son).

140. In fact, the dentist to whom Eric "spread the Gospel of Welch" proved to be "the best dentist" Denton had been to (*Journals*, 166 [October 11, 1944]).

141. See note 136.

142. Denton has throughout been ambivalent about Eric's continuing to stay with him, vacillating between worrying about their menage being "terribly dull" for Eric and his own relief at having his friend off his hands for a while.

143. Though this letter is partially ink-blotted, Welch is apparently referring to Jean Timbrell-Fisher, an admirer and correspondent of his. Denton's voyeuristic and gossipy propensities probably made it quite easy for her to discuss her "new" and old Johnnies alike.

144. See note 133. Most poignant is Denton's recurring regret that he had not been able to share in Eric's childhood experiences: "In the picture [accompanying a newspaper article on Eric's saving a cat from a burning factory] a young Eric with diffident face, holding the cat lovingly. Something different, all strange over those years. I had a mourning feeling. To feel that I could never know any of that now" (*Journals*, 162). As has been noted earlier, Welch felt that his accident had deprived him of his youth and vitality, and that he could never experience the fullness of an emotional, sexual relationship with Eric as a consequence.

145. Again the problem of dealing with the demands of writing and painting, and with actually living with Eric, present themselves in Denton's rumination over whether his companion will be able to avoid "champing & chafing & feeling like a fish out of water." In two separate journal entries of this period, Welch lays out his concerns more clearly:

> In so many ways it is lovely to have Eric living with me here for the winter in this tiny garage cottage with only this one room, but I find myself getting swallowed up only in living with him. It changes my feelings about work. I want to work so much now. But I haven't yet readapted myself. (*Journals*, 166)

When Eric was away and I lay in bed so still with books, my thoughts, the pretty things I have collected, I thought that all I really wanted was to be alone, to think and to dream in a daze of work I shall do. But now that he is asleep on the bed, I find I can still think and dream, and I even feel better physically because someone is there if I should not feel well.

There is always this question with me, to be alone or not. Really, to be alone is my nature. If it were not so, I would not have been alone as much as I have. (*Journals*, 173)

It must be mentioned that Welch was now working on another novel, *A Voice through a Cloud*, and on illustrations for *Vogue*. The concerns he voices in his journal and letters would be those of any artist besieged by a demanding publication or completion schedule. However, when this is combined with the urgency and uncertainty caused by Denton's precarious physical condition, as well as his background as a contemplative loner, all criticism of his ambivalence is silenced.

146. Mary Sloman (Denton's landlady at Pitt's Folly) and her friend Brenda Cobb; Gina was Mary Sloman's dog (*Making of a Writer*, 126).

147. A new nickname for Eric, presumably based on that of General Dwight D. Eisenhower. Eisenhower would have been much in the news following the Normandy invasion of June 1944.

148. Possibly a pair of corduroy riding breeches Eric had bought for Denton in London (*Journals*, 165).

149. This was a feature for *Vogue* to be entitled "Ghosts and Dreams." Just how agitated Denton became with the effort of producing the article with accompanying illustrations is demonstrated in his journal entry of October 8: "What am I to do? I wish it would all come in a flash but it won't, and I must begin to evolve something. Always the actual subject before one stimulates and then flummoxes" (*Journals*, 166).

150. This is the "Aircraftman Parker," from whom Welch would hear directly in a letter of November 30, 1944. Curiously, this serviceman was the first real collector and critic of Welch's literary and artistic work, from what we would now call a gay or queer studies angle. Denton's journal entry of the same date is illuminating:

I had a letter from an Aircraftman Parker in India, who apparently read *Maiden Voyage* and then started to track all my other work, writing and

painting, just as [A.J.A., or Alphonse James Albert] Symons tracked
Corvo in his book *The Quest for Corvo* [Baron Corvo, whose homoerotic photographs of Italian and Sicilian youth were current in homosexual circles in the early twentieth century].

This Parker has been amazingly persevering and has almost found
out everything there is to know about my published things, even down
to little poems in queer magazines!

He has been undertaking the search with another friend. And everything they found about me, they put into a book labelled "Denton
Welch—His Book."

Now he wants to buy a picture to round off his search! He wrote to
the Leger, the Leicester, the Redfern. And the Redfern forwarded his
letter to me.

Isn't it crazy! I wonder if he will have the determination to do anything like it again! He might do some quite interesting research on a
dead and gone obscure author.

It made me feel, when I heard of it, as if I had been preserving myself on a top shelf for years, waiting to be discovered. As if I were dead
and done with, and watching some future person ferreting me out.
(*Journals*, 173)

151. "Frankie" refers to Francis Streeten; see notes 1 and 63.

152. This is the same Mrs. Littleton with whom Denton had visited in
August 1943. Her collection of bookplates piqued Welch's fascination with
minutiae, as well as his tendency toward imaginative wandering: "She showed
me book plates and the little round wafers of her husband's grandmother.
'Duchess of Northumberland, Syon House' the book plates had on them, and
the coat of arms and coronet. The little wafers were all different colours, pastel
salmon, strawberry, apple, lime, larkspur, lavender, citron, marguerite. I imagined the duchess in the 1830s putting these little wafers on her notes and then
pressing the seal on them. I saw her sticking her bookplates in her own books.
They struck me at that moment as most charming relics, fragile, of no money
value. There were also many old French bookplates that their Uncle Henry
had collected. They were on coarse paper—delightful rococo, beautifully engraved yet archaic" (*Journals*, 97–98).

153. Possibly one of Eric's mates at the Appledore hostel, killed in a rocket
blast in July 1944. It was this incident that determined Eric upon staying with
Welch; see note 131.

154. A study for her portrait of Eric; see note 56.

155. John James Bloom. His old job was with a music publisher in Charing Cross Road.

156. One of Rosalind Welch's Christian Science entourage, with whom Welch had been acquainted as a boy. The book is *Maiden Voyage*; the homoerotic episodes would indeed have "opened the eyes" of his mother's old friends.

157. "Myrtle" was one of the nicknames given to Evie Sinclair, Welch's longtime friend and housekeeper.

158. Apparently a request that Eric bring certain items from London; part of the text is obliterated by inkblots.

159. An unflattering reference to Peter Cromwell; see note 116.

160. Eric returned to Pitt's Folly on October 7. The next day was Eric's birthday, so he and Denton went once more to Penshurst Place, the manorial estate of Sir Philip Sidney, Elizabethan courtier and poet. Welch recorded his impressions, now laced with the poisonous impact of war:

> Later we went back to Penshurst Place and walked round it in the wild windswept grass and Eric showed me where he had won the prize for running when he was twenty-one. The house looked utterly blank and dead, because so many of the windows had been smashed by a flying bomb, and boarded up. We couldn't get in at all and so we left it and went into the church, where the windows too were broken, and the wind whistled through the beams, soughing and whining. In the Sidney chapel, the important tombs somehow deserted and not considered any more. A feeling of pastness and dulled memory, no kindling. (*Journals*, 165)

The couple went to lunch at the nearby Leicester Arms, where Denton's recollections mix pastoral and wartime images: "[W]e left our bikes near a crate of champagne cider bottles. We went into the outside lavatory and there was written 'Down with the Nazi Bastards'" (*Journals*, 165).

By October 26 Eric accompanied Denton to London, in order to take some of the artist's paintings to the Leicester Gallery and to show Julian Goodman the portrait he had done of her; see note 83. Welch's description of the visit evokes the cruelties of life in London during the blitz:

> It was a year since I had been to see her [Julian Goodman] last with the picture of her pug. When I got to Ottoline Morrell's red door in Gower

Street I saw that the windows were smashed and boarded. I rang twice, then knocked, and at last Julian came to the door dressed in green, attractive, high-coloured, and with new shoes on. We went quickly into the hall and I saw that the house was quickly becoming a slum. John drawing [Augustus John's portrait of Ottoline Morrell], Condor lithographs, old tortoiseshell cabinets, and the chipped paint, torn curtains, grime of war-time London.

Julian took me into what had been the dining room and told me that they were living in that room only, the others uninhabitable through smashed panes. . . .

I undid the picture and we all made remarks. I had made brown eyes when Julian's were grey-blue. . . .

Nervous smiling, talking about Julian's son's first term at Eton and the other little one's unhappiness at his school. The pug there on the floor, looking awfully like my picture of him. The great drooling, weeping eyes rolling. . . .

She began to tell me about the boys, fifteen and sixteen, who broke into the house after the doodle-bug had broken all the windows, and lived there for two or three days. They left their filthy shirts and trails of burnt matches wherever they went. They had only just come out of an institution. They broke an ebony cabinet to pieces because they found a letter saying it had a secret drawer. They also took some little trinkets and a suitcase full of silver, but when they found it was covered with crests they left it just by the Queen's Hall, and by great good luck a policeman picked it up. So after two month's of waiting to be claimed, Julian's family silver was returned to her in this strange way. . . .

In Murray Maclaren's bedroom the leg of the old French harewood commode off, supported by a pile of books, the paintwork dingy and cracked as transparent as dragonflies' wings, the bedspread Julian's grandmother embroidered in 1890. Everywhere a mixture of squalor and interesting or beautiful objects . . .

When the doodle-bugs began, Julian had gone down to the country with an Augustus John under each arm, which she hopes are worth £1,000 apiece. A little bit of dust stuck to the portrait of her mother and pulled a piece of paint off. Small and insignificant, Julian thinks. (*Journals*, 168–69)

161. Presumably, the fact that Eric's aunt Rose was moving in with his mother was good news, as there wouldn't be room now for Eric to stay with his mother for any length of time. This would ultimately facilitate Eric and Denton's permanent cohabitation. The American party is unidentified.

162. Bernard Adeney had delivered Noël's portrait of Eric Oliver.

163. Robin Cornell was an Australian fan of Welch's homoerotic writing. Denton's journal entry of October 11 refers to Cornell's correspondence: "Letters yesterday from Robin Cornell, four air ones, all saying that he's rather 'thrilled to have found you!' Australia has no intellectual life. What does this mean? Professorial people are cold. 'They talk about classical philosophy and then want to whip you into bed.' (This doesn't sound cold to me at all)" (*Journals*, 167). The tenor of Cornell's letters indicates that he was probably an undergraduate student. The naval friend probably refers to Ted Nichols, who would accompany Cornell on a visit to Welch on July 18, 1945.

Denton's journal entry dealing with the visit is, as De-la-Noy points out one of his "most vicious":

> Well, the next day Ted Nichols and Robin Cornell arrived for lunch, late, and Robin, in his pathetic, arrested-development way, had to explain that they were late because they had drunk too much the night before, and that had made them sleep late and miss the train. It was sordid. And all through the afternoon we had to listen to his disgustingly commonplace tidbits about his own fascination and charm. (He had one of those fish faces and underwater eyes which *always* are trimmed with thick horn-rimmed glasses.) This sort of person should be smacked and put to sleep forever, but I suppose they live longer than most people and burden others for years with their extraordinary pretension and mental squalor. (*Journals*, 205–6)

Welch's distaste for academics and intellectual pretension is often mixed with a kind of star-struck fascination with a world he opted out of in his own student days. For instance, on October 26, 1944, he writes: "[O]n Tuesday, I had a letter from King's, Cambridge—would I go talk to them on 'Contemporary Literature'!! Delightful if I could be persuaded. What would I feel like, talking to and looking at undergraduates? Imagination falters. They say nothing about lodging me or anything of that sort. Do they ever get any writers to go, I wonder?" (*Journals*, 170–71).

On December 18, 1944, he again shows disgust with the affectation of intellectuals:

> On Saturday came John Butler from Cambridge, tall, skinny, bearded, smelling of scent, too stupid to be interested in life—everything I dislike mentally and physically. We sat through lunch—me in my cassock [an acolyte's cassock that Denton wore as a kind of casual dressing gown] offering him rice, sardines and raisins with hard-boiled egg, he with his legs cocked up, his hands drooping and twisting. Tiresome is the only word for it all.
>
> Then, the night before, an Eton boy, Robin Hamilton, came with his poems all based on Hiawatha. He was rather nice in spite of them, and talked about mountains, Scotland, castles with curses, and sleeping in tents on moors. (*Journals*, 175)

And, on August 9, 1945:

> Yesterday I had a letter from Syracuse University, asking me about my story "When I Was Thirteen" [see note 18], saying that I had a following there amongst several of the younger members of the staff. The Librarian, it seems, gave his copy to a friend who was on a boat crossing the Atlantic. The boat went to the bottom of the sea and my story with it.
>
> Now I am trying to find the manuscript of the story. I have found every other manuscript but that one. Could I have destroyed it? I wanted to send it to Syracuse University; then they could bind it in gilt morocco and keep it on their shelves for ever.
>
> When I saw Syracuse on the envelope I felt quite confused. I thought it had come to me from the past, from classical times. (*Journals*, 213–14)

Editor's note: in fact, the manuscript for the story was recovered, as it is now at the Ransom Center, University of Texas.

164. *Maiden Voyage.*

165. Welch had three days earlier had a temperature of 103 degrees, one of the recurrent bouts of the illness that would eventually claim his life. He was at work on his third novel, *A Voice through a Cloud.*

166. No reference to the ring is found in either the correspondence or the journals. It seems that it was intended as a Christmas gift for Noël Adeney.

167. "Doodlebug" rockets.

168. This number of *English Story* included Denton's story "At Sea." De-la-Noy points out that the periodical also included stories by Elizabeth Bowen, Rex Warner, and Henry Treece (*Making of a Writer*, 239).

Ironically, it was Henry Treece who, in his capacity as editor of *Kingdom Come* (another English literary publication of the period), had in 1943 rejected for publication Welch's story "When I Was Thirteen," on the grounds that it was "too amoral" (*Making of a Writer*, 185). It was also Henry Treece—then serving in the RAF—who in a letter of January 1943 had lectured Denton to "stop your narcissistic twitterings, jump on to a 4-engine bomber and have your face blown off while flying over Berlin." Welch wrote Treece a blistering response in which he explained his physical handicap and why he was ineligible for military service. Welch ended his letter with: "Don't write to me again unless you can be civilized."

It is worth noting here that Welch possessed an extreme sensitivity to combatant suffering in war. Methuen-Campbell quotes at length from Denton's comments of January 6, 1943, written on a loose sheet of paper among his manuscript material:

> I always remember the first war-joke I saw. It was in an old *Punch* and I was a little boy in my Grandfather's drawing-room. The *Punch*, unusual and therefore fascinating because it had no colour on its cover, I had picked out of the cupboard under the stairs. I took it with me and sat down by the bow window.
>
> Then I opened it and I saw the war-joke. I think some wretched soldier in slovenly rolled puttees groped and slopped through the mud while Very lights or shells burst above him. Underneath was something incomparably British, middle-class, sordid, manly, and false—stinkingly false—something jolly and vomit-making.
>
> I stood up in amazement. It seemed horribly dirty and wicked to me—another example of the horrible devil-worship of grown ups. I am not exaggerating, only the words are too flashy but there are no others.
>
> I was frightened and I always shall be at that sort of thing.
>
> Why don't they laugh and joke when the torture of the boot is applied—when the trap-door opens and the "last offering to Venus," so beloved of novelists, is made by the kicking victim? Why don't they laugh and joke in the hospitals when the patients scream and vomit? Why don't they laugh when the poor lunatics sit in trances of

melancholy for days or when the homosexuals and other unchangeable
neurotics weep and shout and build new facades even more brittle,
more ginger-breadish than the older ones?

Now this stinking broadcast shoots its obscene pantomime. Slimed
over with this filth everything is Gilbertianly villainous and oh so
good-humoured.

This is what makes the war possible. We have such a wonderful
sense of humour. So wonderful that it is quite grisly. (quoted in *Writer
and Artist*, 107)

Welch clearly identifies living as a homosexual and an invalid with that of the
trench-bound combatant in the Punch cartoon, with having to endure malicious
comment and ridicule masked as "good-humour." Methuen-Campbell concludes, "For Denton the whole affair of the war was something so meaningless
that it did not deserve the attention of a person who had dedicated himself to
art. The idea that young men in their prime should be sacrificed in order to
maintain the status quo was deeply offensive to the homosexual side of his
nature and he could not understand how armed conflict could be viewed as
anything but profoundly evil" (107).

169. Denton's desire to either refurbish or build a house would intensify
through the spring and summer of 1945. His journal entries of July 23, July 31,
August 3, and August 9, underscore his hopes in this regard:

23 July, 7.30 p.m.

And there we were before an empty Victorian house with generous
bays and wide windows. Inside, the rooms rather low and long. Something extraordinarily attractive about it, and also about the garden and
its monkey-puzzle tree, its little terraced lawn, paths and greenhouse.

We could not understand why such a house in the heart of Tunbridge Wells could be empty at such a time. We suppose it had been
requisitioned by the army and was still held by them.

May [Walbrand-Evans] wanted us to divide it in half and share it.
She was going to the agents but then forgot. I would not have wanted it
in the town or with her, but it was good for what it was—delightful
that there was only the bricked footpath in front. (*Journals*, 207–8)

31 July 7.5 p.m.

On Thursday we went over to Trottiscliffe to look at Ivy Cottage which Mrs Carpmael offered me for 14s 6d a week—amazing rent for nowadays.

I remembered it on that half-term when I was eleven and at St. Michael's. She and Irene had driven over to fetch me [Cecilia Carpmael and Irene Dallas were Christian Scientist friends of Denton's mother Rosalind Welch], and then we all sat in Ivy Cottage in the pouring rain and listened to the chicken roasting in the oven in the kitchen. The walls of the front room were (and are) panelled in a sort of lincrusta cardboard, and I remember so well the terrible consuming depression and excitement mixed, of the day, the darkness, the good food, the constraint with the elders and the dark threat of returning to school in the evening.

Then, in spite of its gloom, Ivy Cottage was a refuge, a haven of civilization and comfort, but when I saw it last Thursday, squalid after the last derelict old father and daughter had left it, I felt that I would be foolish to move there. Chief objections are that it is right in the village and that it is semi-detached, the gardener's widow having the other half.

And there was the feeling too that even if we could get the builders to put in electrical fittings and repaint it all, it would still be only a makeshift, a temporary place, a mistake.

I would go with pleasure, if I had nowhere else, but that feeling is not strong enough. C will be offended, I'm afraid, and think that I am foolish to turn down her lovely offer. She would find it difficult to see that what was her was not found suitable by someone else. She is a very strange mixture of kindness and complete egoism. (*Journals*, 209–10)

———

3 August, 3.40 p.m.

There really seems some chance now that I may be able to build a tiny house, and I keep seeing in my mind exactly what I want. A long room downstairs with three french windows from floor to ceiling along one wall, a fireplace and an old mantel at one end, and at the other a blank wall for my tapestry cartoon. Upstairs three small bedrooms and the bathroom. (*Journals*, 212)

———

9 August

In the evening we went up to Crouch to fetch the milk in the car; and after we had escaped, we parked the car on the ridge just above the early fourteenth-century manor, "Old Soar." . . .

Round at the front we saw the red Georgian farmhouse which has
been built on to it. The fanlight over the door has little Gothic arches —
suggested clearly by the Gothic building. The woman let us in a little
grudgingly, and we went alone up the spiral staircase into what I suppose
was the solar; from it led the little chapel, and what the farmer later
told us was the garde-robe (but I always understood that garde-robe was
a polite medievalism for W.C., so I feel perhaps that he might be wrong).

We climbed up to the top floor, the floor that has been inserted in
the hall or solar, cutting the charming pointed windows in two, and
saw there the amusing early nineteenth-century drawings that have
been done in red chalk on the ceilings. Childish little sash-windowed
houses with belfries, trees with large leaves, horses, a man in a swamp
shooting duck perhaps — and then two fat little pugilists with their fists
up in the old-fashioned way. (Someone had been rude here and had
pencilled in a long thin phallus that jutted out from one and poked the
other in the ribs.)

The doodle-bomb of last year that burst near the gypsies in the
orchard above has made the ruinous conditions of some parts worse
than it was, as well as breaking all of the windows.

I longed to be able to buy the place and very, very carefully restore
the manor part and live in both it and the red farmhouse.

I am going to write to the Society for the Protection of Ancient
Buildings to see if they will do anything about it. (*Journals*, 214)

Although income from his writing and art work was not insubstantial, Denton
envisioned a much greater inheritance from his father's estate than would actually be realized. Limited financial means as well as deteriorating health unfortunately prevented Welch from realizing his dream of a house of his own.

170. Welch had begun growing a beard, which he described in his November 30 journal entry: "I have grown a beard in bed, which I have kept. I think it
looks nice and it is so natural and easy. It quite changes me, makes me look
from another age" (*Journals*, 172). The "Bearded-Queen-Bee-D" valediction
obviously refers to his new growth, with a touch of camp.

171. By the new year, 1945, Denton was feeling confident in his relationship with Eric; a level of easiness and trust had developed between them that
could not have been anticipated from the nature of their early acquaintance.
They had spent a quiet, comfortable Christmas together. The delight Denton
felt at finally having found a life mate can easily be discerned from his journal
entries:

31 December
All still in the moonlight, stifled, spun into a glass picture.

Now we are by the gas fire here on New Year's Eve—Eric sleeping on the bed, me writing my book, trying to pick my own brains. . . .

This year [1944] has taken a stranger turn than any I expected. If someone had told me at the beginning that I would share everything before it was out, I would never have believed it.

It had seemed something so impossible for my temperament that I would have laughed. (*Journals*, 176)

———

8 January, 5.20 pm. Grey half-light
My life is a great unfoldment with many marvellous things about it. I would not have thought that I would be damaged and ill so soon (twenty) or that so comparatively late (twenty-eight and a half) I should have found someone with whom I could live in almost complete peace. All of life before that had seemed quite necessarily a solitary affair— and so it still is, but with an utterly different quality of solitude.

In my heart are hung two extraordinary pictures; one called "Accident and Illness" and the other, exactly opposite, tilted forward as if to meet it, is called "Love and Friendship."

Now they play Bach concerto (for harpsichord, but on a piano wonderfully) on the wireless, and the gas fire, with steel blue and orange flames, roars. Down the windows dribble long tears of condensation. The birds are snapping and creaking out their calls before bed. (*Journals*, 181)

172. Denton had begun the practice of affectionately calling Eric after types of food; "Tunyer" is a version of "Tuna" used in later correspondence.

173. Evie Sinclair, his landlady, Mary Sloman, and Brenda Cobb. Here Welch makes a campy innuendo concerning the "frightening" idea of sex with a "Lady." Eric had gone to stay with his sister in London.

174. Guy Allan; see note 82.

175. During his stay in London, Eric had been doing some antique shopping for Denton.

176. "Ghosts and Dreams"; see note 149.

177. One of the three London galleries at which Welch had placed paintings. The others were the Redfern and the Leger.

178. Francis Streeten; see notes 1 and 63.

179. Priestley's novel is *Angel Pavement* (1930).

180. Denton describes in detail his refurbishing of a Georgian-style doll-house in his March 26, 1945, journal entry. As the following excerpt demonstrates,

the detailed construction of the house appealed to Welch's fascination with minutiae, a characteristic aspect of both his writing and painting styles:

> For the last few weeks I have been mending the mid-eighteenth century doll's house (which Mrs Bosanquet of Seal [see note 113] handed over to me in 1941). It has been in her mother's family (Littledale of Yorkshire) since it was made. Mrs B said glibly, "I suppose it was made by the estate carpenter." . . .
>
> When I stripped the rooms I saw how coated with ugly pink and green paint each delicate moulding was. Even the floors were painted pink and green. (Perhaps by some child with two pots of bright enamel.)
>
> In the bedroom were two delightful cupboards, one on each side of the mantel, and they had been fixed with brutal brass hinges (the old leather ones having perished).
>
> Nothing was left, scarcely, of the banisters. The classical pediment that went over the arched central window of the house was luckily in one of the drawers of the stand. . . .
>
> With a lot of work I gradually scraped nearly all the front and also the inside. It took months and covered everything with dust.
>
> Inside I found that every room had originally been wall-papered with different patterned papers. There were fragments left in the hall (where I actually uncovered some delightful sprig, a sort of stiff tulip); also in the drawing-room, but these I did not uncover, as there was too little left. . . .
>
> I painfully scraped down to these, scraped the floor to its original plain wood, and found that the doors were meant to be bare mahogany and white surrounds. . . .
>
> Then I did more stripping. The top landing to dark blue (the first and original coat) with white mouldings, and the wainscoting in all the rooms. I made little leather hinges, just like the originals, for the doors, and I began on the staircase, doing the chief newel posts in cedar, attempting to match the three originals left. The rest is left to do. . . .
>
> Nothing will look grander than the doll's house, with its perfect classical door, window proportions, heavy Palladian coigning, cornice, and then the pediment and the reconstructed balustrade, all standing on the stand with its fret pattern revived.

All these weeks I have been doing it every afternoon (after writing) in May's garden. One has the feeling that slowly the house is coming to life again. (*Journals*, 182–85)

The dollhouse is now in the Museum of Childhood, Bethnal Green. It is illustrated in Constance Eileen King, *The Collector's History of Dolls' Houses* (London: Robert Hale, 1983) (*Writer and Artist*, 233 n20).

181. A reference to Noël Adeney's embarrassing and hopeless infatuation with Welch; see note 93.

182. A German long-range V-2 rocket explosion.

183. Welch unfortunately would never "beat down" his bouts of fever. They were related to a tubercular infection in his spine and pelvis.

184. Mary Sloman and Brenda Cobb. As earlier episodes make clear, Welch often wearied of the company and nosiness of his landlady and her friend. In fact, by May 1, the "smooth and affable" had changed to:

There have been upsets and troubles with Sloman, our landlady. She was insolently trying to make use of Evie and Eric. Evie was violent and told her not to dare to interfere with my morning's work, and I got so disturbed by it all that I wrote a note to say that we could not look after her dog and her house while she was away, I did not think that I ought to pay any more rent and that Eric could not help her in her garden for "pocket money," and that it had, of course, not been meant seriously and therefore I must not be annoyed. . . .

In my excitement I had written to everyone about finding a place for me, and Julian [Goodman] writes this morning that she has been trying to telegraph me all the weekend as she thinks she has just the thing for me at Garsington [the estate of Lady Ottoline Morrell]. Home Close—three guineas a week and she will dislodge the Colonel who has it now! . . .

Needless to say it is not just the thing at all. But it is so nice to know that people are looking, and I am wondering too if it is the cottage that Ottoline offered [D. H.] Lawrence. I think it must be and that interests me, as I always remember reading his letters when he was eighteen and thinking how foolish he was not to accept her offer.

Julian has also told me of a thatched cottage that may be empty in the summer, near her place at Newbury, but rich and semi-rich people never realize that a rent that is half or less than half their own is still "expensive" to someone else with less money. (*Journals*, 189–90)

185.   A review of his novel *In Youth Is Pleasure*. Denton refers to other reviews in his journal of April 9: "I have said nothing about *In Youth is Pleasure*, and it has been out since 22 February (I think). So far everything is so much better than I thought it might be. Good reviews, except for Kate O'Brien in the *Spectator*, and quite long ones and lots. It was sold out before publication, so now they are bringing it out again" (*Journals*, 186). In April, W. H. Auden reviewed the novel for the *New York Times*; shortly thereafter, it sold out in first American edition (*Making of a Writer*, 247). "Despite advance sales of nearly 5,000 copies and an exceptionally favourable review from W. H. Auden in *The New York Times Book Review* (18th March 1945), on 28th September Ragg [T. Murray Ragg, Routledge managing director] wrote to DW [Denton Welch] that the American publisher Fisher had 'got stuck' with a great number of reprints of *Maiden Voyage* and that Routledge were taking 2,000 to sell in the UK" (*Writer and Artist*, 234 n43).

186.   Denton now also refers to himself, as well as Eric, in gastronomical terms.

187.   In May 1945 Denton and Eric went to stay once more at Middle Orchard, Noël and Bernard Adeney's home near Crouch. They had stayed there briefly the previous summer (see note 131). Noël's making the house available was fortunate for Denton, who was having a difficult time working at Pitt's Folly, with the more-or-less constant irritations caused him by his landlady, Mary Sloman. In fact, Eric wrote to Noël inquiring whether they could let the house permanently (*Making of a Writer*, 250).

188.   Eric had gone to London for a week. He was to deliver Welch's finished portrait of Julian Goodman; see notes 81 and 160.

189.   Denton jokingly refers to a "silver-gilt" snuffbox belonging to Julian that he coveted. Did he really wish that Eric would snatch it for him!?

190.   "Mrs. A." Noël Adeney. This seems particularly rude in light of her kindness in allowing Denton to temporarily relocate to Middle Orchard.

191.   Welch gained this tidbit of information during his visit to Julian Goodman on October 26, 1944.

192.   Director of the Leicester Galleries, where Welch placed paintings for sale.

193.   Welch's bouts of illness considerably abbreviated his patience with "drop-by" visitors such as John Bloom. Denton had also begun to tire of the

young man's company once the physical attraction he had felt earlier had
abated. See note 118 for their first encounter.

194. The only note on Amy Oliver's latest tenants is found in the journal
entry of July 8, when Denton relates that he and Eric ate tinned "American
shrimp paté (from the U.S. guys at Eric's mother's flat)" (*Journals*, 204).

195. Phyllis Ford, a neighbor and tenant of Peggy Mundy Castle. Welch
records an amusing anecdote concerning Ford in his journal of March 28, 1943:

> I spoke all day to Noël Adeney. Lying in Hurst Woods we ate our hard
> boiled eggs and talked about homosexuality. Her probe is so uncom-
> fortable; she tells you just the things that ruffle you. And yet all the
> time you think she rather admires, or at least likes, you.
>
> She ate my chocolate, which I resented although I broke off large
> pieces for her. Then Sir William Ceary and Phyl Ford rode by on
> horses. I think they thought we were lying in the leaves making love.
> Wasn't that queer! Quite gruesome. (*Journals*, 61)

196. An iron supplement for Evie Sinclair.

197. De-La-Noy refers to the sexual attraction and tension that existed
between Evie Sinclair and Eric. In quoting from Denton's March 9, 1947,
letter to Noël Adeney: "Things have been in rather a turmoil here . . . on top of
everything Evie has thrown a cup of hot tea at Eric and been thoroughly
spanked for her caprice. She is still in a towering rage, swearing that she will
'have the law on him.' She bangs doors all the time and kicks E.'s shins when
he has a tray in his hands, and E. only turns round to say that next time he
will take her trousers down! in true macabre low comedy vein. It is all quite
grotesque and peculiar, really like a Punch and Judy show" (*Making of a Writer*,
277).

Eric—in the end—did much more: "But by far the strangest turn of events
had occurred shortly after Denton's death, when Eric Oliver, despite his pro-
fessed dislike of middle-aged women, proceeded, in the bath, to divest the
fifty-five-year-old Evelyn Sinclair of her virginity" (*Making of a Writer*, 294).

198. Phyl Ford's son Michael.

199. *A Voice through a Cloud.*

200. Mary Sloman and Brenda Cobb.

201. Short for "Tuna."

202. Denton's worries concerning the chronic nature of his illness—the re-
currence of severe fevers and headaches—are echoed in his journal entry of July

13, 1945: "I longed so violently to be strong again that I thought something must happen. Something in me, or outside but in me too, could withstand. But I think really that I get worse all the time, so that I have a picture of myself draining away. The only thing that can withstand is the will, in its own weak, shabby, obstinate, joyless way" (*Journals*, 205).

203. Some delicacies, including shrimp paté, obtained from Amy Oliver's American tenants; see note 194.

204. Another spat with Noël Adeney, which has little to do with their obtaining milk from her and much with her jealousy of Denton in his relationship with Eric.

205. Denton and Eric did stay at Middle Orchard for twelve days, July 5–17, 1945. On July 15, Denton described a summer storm that he watched from the "white balcony" at Middle Orchard:

> Last night was the most tremendous storm I have ever been in. Lightning continuously from perhaps nine-thirty to four o'clock in the morning, and lightning that appeared like violent cracks in the curved sky bowl. Flashes of pink light that showed the orchard trees up in a sort of ghostly powder blue grey. Thunder crawling all over the sky. Two moths fluttering madly against the window pane to get out of their deaths, while we watched from the top windows for hours, drinking tea and exclaiming. Once I went to shut the metal fitting of the window, and felt what seemed like a vibration through my fingers as a lightning split the clouds.
>
> There were lights over towards Wrotham and the red flashing of the aeroplane signal tower, hailstones smacking on the balcony, the injured telephone ringing helplessly in little bursts.
>
> At last we had to go to bed, we were so tired, and my ankles were aching and burning as if from the storm. (*Journals*, 205)

206. Glinn-Jones (to whom there in no further reference in the letters, notes, or biography) was apparently at Repton School at the same time as Denton, from 1929 to 1931. The "girl" obviously had only a passing knowledge of the Welch family. Although in his journal entry of December 4, 1942, Welch recalls his preparatory school days with a mix of disdain and anxiety, he does admit to being drawn to the exclusively male atmosphere of his old school:

> Nine years ago, in November 1933, I went back to Repton for an Old Boys' Celebration Day or whatever it may be called. It seems perhaps a

curious thing for me to have done, and yet not curious at all. Although I ran away and hated it so much, my eyes and my heart often looks that way. At any moment of the day a picture may flick up in my mind of the street outside Brook House with the high wall of the games yard and the little gate piercing it. The high wall looks like a prison wall and the little gate is wicked too, yet they still hold their sort of frightening glamour. . . .

It is difficult for anyone who has not experienced it to realize the cast-iron convention of submission in English schools. If you do not bow the knee willingly and with good grace you are an outcast and a cad. In some subtle way, independance is made to appear low, "canaille." Hence, if you are a prefect (or an old boy down for the day) you have the extraordinary and rather wicked pleasure of being waited on by boys who are in every way your "equal" except for the number of years they have lived. Their deference must make after life seem flat and rough to the person who has been successful at school. (*Journals*, 30–31)

The atmosphere of repressed homosexuality in the English public school experience, so vividly portrayed in Welch's story "When I Was Thirteen," is once again demonstrated in Denton's recollection of how a fellow "old boy" made sexual advances toward him during his 1933 visit to Repton:

In the early hours, I heard Riley tiptoe across to me [in the dormitory room] and say, "Let's go to the bathroom before the others wake up; there'll be a terrible crush."

I was most unwilling to do this, but I had to be amiable.

"Shall I go first," I said firmly, "or will you?"

This was clearly not his idea, but he appeared to fall in with it.

"All right, you go first, if you're quick."

I got up hastily, taking my clothes with me to the bathroom.

As I stood up in the bath naked (for the water had not yet warmed the cold enamel) I heard the door being tried.

"Let me in, let me in," Riley said, "I want to get some water for shaving, while you're bathing."

I turned the key reluctantly and jumped back into the bath. He came in muffled up in his dark camel-hair dressing-gown, and bent over the can as he held it under the tap. Something was going on within him and he would not talk, but seemed to be fuming and fretting. He spent far too long over filling the can and still would not go. At last the situation petered out in complete anticlimax. Something went quite hard and stern and loathing within me. I would not even look at him until he gradually, weakly withdrew from the room.

Then I became quite sorry for poor Riley, who must be hated quite as much, now that he is at Sandhurst [military academy], as he had been at Repton. (*Journals*, 35)

207. The "millionairish pool" at Merstham is unidentified.

208. This refers to an interior scene Welch did for *Vogue* in 1944:

I have had to do a picture of an interior for *Vogue*'s Victory Number and have chosen the end of my own room with the baroque angels and the iron table. It will be reproduced in full colour with four other painters' work—Julian Trevelyan, John Armstrong, Francis Rose and Kenneth Rowntree.

They have also asked me to do a "feature" and decorate it myself with drawings. (*Journals*, 162 [September 13, 1944])

209. Hector Bolitho was a native New Zealander who was the official biographer of the English royal family. He had met and traveled with the Prince of Wales, later Edward VIII (who abdicated the throne in 1936); he wrote biographies of Queen Victoria and Prince Albert, and of Edward VIII (*Making of a Writer*, 251 n7).

Bolitho was commissioned to write a feature on Denton Welch for the American publication *Town and Country*, and on June 16, 1945, visited him at Pitt's Folly in order to interview him. He would become one of Welch's literary champions.

Fragments of Bolitho's visit are culled from the writer's journal of June 17:

Hector Bolitho came yesterday, rather early for lunch, while Evie and I were still getting things ready. I had lain the little marble-topped chess table with my mother's very flat, delicate Italian lace mats, the small squat cut-glass tumblers, the old straight-sided white-and-gold sugar-basin in the middle with a poppy, a marigold, briar roses, cat mint and some magenta star flowers in it. . . .

At last he was walking up the dark stairs. I switched on the light and saw a small tubby man with large heavy rimmed glasses and a rather square "German" head with bushy white-grey hair.

At once it was really very easy, ordinary. I curled up on the bed and he sat in the armchair. I offered him a cigarette and he began to tell me that he was just out of the Air Force and he felt like a newborn child. . . . I listened, then said that I could not know what any of the services were like, because I had been entirely out of the war, because of my health.

"Isn't that strange!" he said, "for I had the idea that any young writer, who has not been involved in the war, would be very old-fashioned— but you had not struck me as in the least cut-off, and so I thought that you must have seen quite a lot of service somewhere."

I did not know what to make of this. Is it that I look as if I had been made to put up with a lot—accident, illness, pain, discomfort? . . .

Then he said, "But I am talking all about myself, and I came to interview you!" He asked me if I knew what sort of magazine *Town and Country* was, and explained how much better the letterpress was than what one might suppose! He explained that two other books of his had been serialised in it and added that the editor now wanted him to write an article on someone, and had told him that America was talking about me and wanted to know something about me. (Here I imagined an extraordinary sort of monster with a very large mouth asking—no, demanding—straight answers to the most embarrassing questions. Or perhaps was it a figure with a million, million mouths and one tail who was doing the demanding? Anyhow, my imaginings were as fantastic as his statement.) . . .

It was soon after this that he said, "After I had written to you I regretted it, and I will tell you why now, although it may embarrass me."

He told me that the night before, he had been reading *In Youth is Pleasure*, and although he had felt that by now he had defenses against life so that things could never hurt as they had at first, the reading of the book seemed to break all his shell, so that when later that night he had a quarrel with his host [Beverly Nichols, with whom Bolitho had been staying since his discharge from the RAF] and the man was venomous and cruel, he retreated to his room and sobbed. "And sobbing is different to crying," he added. Later the wife of the man came in and all was made up because she was so charming.

He said impulsively, "I think I am devoted to the man too." Then he dashed it away by, "But I don't know whether I am, because he is so cruel." There seemed bitterness and a wound there, and I wondered what else he would say, but he suddenly switched back to my book, saying, "But the quality that I was afraid of in you was the absolute honesty that strips away one's barricades, so that one can be hurt, just as one was as a child. I would not have sobbed last night, if I had not read In Youth is Pleasure before."

"How awful," I said, "that my book should do that." I was at a loss, not knowing how to take his tribute. Was it all a fancy thing, not genuine?

"It isn't awful!" he answered, "but that is why I regretted writing." . . .

He spent a lot of words on his desire to have money, his willingness to be a "hack" as he called it, to earn enough for comfort and luxury. He seemed to treat me as someone who would never behave in the same way. It is difficult to know whether people are really complimenting you, when they take up this attitude, or whether they are just thinking you a poor incompetent. They are doing both, I suppose—praising and blaming your supposed unworldliness.

The taxi was late in picking him up, so about three I took him into the wood and round in a circle. Talking out of doors was stiffer, more pointless. . . .

Eric was there when he came back from the wood, and when I went out of the room to talk with Evie, Bolitho said to him, "How nice it is to meet someone who is unspoilt by his success." And he said to me, too, "Your vocabulary is so unpretentious." What did he expect!

When the car came at last, we took him out to it, and he pressed both our hands with a meaning look. Something most understanding—put on, of course, but likeable, for in spite of all the little insincerities, that even a great person can't entirely weed out, he seemed to wish one well, "to want to live and let live," as Eric put it.

Eric said, the moment he was gone, "Well, that went off like a house on fire. What do you think he'll write? Something pretty good."

And we talked about it all, and I suddenly felt quite exhausted. (*Journals*, 199–203)

In July 1945 Hector Bolitho sent Denton a copy of his manuscript for the article, to which Welch replied: "I have absolutely no criticisms to make. I like it all very much. Perhaps it has made me too equable and controlled, but I am very pleased you have. I should hate the readers of 'Town and Country' to learn everything" (quoted in *Making of a Writer*, 253).

Bolitho's published article arrived in time for Christmas 1946. Welch mentions it in his journal entry for December 17:

> On Thursday, I had a letter from Hector Bolitho, with the article that he had written about me for *Town and Country*. They had called it "In Welch is Youth"; he explained that it was not his title. He wrote from the Mayflower Inn, Washington, Connecticut, and said he was lecturing, trying to make enough money to buy a house on the York River.
>
> The article is buttery, and they have reproduced quite well, my pen-drawing fancy portrait of myself. (*Journals*, 314)

As the letter of June 26, 1945, indicates, Bolitho was also kind enough to have Denton's cuttings of articles and reviews of his work mounted for framing.

210. Welch promises not to overexert himself by hiking or bicycling. These physical exercises were now almost invariably followed by bouts of fever and headaches. "Scouting days" refers to Denton's periodic adventures with young men he met while on his riverside walks.

211. A comical misspelling of his name?

212. Short for "dumpling"?

213. Probably referring to a meeting between Welch and Peggy Kirkaldy, one of the writer's many "fans." She had visited him on July 31 and had brought him a "cucumber, tomatoes, large cake, book on china, and two pretty George III teaspoons, the engraved sort, datemarks 1801, 1802" (*Journals*, 209).

214. Welch may be confusing the visit with Kirkaldy with another picnic outing he had with Eric at Peckham Old Church on September 1, 1945. This would explain the reference to sewage: "As we were eating, the rural district sewage tanks drove up and emptied their loads straight into the woods. We heard sewage swishing and gurgling and then the smell struck us in the face with sudden gusts. We shut the car window on that side and soon it dispersed; but surely this is a very extraordinary thing to do, to empty sewage straight into a wood" (*Journals*, 215–16).

Denton seems to have experienced other imaginings (as well as vaguely erotic encounters) while at the Mereworth estate. One can't always distinguish the actual occurrence from his literary reworking of it:

> Afterwards a fair-haired youth, with a darker, very faint beard just sprouting, told us that they sometimes just emptied the sewage into a

field, although people complained, so he supposed they now came and dumped it into this lovely wood. He was gentle and docile, and so rather likeable and sad. One felt he was soon going to be ground down. We left him and walked down to the War Memorial [Great War] lych-gate, where we sat on the stones in the sun and looked down on to Hadlow Tower, seemingly so far away.

Eric's shirt had split right down the back, so he took it off and sunned himself. . . .

After some time in the sun we left the church and drove slowly down the tiny rough lane towards the ruined arch with Corinthian pilasters on the edge of the Mereworth estate. . . .

When we got to the ruined arch, we found that gypsies or soldiers had demolished most of the wooden fence and we could walk right into the grounds. This we did, I rather nervously, expecting to be turned out or seized by guards. The army had put a hideous little field telephone right through the arch and down the ancient, dangerously ruinous beech avenue, but even this could not spoil the absolute romance of the lovely villa seen far away, with rough ground and banks of bracken sweeping down on each side of it.

The picture was fine because the warm dust-coloured porticoes, dome and pavilions were set against a deep background of sage-green trees and hill. We sat at the end of the avenue and gazed for some time at this house, perfect of its kind and time. The old-fashioned architecture books point out disparagingly that it is a slavish copy of one of Palladio's villas, but yesterday it looked quite perfectly eighteenth-century English. It seemed as if the countryside cried out for it, and after we had left it I felt that everything else seemed unrealized and insipid.

At last, after I had said how much I wished I could have it to look after it and live in, we went back to the car. Eric had found some mush-rooms and I had eaten a few autumn blackberries and tasted their mys-terious juice, delicious and bitter and sad. (*Journals*, 216–17)

215. "Right through" the estate grounds.

216. Denton's deteriorating health no longer allowed him to exert himself. The onset of "peculiar" feeling often led to his being bedridden for lengths of time.

217. Though Denton had sold his Austin 7 in 1943, he was now using an automobile belonging to May Walbrand-Evans (*Making of a Writer*, 257).

218. Welch seems to have experienced a certain frisson in relation to POWs: his previous visit to Yalding—including another encounter with Italian prisoners of war—is described in his journal entry of June 26, 1944:

At Yalding I sat down in the long grass, close to the medieval bridge, where the water falls away in a thunderous roar; and an Italian prisoner in pinkish chocolate battledress came up to me and asked if one could bathe at that spot. We got talking and he told me that his brother was a postman in Sicily and he himself was captured at Tobruk in 1941. He was nice. His face was brown and coarse and good-looking and his body thick-set.

Another prisoner approached, a more Egyptian-looking type, and the first one said, "He is my cousin; caught on the same day."

We all sat together in the grass until about four-thirty, when they went to get back into their lorry to go home.

Then I walked up on to the bridge and gazed down at a young man in a white singlet who was trying to catch fish in a bag of wire-netting on the end of a long stick. He had a large wad of bread and he threw bits of this into the water.

He must have seen my shadow far above him, for he suddenly looked up and smiled shyly and flashingly, wiping it off in a moment. It was a surprise to me—his face I mean—for it was strikingly handsome, not just ordinarily so, but regularly beautiful, the hair springing from it harshly and exuberantly. I wondered if he too was an Italian prisoner. (*Journals*, 157–58)

219. Harmston is unidentifiable from either the letters or journals. Apparently a mutual acquaintance of the Adeneys ("he burnt the mantelpiece at M. O.") and Welch, he had—if Denton's comments are to be trusted—struck up a relationship with Peggy Mundy Castle. Peggy Mundy Castle had been staying at the Oast House, Trottiscliffe ("Trot's").

220. Howard Oliver. There exists no other reference to an Oliver "family reunion."

221. May Walbrand-Evans.

222. Peggy Mundy Castle.

223. Only one more reference is made to this story for *Harper's Bazaar*, in his journal entry of November 20, 1945: "I have my story to do for *Harper's*, another to do for *Kingdom Come*, my *Vogue* drawing to do in four days, my

192   Notes

book to finish" (*Journals*, 229). The *Harper's* story was never completed; in fact, by December 4, he reports in his journal: "Yesterday I did no work because my story had gone all to bits" (*Journals*, 233).

224. A reference to Eric's frequent "pillaging" of his mother's belongings for the Welch/Oliver/Sinclair household. The literary connection is with Charles Dickens's *Oliver Twist*.

225. Violin impresario whose interpretations of Beethoven and Mozart were current during the Second World War.

226. Fillings.

227. As De-la-Noy points out, Denton's purchase of a home such as that at Little Hawkwell was "fantasy" (*Making of a Writer*, 260). He had just learned from his brother Bill that his father's assets had been almost entirely left to his stepmother and that it would be an arduous process to obtain the brothers' share in the estate:

> On Sunday, Bill and Anne came. My brother had grown grey hair at the sides and he told me all about our father's latest Will. It appears now he has left everything to my stepmother unconditionally. She is sole executrix too. This, which seemed so very bad on the surface for us, is apparently not quite so bad, as Bill thinks the whole thing can be settled, if he offered her an annuity on condition that she gives over the shares [stock in his Shanghai rubber estate management concern] to our keeping. At present she is staying in Shanghai and swearing that she is going to run the firm herself. It is just like a wicked stepmother in children's stories. Bill says that in a year or two we should have quite a comfortable amount. But I suppose Ada knows this too, and so I can't help feeling that she may be very difficult.
>
> There is also the question of money of our own mother's that may now go into her pocket. For our father sold the house [585 Avenue Foch, Shanghai] (bought with our mother's money) for about £15,000. This should really have been divided between us instead of going to our father's estate. Bill says that he will rake this up if Ada will not agree.
>
> I suppose money is so fascinating, so repelling and so tiring because it has the power to draw all forms of ingenuity out of people. (*Journals*, 225–26 [October 18, 1945])

The journal entry for September 9, 1945, also mentions Denton's hopes in regard to his father's legacy:

Last Sunday Paul [Denton's brother] came and told me that if we get nothing else, we will eventually get eighty shares in Wattie & Co. and if the firm gets going again [after the Japanese occupation] and is moderately successful, we should each get about £300 a year. But there is the mystery of what has happened to the rest of our father's money. Did he spend it all? Will our step-mother be able to throw any light? It is all peculiar and just what one should expect, I suppose. He had about £4,000 a year in director's fees alone. (*Journals*, 217)

By July 1946, Denton knew the disquieting truth concerning the estate. As he confided to Noël Adeney, "his stepmother had sold everything, even his brothers' clothes, and was very disappointed that her husband had left her less than she had expected. Although she had made a Will 'leaving everything to us that was not already tied up,' Denton was 'sorry that Paul could not even salvage some of our possessions, for I might have been able to have some more of my mother's family things'" (*Making of a Writer*, 257).

228. A reference to assets belonging to his father's estate. It is well worth mentioning that Denton's brother William, or Bill, was an indefatigable financial advocate for him. Denton had been afraid that his unflattering portrayal of his eldest brother in "When I Was Thirteen" would be met with resentment, or worse; see note 35. When Bill returned from service in North Africa in March 1944, Denton had written anxiously to Noël Adeney: "Do you think Bill will arrive? This is pure horror to me." He also wrote to Eric: "Isn't it frightful? He'll be down here any day now, because I've written to say I've not been well. He read both my new book [*In Youth Is Pleasure*] and the Horizon article ["When I Was Thirteen"] which comes out in April. This worries me far more than it ought to, I suppose. I feel very guilty about maligning him in print. I think it will hurt his feelings more than it was ever meant to; I thought that he would be out of the country and that he'd never read anything I wrote" (quoted in *Making of a Writer*, 211–12).

Denton's trepidation was entirely unfounded, as Bill gave him only congratulations on the success of his writings and continued to look after his younger brother until the latter's death. In July 1947 Denton told Noël Adeney that Bill had been "extraordinarily good. In his last letter he offers to send me 'a few hundred pounds' as he puts it, whenever I need it; and he also wants to know what it costs to keep E. [Eric] and Evie and me, so that if I am ill again for a long time and not much coming in, he can come to the rescue, and I won't feel that I might have to delve into my capital" (quoted in *Making of a*

Writer, 278). William had also made a birthday gift of his £100 army gratuity to Denton in March 1946.

229. Alethea is unidentified. Perhaps one of Amy Oliver's friends.

230. The address for May Walbrand-Evan's sister, Miss D. Morgan. She had wanted Eric to pick up some "Mates" for her, before he returned to Pitt's Folly.

231. Much—both good and ill—occurred for Denton and Eric during the first half of 1946. Noël and Richard Adeney purchased the property belonging to Evie Sinclair and her brother at 34 Croom's Hill, Greenwich. This was the house where Denton had stayed while an art student at Goldsmiths and where he had first met Evie, his future housekeeper. The Adeneys' move to London facilitated Denton, Eric, and Evie's long-awaited, permanent move to Middle Orchard. However, before Denton made the final lease arrangements with Noël, his health took a serious turn for the worse. On December 20, he described the onset of new complications:

> Then, just before Evie came up to read, and as I was sitting on the arm of the chair looking down at a picture or book, something seemed to shift delicately in my eye and there was a slight swimming of which I took little notice.
>
> I settled myself on the bed with Eric, about to listen to the reading, but before it began I said something about my eye, which he pooh-poohed rather, telling me that I was a little neurotic.
>
> As Evie's voice, reading [Siegfried] Sassoon, lulled on, I shut my eyes, thinking that the cloudiness might lift when I opened them; but it didn't. It seemed to grow, and I saw two teapots, two Evies and two warm lamps. I still did not worry too much.
>
> There was an amusing piece about Ronald Firbank, fruit from Belheim and rich chocolate cake [refers to an excerpt from Sassoon's autobiographical *Memoirs of George Sherston*]—and after that I jumped up, not being able to stay still any longer, and went into the bathroom.
>
> I saw there that my lid dropped down and that the pupil underneath was huge, velvet black, almost swamping the tiny coloured rim. The other pupil was normally small. The whole effect of my face was wickedly languorous and lop-sidedly un-me. I went down to the others to tell them and to show them, but they still pooh-poohed comfortably.
>
> And so I settled down to a night of deep pain in the heart of my head like a little tight walnut. I took a Veganin tablet, and after that I

seemed to be still in pain but too lethargic to be as restless as I wanted to be. My eye was weeping all on its own, apart from me, the water coursing down my cheek, and my heart was frightened. I felt abandoned. The watering of my eye seemed as gruesome as the dripping walls of the lavatory in an Industrial Revolution slum.

In the morning, the lid and the eye on my left side all seemed to be sinking down to the left—everything left, hooded, wilting. (*Journals*, 241–42)

That morning, Eric called in Jack Easton (Denton's doctor from Broadstairs, and the object of his youthful infatuation) to examine him. Welch recalls his reaction:

He was more or less the person that I had first seen ten years ago in the garden of the nursing home at Broadstairs; there was less hair on the top of his head. He was tireder, and I thought of all the disgustingness that he had had to deal with in Egyptian hospitals for the last four to five years [Easton had served with the medical corps in North Africa during the war].

The meeting would have been much more graceful if Jack had not suddenly said in a too social voice, "How are you!" What was I to do? Respond in the same tone, or at once plunge into my anxieties over the eye? I compromised and said with rather a giggle, "I'm quite all right if it weren't for this peculiar eye surprise." There was a tremor of dislocation and surface silliness, then I told him just what happened and waited. . . .

Then he told me that he thought it was a temporary paralysis of the third nerve, and that it would get better but would take some time. First he said a few days, then six weeks or perhaps two months! . . .

He said that I should wear a black patch over the left eye to stop me from seeing double. He said it was impossible for the other eye to be affected at the same time. (*Journals*, 242)

By the end of March 1946 Denton was celebrating the move from Pitt's Folly Cottage to Middle Orchard, and the redecoration project he and Eric had undertaken:

It's happened, we are here. I'm in the quiet room all to myself and Eric is in his, sleeping already. The stiff new red, grey and fawn striped curtains are round me and I smell paint from downstairs. I ache all round the middle of me in a broad belt. There was an owl just now calling and calling. (*Journals*, 261 [March 25, 1946])

———————

To go back to the house here; we have now put the eighteenth-century cartoon for a tapestry that I have had rolled up for four years. It came about twenty-five years ago from a château in the south of France. It is all faded blues, greys, pinks, creams and greens, and in it Venus is leaning down from her chariot and her doves and blessing a young girl whom Cupid is fixing with a dart. An older woman looks on with an expression of amazement on her face. It is framed in a lovely rococo border of shells, wreaths and spiky fins or wings.

It is ten feet square so we had to fold two feet up and put one side a little round a corner. It has been backed with some finer material which is stiff with glue, so it crackles and is difficult to handle. When we folded up the two feet at the bottom, we had already hung the cartoon, therefore I had to pin it first, creeping all behind in the dark, then I had to thread a needle, sit on the inside, with Eric on the outside, and we had to pass the needle back and forth, through the stiff canvas, till we came to the end.

The walls of the living-room are light blue-grey-green, woodwork white, floors natural wood waxed; then the two terracotta rugs are in there, the little Regency rosewood side cupboard with mirror doors and ormolu gallery and pillars between the windows, curtains the old deep green velvet ones I had in my first flat, the Hadlow Row one, when I was twenty-one. (*Journals*, 262 [March 30, 1946])

However, by April 7, Denton reports another unsettling development in his condition: an episode of internal hemorrhaging. This awakens again his resentment for having been injured in the accident of 1936:

I bleed inside; and when it comes out of me, almost fascinating in its disgustingness, I feel full of snarling that I am spoilt. To have always to do every fragment of work with the gloves of sickness sheathing each finger, to have that added! The glove of flesh is thick and deadening enough, without the bewildering adventure of illness never-ending. And if a silly woman in a car ten years ago had driven straight instead of crooked, I should not be whining till I'm stiff all through. (*Journals*, 263)

Nonetheless, despite or perhaps because of this episode, he describes one of the little quarrels that inevitably takes place while setting up housekeeping with a partner:

> We quarrelled because I did not quite like the shape he was cutting round the honeysuckle hedge. He [Eric] was changing a gentle curve into an angle. The verge cut in this way seemed to have much less reason and meaning; just as a bow window that is three flat sides and not a segment of a circle is usually much less pleasing. He did not like me to say this and told me that people must be allowed to do things in their own way. I then said that I had spoken because otherwise I should have resented the shape of the lawn every time I looked out of my window.
>
> How tedious the little details seem, written down, yet it is always this littleness that seems to have, banked up behind it, great walls of fight and resistance. I think it is true to say that criticisms on matters of "taste" bring out of children and ancients, simple and complex, the interested and the uninterested, great waves of animosity. It is as if each person feels insulted when his judgement on artistic things is questioned.
>
> When there is resentment in a house, however passing, the walls seem thick with it and the floors muffled. The weight of it is like stone beads. (*Journals*, 263)

232. Welch's irritability with Noël Adeney (Rich was her son) for disturbing his work, although her visits to Middle Orchard were well-intentioned, had much to do with the growing popularity of both his literary and illustrative work. The *New York Post* as well as the *New Yorker* requested stories from him. He was asked by *New Writing* to "do some little headings and tailpieces" (*Journals*, 293) and to illustrate Katherine Mansfield's "The Voyage" for an adolescents' magazine, *Junior*. His first novel, *Maiden Voyage*, had already run through four editions in England and two in America, and it had been translated for Swedish, French, Italian, and German editions (*Journals*, 294).

Although all of this attention flattered the writer, he was—due to precarious health—hard pressed to attend to any of the new offers: "I would like, whenever I am asked for something, to be able to do it; but I cannot, and so feel confused by requests and wish to be left alone to finish my book [*A Voice through a Cloud*]. . . . It would be lovely to have the health and vigour to do all these things one after another smoothly, in the moments that I spared from the book. I have always this tantalizing picture of happy busyness to goad me" (*Journals*, 293).

One of the more exciting projects he was asked to undertake had been that from Jose Villa, editor of the *Harvard Wake*. Denton was asked to write an essay about his first meeting with Edith Sitwell for the journal. He wrote to Sitwell asking her permission, to which she enthusiastically replied: "I am filled with a mixture of really *extreme* delight and some trepidation at the thought of your describing that lunch party for two. (Trepidation remembering your description of Mr. Sickert [the 1942 article for *Horizon* describing Welch's visit with the painter, Walter Sickert, which launched Welch's literary career]. But at least I did not, as far as I remember, dance or sing. Oh, how Osbert and I laughed over that description.) Well anyhow, trepidation or no trepidation, I am *enchanted* that you are going to do it, and look forward to it greatly" (quoted in *Making of a Writer*, 269).

The trepidation was not all on Edith Sitwell's side, as Welch's journal entry of July 15, 1946, indicates: "It is so difficult to write this article, for so many things cannot be repeated. Edith said she thought Vita Sackville-West and Rosamund Lehmann poor writers. Dorothy Wellesley also. These names I have to wipe out. There was also the amusing part too about Dorothy Lady Gerald Duchess of Wellington that is arriving drunk at a poetry reading and not being allowed to recite. I long to travel over this forbidden ground. But all the time I have to think if my words will cause mischief between these people and Edith" (*Journals*, 285). Welch did complete the article, entitled "A Lunch Appointment." Although approved by Edith Sitwell, it was never published (*Journals*, 285 n22).

233.   Among the requests for contributions was one from a nudist association publication. Welch's reaction is one of the more hilarious of his journal entries:

> Now today I am sent the *Sun Bathing Review* and told that Bernard Shaw, Laurence Housman, Naomi Mitchison, Vera Brittain, A. E. Coppard, J. C. Flugel, Robert Gibbings and C. E. M. Joad have written for it and will I write too — a likely theme, the value of nudity in schools "as a means of countering the unhealthy practices with which anyone who has been educated at a boarding school is familiar."
>
> I think the only thing I can truthfully say in reply is that I feel that nudity would increase the "unhealthy practices" whatever they may be, perhaps set a fashion through the whole school for them — that is "nudity" of this magaziny-shiny-photograph sort. The booklet is uncomfortable. I know that if someone came into this room at this moment, I would hurriedly explain that it had been sent to me, and that I had not bought it for my own delight. Why do other people's fetishes

seem ugly and improper? I am fond of naked people, but not of a great
to-do and business of nakedness. To read this magazine is to be half
told that if everyone would suddenly strip off their clothes the world
might be made quite wonderful.

The articles are very like the tracts Evie's sister brought me from
the Bible and Tract Society. God and Jesus are replaced by Sun and the
Naked Body. (*Journals*, 294)

234. One of Welch's unreasonable frustrations was that he was not com-
pensated for reprints of his work, which had already been sold to various
journals and publishers.

235. Ted Nichols; see note 163.

236. Friend and biographer of the Sitwell family. His biography of the
three Sitwells (*Facades*) was published in 1978 by Macmillan (*Making of a
Writer*, 159). See note 208 for *Vogue* illustration reference.

237. Short for brewing hops?

238. No references in the journals or correspondence.

239. This page of the letters is clearly out of sequence. His reference to Eve
"busying about" at Middle Orchard would not have been possible, as she had
already moved to Cornwall, where Eric was then visiting her. His journal entry
of August 8, 1946, describes a telephone call he received from Eric and Evie,
that evening:

The telephone rang and I have just been talking to Eric and to Evie. I
ran downstairs believing it was Eric, yet wondering if it could be anything else. The bell's ring was in those little gusts, frightening, exciting
in an empty house, like a mad doll bouncing.

Then the request, "Hold the line, please," the wait, and at last Eric's
voice.

He had just arrived and was still eating his supper. He had been
given Dr Wood's [the sisters' father] bedroom, and they were thinking
of going to Land's End tomorrow. He had a delicious ham sandwich in
cellophane at Paddington or Victoria. The journey was very easy. Evie
met him, timing it perfectly.

I spoke to Evie at the end. She remembered the cat postcard I had
sent her, as it lay about for months in my room at Pitt's Folly. I seemed
linked with peculiar minute links. (*Journals*, 292)

This page belongs somewhere in the correspondence between March and May
1946, when Evie Sinclair was still living with Denton and Eric; however, it

can't be accurately placed with any of the other letters. Perhaps this was a discarded page from one of Denton's letters to Eric when he was visiting his mother in London.

240. Unidentified gardener or handyman for Middle Orchard.

241. Probably refers to the "help," a Mrs. Reffold, identified in the journal of February 25, 1948, as "turning out the furniture and mopping up," after a plumbing mishap (*Journals*, 353).

242. Unidentified.

243. On Eric's periodic visits to London, he was usually asked to check whether any of Denton's paintings at the Redfern and Leicester Galleries had been sold.

244. See note 232.

245. This letter was to his brother William, who had returned to Shanghai in an attempt to settle their father's estate; see notes 227–28.

246. He was taking M&B tablets (a sulpha drug for bacterial-tubercular infections), which he described as making "me feel even worse—black, dead, inhuman as a boulder—telescoped into myself till nothing could come forward" (*Journals*, 214 [August 26, 1945]). This may be the "new treatment" referred to. Whatever the case, Denton's health had begun seriously to deteriorate. He had been invited by Edith Sitwell to a lunch party and a presentation of Façade (a series of Edith Sitwell's poems, set to music by William Walton), but his journal of that day indicates he was unable to attend:

> This is the day that I should have gone to London to have lunch with Edith Sitwell, and afterwards to be with her at what she called a big tea-party!
>
> But I could not face going in my precarious state. This is the first day— except for the dentist on Saturday—that I have been out of my room for three weeks or a month. I wish I could have gone to Edith Sitwell's. (*Journals*, 301)

247. This request from the noted art critic Michael Ayrton indicates the level of recognition Welch's painting was beginning to attract. The journal entry describing Denton's reaction to Ayrton's letter is included below:

> This morning I had a letter from Michael Ayrton. The notepaper rather peculiar, or isn't it all peculiar nowadays? MICHAEL AYRTON in Roman letters, then 4, All Souls Place. W.1. in small type. He wanted me to submit some small pictures to him for a show he is organizing at

Heal's [Gallery]. He begins, "So much steam was generated by a chance remark I made on a B.B.C. Brain's Trust [a program dealing with topics from the art and literary world] about the comparatively low prices at which good pictures by young painters could be bought, that Messrs. Heal & Son have asked me to sponsor and select a small exhibition of pictures below £40. Heal's are to buy one picture outright, the rest to be on sale-or-return basis. In order to make a really good show, only about sixteen artists will be asked to submit work. I very much hope you will be able to co-operate in this venture."

There is a postscript at the bottom, in his own writing (the rest in type): "I hope this will give us an opportunity to meet, as I am an admirer of your work."

Does he mean writing as well as painting? And would I dislike his conversation with me as much as I dislike it on the wireless? I suppose so much of his pleasantness would depend on mine. But on the wireless he seems quite spoilt by a distressing parade of youth and talent. He seems to be insisting rather school-girlishly on his charm, when all the time I feel quite unwilling to give him any credit for any charm at all.

But the wireless must be such a horribly deep vanity probe. One could not hide one's weakness or help slipping into some falsity, or being twisted into it. So really I feel that I would like his true self much more than the wireless voice; but even then, it might not be so very much.

I feel happy that he wrote to me though, it made my breakfast of toast and honey and coffee happy. (*Journals*, 296–97)

Welch painted two pieces for the Heal's exhibition, *The Coffin House* (later purchased from Leicester Galleries by novelist Rose Macaulay) and *The Woodman's Cottage* (purchased by John Lehmann). Macaulay wrote to Welch on February 10, 1947, describing the painting:

I have found the signature in the top left corner; quite legible; but the one on the leaf in the bottom right corner seems to have got overgrown with leafage and acorns since you did it, and though, helped by your drawing of the leaf in your letter, I searched diligently among the under-growth, I couldn't be sure I had found it, tho' I saw one or two possibili-ties. If ever you are able to come here (which I very much hope, and I am sorry to hear that you are house-tied for the present) please identify

it for me. I find the picture more and more fascinating, as I knew I
should when I failed to resist it at the Leicester. The detail is so exquis-
itely mortal and corrupt, the robin singing against it with such brave
larger-than-life protest. I especially like the blind white hare pawing
the toadstool; and the clawing tree-trunks like dendrofied ghosts or
dragons reaching for the sky. Your pen-work is so beautifully precise
and strong; and all the colour is good. I should like some time to visit
the scene myself. When or if I do (perhaps when there is petrol again) I
shall certainly let you know, and come and visit you if I may. The
picture also smells of fungus and the damp wood; I know the smell so
well. It must have been exciting to do. It seems to me unusual to be
able to do two things so well as you do, writing and picture-making.
(quoted in *Making of a Writer*, 273)

De-la-Noy notes that the current whereabouts of the painting is unknown,
though it is reproduced in the short-story collection *A Last Sheaf*. *The Woodman's Cottage* is in the collection of Mr. W. H. Boomgaard (*Making of a
Writer*, 273 n2).

Michael Ayrton's identification of Denton Welch with a new "school" of
young postwar artists (later known as the Neo-Romantics) was prescient. An
exhibition entitled *A Paradise Lost: The Neo-Romantic Imagination in Britain:
1935–55* was presented at the Barbican Art Gallery in 1987. The exhibition included paintings by David Jones, Graham Sutherland, Alfred Thomson,
George Warner-Allen, Rex Whistler, Gerald Wilde, Bryan Wynter, Doris
Zinkeisen, Robert Colquhoun, Keith Vaughan, and Denton Welch. The Welch
paintings exhibited were *Hadlow Castle* (1937), *A Lion and a Pilgrim* (1944), *By
the Sea* (1940), *Flowers* (1943–44), *Flowers and a Demon* (1943–44), and *Fantastic
Portrait of a Cat* (1940). First editions of his novels and short story collections—
Maiden Voyage, *In Youth Is Pleasure*, *Brave and Cruel*, *A Voice through a Cloud*,
A Last Sheaf (with illustrations)—were also part of the exhibit. Interestingly,
some of these books were lent to the Barbican by Michael De-la-Noy.

248. Keith Vaughan, a fellow exhibitor at Heal's (also included, along with
Welch, at the 1987 Barbican exhibit; see note 247), visited Denton and Eric on
August 30, 1946:

The telephone rang again on Monday and I heard Eric talking to an
unknown. It turned out to be a Keith Vaughan, who had written to me

about *Maiden Voyage* when it first came out. He is a painter. We asked him to appear for tea, since he was going to be in Sevenoaks and would like to come over.

I didn't really expect him to find the way, but almost exactly at four I hear someone walking up the path to the front door. Eric ran down and said, "Hullo." The next moment he was up here beside my bed—he being Keith Vaughan.

He was fairly small and slight, very smiling, hair a little thinning, dressed in corduroys and a sort of policeman's jacket, which I rather liked. He had an open neck and wore a broad leather belt.

Almost at once it was friendly and easy. I thought that he was one of the pleasantest of my chance guests. He told us that he walked all through the lanes and that at last he had found someone and asked the way to the house only to be told a little vaguely that it was past "Grandad's" house. He found the footpath though and came to us that way.

He talked about his time in Yorkshire guarding German prisoners, how much he liked them. He talked about that part of a house which he and John Minton were trying to get repaired and converted for themselves [Minton was another of the artists included in the Barbican exhibit; Minton and Welch had contributed decorations for a book called *Contemporary Cooking* by Doris Lytton Toye (Conde-Nast, 1947) (see *Journals*, 299 n25)]. At present he was living with his mother in a flat at Hampstead. He began by telling us what an excellent manager she was, but before the end of the visit he told us more.

Tea, which I had put together quickly on one of my rare visits downstairs, was nice. There were water biscuits, plum jam and butter, dried bananas, almonds, a plum cake Eric's mother had made and two ginger and one chocolate biscuit.

K. V. ate in that way which is not quite discriminating, yet certainly not uninterested. A sort of stolid way of eating.

At six o'clock he jumped up and said he must be going. I let him go, not wanting to make myself tired. But as Eric walked down the drive with him, they came upon our neighbor Mrs Potter and her son cleaning the car.

The son, Ian, mistook both Eric and K. V. for me, one after the other. He then, when he knew that K. V. was going back to London, offered him a lift at eight o'clock. So Vaughan came back again.

I heard the voices and wondered what had happened. Eric hurriedly got together soup, omelette and plums for supper, and we began to talk again.

This time we heard how difficult it was for a grown son to live with his mother, how unsuitable it was, how irritating, how bad. There was a lot of this, and it gave me a feeling of sadness. I saw how many people must despise their parents.

Vaughan's mother was a "good manager" and was very fond of him—too fond and doting—but she had no money and he had to keep her. She could share none of his interests. She questioned his movements. Her friends were dreadful. He wished he could admire the wisdom of the old, but he had never known an old person with wisdom. The ideal mother would be someone with a comfortable home and a husband. Someone who had a life of her own. Someone who did not live only in her son (and *on* her son).

Now we were seeing a little more of the leathery side of K. V., the desire for comfort and money, and the greater respect he gave to those with material advantages. He blamed his mother for the lack of them.

I suppose we would all like our relations to be as rich and as comfortable as possible, if we could choose; but we would like riches for the whole world too. I wondered if most people resented supporting their parents—regretted so much their lack of money and importance. I wondered if I often felt pleased with my father whilst he was alive because he was rich enough to promise comfort to me and not responsibility.

Keith Vaughan told me that my last little picture at the Leicester, the "Woodman's Cottage" one, had been bought by John Lehmann. (*Journals*, 299–300)

On August 17 Denton had been informed by Eric that his paintings *Spirits above a Flower*, *A Cat Waiting for Its Master*, and *Woodman's Cottage* had been sold by the Leicester Galleries.

249. Ted Nichols; see note 163.

250. Money. Eric was still visiting Evie Sinclair in Cornwall.

251. Mildred Bosanquet, from whom Denton had received his Georgian dollhouse; see note 180.

252. The progressive deterioration of Denton's health "now made it imperative, should Eric ever be away for any length of time, to have someone else there permanently to help with the house. Evie had paid a brief visit to Middle

Orchard in August, and Denton was trying to persuade her to come back"
(*Making of a Writer*, 273).

De-la-Noy continues this passage with a quote from Denton's letter to Noël
Adeney of November 11, 1946: "We have been in a state of siege here—both in
bed at the same time; but now we're better and E. has gone to do some shopping.
It grew so gruesome last Sunday that we sent a telegram to Eve, but luckily she
was away in Bath so was not disturbed, and E. got quickly better the next day.
But we have since asked Eve to come back at least for a little time at Christmas
and she seems quite keen. We are going to work it this time very firmly with
strict days off and holidays away, so that she remains linked up with the outside world. It is all to be written out for her, before she returns!" (*Making of a
Writer*, 273–74).

Evie Sinclair did return to Middle Orchard on a permanent basis on November 18, 1946. Denton reported that she "has been cooking really delicious meals
for us. In spite of bad beginnings over time—everything late and the clock
looked upon as a useless ornament—we now feel glad that she is here. She does
make life easier, and I have got beyond worrying over her eccentricities"
(*Journal*, 313).

In his journal entry of December 4, 1946, the intensity of Denton's struggle
is laid out in wrenching detail:

> After almost a month in bed, I got up on a fine day, last Tuesday, and
> went with Eric to picnic in the car. We were on the way to Maidstone
> and we stopped in a clearing where hop-poles were to be dipped in
> creosote. There were logs, poles, palings and twigs all about us—nothing
> but wood—even soft sawdust instead of earth.
>
> When our picnic was over we drove on to Maidstone to find a
> christening present for Paul's [Denton's brother] godchild. To pre-
> serve me as much as possible, we only went to one shop, the Malt
> Shovel, and there I chose a little cream-jug, George II, 1759, £8.10s. . . .
>
> When I was home, I realized how tired I was. I woke up in the
> night and felt that my temperature was rising. In the morning I was
> really ill again—aching all over, but I always prefer this to only aching
> in the head. I drowsed and lay there all day and the succeeding days,
> and when the temperature subsided I caught the cold which Eric had
> had! So I am still here in bed, with nothing done for over a week.
>
> Lying here, able to do nothing, I have realized that all the year has
> been a sinking into bed and a painful rising out of it, only to be dragged

down again before I could breathe or spread my arms. I have realized how half-afraid I have been to do anything because of what comes after. How many hours, days have I had to let swim over my head? And I, who could be busy all day long. The feeling has come over me that I must let everything melt away, that I am no longer in command at all. And in my idleness all I can think of are rich strange dishes wonderfully cooked, amazing little houses in fine gardens, rare and lovely objects for these tiny palaces, and then wills and bequests both fantastic and more down to earth. (*Journals*, 312)

Welch goes on to relate that the contemplation of wealth, which he hoped to gain by way of inheritance (either from his father's estate or from his mother's friends) was the unseemly product of his chronic, debilitating illness:

I keep wondering if I shall receive anything from my father's estate, and whether Cecil Carpmael [Cecilia, a close Christian Scientist friend of Denton's mother, Rosalind; see note 169] intends to leave me anything or not. I wonder what she has to leave. Sometimes I work it out contentedly at anything from £50,000 to £80,000; and I go through her possessions too, remembering the few nice things, the Georgian silver teapots and the Persian rugs.

I see now that day-dreams like these, very material—always of things, wealth, security—crowd in as the chance to finish work recedes. Agitation, fear of all things that may never be done, is suppressed. One can no longer plan happily to begin or to complete, so only wealth is left to dream about.

This is the reason people's thoughts, as they grow older, turn more and more to the safety of wealth. Other things cheat them, escape them, are snatched from them, only the fat mountain of wealth remains.

But as this process of decrepitude is so speeded up in me, for that is what invalidism seems, a sort of wicked acceleration of one's life, I feel not happy in dreaming of wealth and security, but curiously fobbed off with wishes that I do not wish for, unconnected with other wishes, that can no longer be entertained. Wealth alone is, I think, everywhere secretly thought of as a second best, a lump of dough that must be lightened with fame, happiness, even rank. It must have some trimming, real or frothy. That is why those only rich faces are so peaked, so cheated and complaining. (*Journals*, 312–13)

From the end of 1946 through the middle of 1947, there would be only brief periods during which Welch felt well enough to leave Middle Orchard. The brutal winter of 1946–47 did nothing to relieve this situation; he vividly describes the semi-hallucinatory impressions produced by isolation and illness.

28 January

After three weeks of bed, able to do nothing, I began to revive again and try to write here first. I have been too sad to want anything, and the snow has been falling for days. It is falling now, there is a great layer on the roof. The wind bites through the apple trees and round the corners of the house. . . . I am waiting now to get back to everything; but my head has been swimming too much for me to do anything. . . .

I wonder all the time I am ill if I shall be able to earn enough money, since so much time is wasted. I am strangely worried and un-worried about it, as if it were only a problem I had set myself. I suppose I feel I shall have the money somehow, that I shall recover in time, that my books will bring me in some more. . . .

All the time I would wish nothing to be done, and yet would give all these things their horrible senseless life. And I even myself grew to a wretched largeness and was invaded too with the activity of nothing-ness. It was an endless toiling and posturing and living for nothing, so heart-breaking and deadening that I longed and longed to be still, to stop churning and to sleep a little.

Sight, sound, touch were all distorted. I was living in a twisted stretched world, where I invaded everything and was the horror that I could not escape. There was no self-love left, only an exhausted disgust. (*Journals*, 319)

———

29 January

There were frost flowers thick all over the panes this morning and the milk was frozen. The pipes were frozen too, and the snow thicker than ever. I have not got out of bed, and will not till I hear the pipes thawing. I have been writing here, then eating chocolate as a reward. The panes are all dripping and splashing in the sunshine now. Eric has gone for a walk in the snow, and I wish I could too. It is the most snow I think I have known in England. (*Journals*, 319–20)

———

2 February, 6 p.m.

The snow is still thick, and it falls fitfully, the flakes floating down, or driving more fiercely mixed with a little rain. As I lie in bed, only getting up twice a day, I feel that I shall never walk about again. The effort seems tremendous. My legs sway and my head swims. In bed I try to write a little and do something to my latest drawing, but my head and eyes do not seem really clear. Nevertheless I do something, and it makes me feel a little more serene. Eric and Evie read to me and I eat to make up for my fasting. I think of food too—of oysters cooked with creamed turkey, of salmon and potted shrimps, of rice with pimento and chickens' livers and peas. (*Journals*, 320)

At this juncture, Welch felt poignantly an intense urge to create, weighed down by his physical incapacity and a concern that his demands were interfering with the lives of his companions:

I wish to have stories and poems in many magazines. I want to finish my story ["Brave and Cruel"] and my book [*A Voice through a Cloud*] and get them to the publishers. I want to be a sausage machine pouring out good sausages, savoury and toothsome, delightful, desirable. I want pleasure and interest to flow out of me, to feel alive and able to bear a heavy load of work to be done. I want to be able to go out and find old books and objects in the promising dirty shops. I want to go down into the house and make it live again with my interest. I want to go out and see different sights . . .

How almost non-existent is my feeling for other people, especially when I am ill! There they are, doing things for me, making life possible, and I am dead to them, hardly even conventionally grateful, almost unable to realize that they have feelings at all. Yet I am dimly worried by them, afraid that they find my illness depressing and gloomy, afraid that there is not enough interest in their lives, that I am dragging them down into my despondency. (*Journals*, 320)

———

3 February, 6.30 p.m.

Rain today spattering on the window, yet the snow does not go, and Eric says that a great tide of slush is mounting up in the road. I wrote a fair amount this morning in a contented sort of daze. What can the result be like? Then this afternoon I tried to cover a picture mount with yellow muslin bandage. The pasting was difficult and I suddenly became very tired.

My limbs ache from lying in bed so much, yet I feel I can do nothing else. I wish I had not the weight of my body to support. It seems like a dead asleep thing hanging on me, bearing me down. (*Journals*, 320–21)

Cecilia Carpmael died on March 3, 1947. Denton's hopes for an inheritance were completely dashed. She had not included him in her will, even though she had been informed of the difficulties he was facing with his father's legacy:

27 March

I have not been able to write in this book, have felt an utter distaste for it. I have felt dull and empty and trivial, and this is due partly to being less well, and partly to the news that Cecil Carpmael has left me nothing at all. Her Will was made when I was nineteen. She must have taken it for granted that I would be well provided for by my father. But of course there has been lots of time for her to add a codicil, after learning that I would inherit nothing until my stepmother's death, and perhaps still nothing, even then. . . .

Before the Will was known, Irene [Cecilia Carpmael's companion and another Christian Scientist friend of Denton's mother] had asked me rather half-heartedly if there was anything I would particularly like of Cecil's. I thought and then wrote firmly to say that I had always been particularly fond of the elaborate late-Georgian tea-pot and cream jug, which came to Cecil from her brother. The surface is all chased and embossed with fruit and flowers and scrolls, and a tiny mandarin perches on top of the tea-pot; a fat ugly cupid's head emerges from the handle of the jug. Its exuberance, its lumpishness and sheer weight, its fine workmanship make the set very attractive to me. It is both frivolous and monumental—surely something rather difficult to achieve. . . .

When the Will was known, the wording of it gave her [Irene] just the authority she was looking for. The silver, together with all the other household things, in trust for Connie [Piffard, Cecilia's mentally ill sister]. She told me this repressively, when she came to tea last Friday. She never mentioned the tea-pot or my wish; but I was to take the hint. I did, and smiled as if nothing had happened. But after she had left, as always happens, my resentment flowered. I realised more completely the unfriendliness, the stupid suspicion. . . .

Somehow this wrangling about a teapot depressed me even more than the news that Cecil had not bothered to remember me at all. I was dirtied by it, turned into a vulture on such a tiny scale. I had thought so often of Cecil's Will, when she was alive, hoped so much that she would leave me a cosy fortune. That had been quite simple and natural and friendly. Now there was a sort of pointless resentment that fixed itself round the teapot, but really spread out far and wide. (*Journals*, 326–27)

Welch had in his words, "always considered myself one of Cecil's closest friends" (*Journals*, 327); she was the person who broke the news to Denton of his mother's death in 1927 and who had taken him home with her from St. Michael's School on that occasion. Denton and Cecilia had maintained a close relationship from that time until her death twenty years later (*Making of a Writer*, 34).

Supplementing this description of Denton's connection with Cecilia Carpmael is the fact that "Denton *was* genuinely upset. Cissie had been the first person to introduce him to painting. She had taken him seriously. She had done her best to make him feel welcome in the school holidays. What lent the news a particular poignancy was that it reached him on the anniversary of his mother's death twenty years earlier. However, once the shock wore off—and it did very rapidly—Denton's mind turned to the contents of the will, and with the snow blowing around Middle Orchard in a blizzard, he lay wrapped up in bed growing more and more obsessed with the matter" (*Writer and Artist*, 184–85).

253. Noël and Bernard Adeney were vacillating on whether to renew Denton's lease at Middle Orchard or whether to sell the property (*Making of a Writer*, 278).

254. Mildred Bosanquet (see notes 113, 180, and 251).

255. The *Orion* poem is "The Trees Were Hung with Golden Chains."

256. See note 240.

257. Denton was once again wrangling with Evie Sinclair, as is indicated by the unflattering sobriquet.

258. Noël Adeney.

259. Apparently refers to a blossoming romance involving Eric's aunt, which is not otherwise mentioned.

260. Another reference to Noël's dithering about Middle Orchard. See note 253.

261. Another frustrated reaction to Evie's frazzled housekeeping.

262. Probably *A Beauty Waiting in the Fields* currently owned by Mr. Geoffrey Parsons; included as an illustration in the posthumous short-story collection, *A Last Sheaf* (*Journals*, 329 n4). Welch refers to this project in his journal entry of April 5, 1947: "I have been doing a water-colour of a big-eyed girl in a large hat for the last two days. I must have begun it some years ago. I suddenly came upon it in a cupboard, and in spite of not feeling well, I was so pleased with it in some way that I began at once to make all sorts of little changes and additions. I want to go on with it all through the day, it would amuse and interest me the whole time; but now I must stop, or I shall have a headache all tonight. If one could have the perfect, untiring head and eyes!" (*Journals*, 329).

263. Braxton Sinclair, Evie's brother, and his wife.

264. Although his "scouting" days were over (see letter of June 26, 1945) it is clear from this encounter that his illness had not dampened his erotic impulse, nor his "collector's eye." Eric and Denton had in fact entertained a German POW at Christmas, 1946:

> On Christmas Day we had a German prisoner to lunch. His name was Harry Diedz and he was twenty-one. He came from Thuringia where he had been a glass worker. He was little, with a flat face and curly hair. He liked Mozart better than Wagner, and football better than boxing. He ate a great deal and enjoyed it, I think. He was in the Channel Islands when he was captured. His brother was captured by the Americans when he was only sixteen.
>
> We sat by the fire smoking and eating sweets and talking stumblingly, until Harry said that he had to go back to the camp to act in some "drama variété." (*Journals*, 316)

De-la-Noy remarks that Harry Diedz appears as a character in Welch's story "The Hateful Word" (*Journals*, 316 n38). Diedz was interned at Meresworth Castle, where Denton had had an earlier experience with German POWs (see letter of October 22, 1945).

265. Apparently a misunderstanding as to whether Eric was to meet Noël in London.

266. Alluding once again to the Adeneys' plans concerning Middle Orchard.

267. This is the last letter Denton would write to Eric before his death on December 30, 1948. From the date of this letter forward, Eric was in almost constant attendance upon his friend and companion.

References

De-la-Noy, Michael. *Denton Welch: The Making of a Writer*. New York: Viking; Harmondsworth: Penguin, 1986.

Methuen-Campbell, James. *Denton Welch: Writer and Artist*. Carlton-in-Coverdale: Tartarus, 2002.

Welch, Denton. *Dumb Instrument*. Edited by Jean-Louis Chevalier. London: Enitharmon Press, 1976.

———. *Fragments of a Life Story: The Collected Short Writings of Denton Welch*. Edited by Michael De-la-Noy. Harmondsworth: Penguin King, 1987.

———. *In Youth Is Pleasure and I Left My Grandfather's House*. Cambridge: Exact Change Press, 1994.

———. *The Journals of Denton Welch*. Edited by Michael De-la-Noy. New York: Dutton, 1984.

———. *Maiden Voyage*. Cambridge: Exact Change Press, 1999.

———. *A Voice through a Cloud*. Cambridge: Exact Change Press, 1996.

———. *Where Nothing Sleeps: The Complete Short Stories (and Other Related Writings)*. Edited by James Methuen-Campbell. 2 vols. Carlton-in-Coverdale: Tartarus, 2005.

LIVING OUT

Gay and Lesbian Autobiographies

David Bergman, Joan Larkin, and Raphael Kadushin
SERIES EDITORS

The Other Mother: A Lesbian's Fight for Her Daughter
Nancy Abrams

An Underground Life: Memoirs of a Gay Jew in Nazi Berlin
Gad Beck

Gay American Autobiography: Writings from Whitman to Sedaris
Edited by David Bergman

Surviving Madness: A Therapist's Own Story
Betty Berzon

You're Not from Around Here, Are You? A Lesbian in Small-Town America
Louise A. Blum

Just Married: Gay Marriage and the Expansion of Human Rights
Kevin Bourassa and Joe Varnell

Two Novels: "Development" and "Two Selves"
Bryher

The Hurry-Up Song: A Memoir of Losing My Brother
Clifford Chase

Body Blows: Six Performances
Tim Miller

1001 Beds: Performances, Essays, and Travels
Tim Miller

Cleopatra's Wedding Present: Travels through Syria
Robert Tewdwr Moss

Good Night, Beloved Comrade: The Letters of Denton Welch to Eric Oliver
Edited and with an introduction by Daniel J. Murtaugh

Taboo
Boyer Rickel

Secret Places: My Life in New York and New Guinea
Tobias Schneebaum

Wild Man
Tobias Schneebaum

Sex Talks to Girls: A Memoir
Maureen Seaton

Treehab: Tales from My Natural, Wild Life
Bob Smith

Outbound: Finding a Man, Sailing an Ocean
William Storandt

Printed in the United States
By Bookmasters